STEPS TO CHRISTIAN UNITY

Steps to Christian Unity

EDITED BY

JOHN A. O'BRIEN

RESEARCH PROFESSOR OF THEOLOGY

THE UNIVERSITY OF NOTRE DAME

73098

"Yet not for these only do I pray, but for those also who through their word are to believe in me, that all may be one, even as thou, Father, in me and I in thee; that they also may be one in us, that the world may believe that thou hast sent me."

JOHN 17:20–21

1964

DOUBLEDAY & COMPANY, INC.

GARDEN CITY, NEW YORK

ACKNOWLEDGMENTS

We acknowledge with gratitude the help of many in the preparation of this volume. We are indebted to all the contributors and to the following: Edward Shea, C.S.C., for translating Max Thurian's article; William J. Hegge, O.S.C., for translating Father Rahner's replies to our questions; to Herbert Vorgrimler for presenting our questions to Father Rahner; to Tanneguy de Quénétain and *Réalités*, Paris, for the interviews with Karl Barth and Hans Küng which originally appeared in the May, 1963 and January, 1964, issues of *Réalités;* to Martin E. Marty and the *Ave Maria,* January 18, 1964, for "Patterns of Protestant Thought"; to Augustin Cardinal Bea for his address, "Liberty of Conscience," delivered at the Eighth Annual Brotherhood Banquet sponsored by the Pro Deo University, Rome; and to Albert Cardinal Meyer for "The Scandal of Christendom," adapted from his 1964 Lenten Pastoral, "Ecumenism: The Spirit of Unity."

CONTENTS

8

GETTING THE MOST
OUT OF THIS BOOK

To enable the reader to get the most out of this work it is well, we think, to indicate its purpose, organization, contributors, intended audience, and the features which set it apart from all the books thus far written on the ecumenical movement. More than a year of planning, study, editing, and work has preceded its publication. Because it embodies the thought of some of the world's greatest theologians and scholars, with which the general reader may not be familiar, a few words as to how it can be read most fruitfully will be helpful.

This book is designed to render a distinctive service to the ecumenical movement and to the general public. Most volumes on this subject by theologians and Scriptural scholars are intended for experts in these fields and are written in the technical language characteristic of erudite dissertations. They advance the cause of research and serve a useful purpose. But little of such findings reach the general reader, and much even of that is inaccurate or superficial, because it comes from news reporters, who generally have but a shallow knowledge of this subject.

Unlike either of such, this book is written *specifically* for the general reader, and it comes from the pens of outstanding scholars in theology, Scripture, and ecumenism: men who are world-famous for their contributions and their leadership in these fields. What literate person has not heard of Karl Barth, generally regarded as the greatest name in contemporary Protestant theology, or Karl Rahner, generally considered the most distinguished and profound thinker among Catholic theologians and perhaps the greatest of the century?

In short, the names of these and the other world-famous scholars and divines who have helped in writing this book are household names on both sides of the Atlantic. They have much of the luster and eminence associated with the winners of the Nobel Prize in the sciences. At our request all have undertaken to tell their fascinating stories in a popular style that brings it well within the ken of the general reader.

Knowing how difficult this is for the specialist, we requested all to illustrate their principal points with examples and incidents. These serve not only to make the points crystal clear but also to weave them into the imagery and memory. That is why the reader will find that the abstract thought of these profound scholars, which previously eluded him, now becomes intelligible, gripping his mind and often stirring his heart. As examples and incidents linger longer in the memory, they will anchor the principles and lines of reasoning more permanently in the intellect and thus bring them more readily to use.

In the cases of Barth, Küng, and Rahner, we deemed it advisable to present their thought in the form of interviews. This enabled them to discuss a greater variety of topics and to come to grips quickly with questions in the minds of millions. It permits the reader to learn in a few minutes the conclusions reached by these scholars only after many years of profound thought and study.

Rahner, Barth, Küng, and Brown typify the eminence of the theologians and Biblical scholars featured in this book. But if actual steps are to be taken toward Christian unity, the thought, views, and suggestions of eminent prelates and churchmen must also be carefully considered. Accordingly, we have supplemented the thought and observations of the research scholars with those of the active leaders in various Christian Churches.

Fortunate indeed are we to share the insights and practical suggestions of such leading churchmen as Dr. Fred Pierce Corson, Methodist Bishop of Philadelphia; of Canon Pawley, observer at the Council for the Archbishops of Canterbury and York; of Frère Max Thurian, assistant prior of the famed

Monastery at Taizé; and of Douglas Horton, former chief executive of the Congregational Christian Churches and later dean of Harvard Divinity School.

Sharing the platform with these distinguished Protestants are Richard Cardinal Cushing of Boston; Albert Cardinal Meyer of Chicago; Augustin Cardinal Bea, head of the Secretariat for Promoting Christian Unity; and Bishop Emile-J. De Smedt of Bruges, Belgium. Occupying high administrative posts, these churchmen of different faiths naturally bring to the discussion of Christian unity the fruits of their long experience, and help us all to appreciate the difficulties of the problem as well as to perceive the initial steps leading at least in the direction of its solution.

As a change of pace from the lengthy articles of the principal contributors, we have run brief articles presenting in capsule form the thought of other leading churchmen on key points. Among these are Pope Paul VI, Cardinal Léger of Montreal, Dr. W. A. Visser 't Hooft, general secretary of the World Council of Churches, Dr. George Johnston of McGill Divinity School of Montreal, Dr. Krister E. Skydsgaard of Copenhagen University, and Athenagoras of Elaia, Greek Orthodox Metropolitan of Canada.

Furthermore, we have selected our contributors not only from the top echelon of theologians, Scriptural scholars, and churchmen of the Protestant, Episcopal, and Roman Catholic faiths, but also from countries on both sides of the Atlantic. The United States, Canada, Great Britain, Germany, France, Switzerland, Italy, and Belgium are among the nations from which our contributors have been drawn. As the ecumenical movement transcends all national lines, so the thinking, work, and prayer which will advance that movement must come from many lands.

Another consideration which influenced our choice of writers was their connection in some capacity or other with the Vatican Council: the great Council of renewal, reform, and unity, upon which the attention of the Christian world

has been focused. Obviously, those who were active participants as Council members or theological or Scriptural consultants, or who were observer-delegates or observer-guests,
or who covered the Council as accredited journalists, such
as John Cogley, were in a peculiarly advantageous position to
report and discuss these new and arresting developments.
Most of our major contributors write from such a background.

Moreover, we have preceded each major article with a
biographical sketch of the writer, covering particularly his
education, training, teaching experience, administrative work,
ecumenical activities, and writings. This will enhance the
reader's interest, for it will enable him to appreciate the experience and scholarship which lie behind the contributor's
words. We hope, too, that the listing of some of the chief
works of the writers will prompt many of our readers to
delve more deeply into the thought and work of these world-
famous scholars and churchmen.

The contributors speak with great candor and freedom,
expressing their honest convictions concerning possible steps
in the direction of Christian unity. Only in such a climate
can the discussion be fruitful. Hence it is obvious that the
views and opinions expressed by each contributor are his
own and do not necessarily reflect those of all his co-religionists. In other words, he speaks in his own name, assumes full
responsibility for the opinions expressed, and does not claim
to be speaking for his denomination or Church.

While speaking with candor and with what the Apostle
Paul calls "the freedom of the glory of the sons of God,"
the contributors invariably strike an irenic and constructive
note. Their concern is to spread light, not heat; they engage
not in polemics but in exposition. Their aim is not to tear
down but to build up, not to divide but to unite.

Despite the wide differences of religious backgrounds, the
contributors are united in the belief that what is needed now
is a more accurate understanding of the faiths of one another and a deeper realization of the possibilities of clearing

away old differences and antagonisms through a new statement of dogmas: one that is adapted to the needs of a vastly
changed world and thus renders those doctrines more meaningful and relevant to modern man. This is the updating or
the *aggiornamento*, which Pope John XXIII stressed so frequently. This calls for increasing use of the dialogue among
all Christians and for face-to-face encounters on all levels.
Crowning all our needs is that for greater understanding,
good will, sympathy, brotherhood, and love. When these are
present few, if any, are the problems which can't, with God's
grace, constant prayer, and endless patience, be satisfactorily
solved. If they are lacking, no problem, no matter how simple, can be solved.

Only incidental references are made to the Orthodox
Churches of the East. This is not because the union of the
Christian Churches of the East with those of the West is not
of paramount importance and concern, but simply because
the factors in that problem are considerably different from
those involved in the West. A whole volume would be
needed to do justice to that problem, and the attempt to treat
it here would only blur the picture of the efforts of Protestants, Anglicans, and Roman Catholics to take at least some
steps toward unity. Perhaps in a later volume we may undertake the other task.

To get the most out of this book and to become an effective worker for the great cause of Christian unity, however,
one must do more than read, study, and reflect upon these
ideas. He must supplement his reading with prayer—sincere,
fervent, and persistent—for only with God's guidance and
infinite help can the consummation so greatly desired by
Christ and all Christians be achieved. What is impossible for
men is possible for God, and through prayer His power becomes our own.

STEPS TO CHRISTIAN UNITY

"We do not intend to conduct a trial of the past; we do not want to prove who was right or who was wrong. The blame is on both sides. All we want is to say: 'Let us come together. Let us make an end of our divisions.'"

John XXIII to Observers at Vatican Council II

John A. O'Brien

Research Professor of theology at the University of Notre Dame, John A. O'Brien took his A.B. at St. Viator College and later studied at the University of Chicago, Catholic University of America, and the University of Mexico, and received his Ph.D. from the University of Illinois. He did postdoctoral work at Oxford University, England. He established the Newman Foundation at the University of Illinois, the largest in the United States, where he conducted accredited courses in religion for university students of all faiths.

Dr. O'Brien is the author of some fifteen books on philosophy, theology, and education, some of which have been translated into many foreign languages. Among his best-known works are *The Faith of Millions* and *Truths Men Live By*. He has edited eight books, among the best-known of which is *The Road to Damascus*, published in many languages. His article, "Fulfilling the American Dream," was awarded the George Washington Honor Medal by the Freedoms Foundation, Inc.

While serving as director of the Newman Foundation at the University of Illinois, he received an award from the Acacia Fraternity, composed exclusively of Protestants, in appreciation of his influence in promoting understanding and good will among students of all faiths on the campus. In 1953 the St. Joseph County, Indiana, Ministerial Association presented him with a Testimonial Letter of Gratitude for his action in defending Protestant ministers against sweeping charges of Communism.

His articles, "Why Do Our Religions Fight Each Other?" in *Look*, "Can Christians Unite?" in *The Saturday Evening Post*, and "Are You Fair to Jews?" in *Notre Dame Magazine* attracted nationwide attention. For a decade Father O'Brien served as Catholic Co-chairman of the Commission on Religious Organizations of the National Conference of Christians and Jews, which seeks to foster understanding and good will among people of different creeds, races, and colors.

A NEW ERA

"We're hearing a great deal these days about Christian unity. The newspapers and magazines are carrying many stories about ecumenical gatherings and the new friendliness and warmth between Protestants and Catholics. A virtual revolution has taken place and we seem to be living in a new era. When did it all start and what's behind it all? Is there any chance of it succeeding and, if so, when?"

Such are the thoughts and questions in the minds of millions of people in all the countries of Christendom. They deserve the attention of theologians, Scriptural scholars, and churchmen. If the ecumenical movement is to succeed, it must be rooted in the hearts and minds of the people. They must not only understand it but also be heart and soul in favor of it.

This fact is demonstrated by the failure of the efforts to heal the Eastern Schism, the separation of the greater part of the Eastern Catholic Church from the Catholic Church of the West under the Roman Pontiff in 1054. Temporary reunions were effected by the Second Council of Lyons in 1274 and the Council of Florence in 1439. The agreement worked out by the theologians and church leaders on both sides was not, however, carried in sufficient detail to the masses on both sides. Neither was it properly woven into their thought, actions, habits, and practices. Hence it did not have the wide and solid base to make the agreement a lasting one.

While the matter was a complex one involving many factors, the factor just mentioned was an important and basic one. It is therefore of the utmost importance, for the success of the current efforts to achieve Christian unity, that the thought, deliberations, and activities of the leaders be explained as clearly and as completely as possible to the rank and file.

Christ on Unity

What is the source of the efforts for Christian unity? It is undoubtedly the clear teaching of Jesus Christ, the founder of the Christian religion. In the tenth chapter of his Gospel, the Evangelist John records the words of Jesus: "I am the good shepherd, and I know mine and mine know me, even as the Father knows me and I know the Father; and I lay down my life for my sheep. And other sheep I have that are not of this fold. Them also I must bring, and they shall hear my voice, and there shall be one fold and one shepherd."

So fundamental and important was the unity of his followers that Our Lord returns to this theme on the night before He died. In His prayer to His Father, as the Evangelist John records it in the seventeenth chapter, Jesus said: "Yet not for these [the disciples] only do I pray, but for those also who through their word are to believe in me, that all may be one, even as thou, Father, in me and I in thee; that they also may be one in us, that the world may believe that thou hast sent me. And the glory that thou hast given me, I have given to them, that they may be one, even as we are one: I in them and thou in me; that they may be perfected in unity, and that the world may know that thou hast sent me, and that thou hast loved them even as thou hast loved me."

These are among the most earnest and impressive words that ever fell from the Saviour's lips. They were uttered at one of the most solemn moments in His life. Their meaning is so clear as to allow no grounds for dispute. They are being read today, as they have been for centuries, from every Christian pulpit. They are taught in every Sunday school and in every Christian college and seminary. They are a basic, integral, and inseparable part of the teachings of our divine Redeemer. They are woven into the consciousness of every Christian and are an inescapable part of the message of every herald of the Gospel.

Running like threads of gold through the warp and woof of the New Testament, this teaching of our Lord concerning the paramount importance and necessity of unity of faith among His followers is echoed and re-echoed by the great Apostle to the Gentiles. Thus in his letter to the Ephesians, fourth chapter, Paul says: "I therefore, the prisoner in the Lord, exhort you to walk in a manner worthy of the calling with which you were called, with all humility and meekness, with patience, bearing with one another in love, careful to preserve the unity of the Spirit in the bond of peace: one body and one Spirit, even as you were called in one hope of your calling; one Lord, one faith, one Baptism; one God and Father of all, who is above all, and throughout all, and in us all."

This then is the teaching of Jesus which provides the *incentive* and the *motive power* for the worldwide movement for Christian unity. His words are indelibly written in the memory of every Christian; they haunt the consciences of all his followers and especially the conscience of every Christian minister. They cause him to squirm and writhe in pain and agony as he looks at the appalling disunity of Christians, which Dr. Peter Ainslee, a Protestant minister in Baltimore, long ago called the "scandal of Christendom."

Striking evidence that the masses of the Christian people are aware that the present disunity is contrary to Christ's plan and are uneasy about it is cited by Hartzell Spence. In gathering material for his book on the different religions in the U.S.A., he spent three years and traveled 205,577 miles. He talked with people of different faiths in all walks of life. What do you think was the question most frequently put to him? It was in substance: "Do you think there is any likelihood of the Christian Churches reuniting into one great

Church, and thus freeing themselves and us from the bewildering variety of denominations and sects which now exist?"

A person who has lost a leg, arm, or hand not infrequently experiences sensations in the nerves at the end of the severed limb, which he feels as though they are coming from the lost member. So the corporate mind of the Christian people experiences sensations of painful regret and wistful yearning, which seem to emanate from the lost members of their body—the fragmented Body of Christ.

Efforts to Achieve Protestant Unity

When did the movement for Christian unity begin? It was inherent in the Church from the day it was founded by Christ and expressed itself all through the centuries. When divisions occurred, they entailed a pain in the Church, the Body of Christ, similar to that of the amputation of a limb. Nontheological factors often played a large, if not the major, role in severing unity. Prominent among these factors has been inflamed nationalism, the great enemy of all international organizations. This was true in the Western Schism, the Eastern Schism, and in the great upheaval and fragmentation of Christendom in the sixteenth century.

The modern ecumenical movement had its beginnings in the concern of Protestant leaders, dismayed at the spectacle of more than 350 denominations, to heal its many wounds. The meeting of the World Missionary Conference at Edinburgh in 1910 is generally regarded as the starting point. This was followed by the Conference on Work and Life at Stockholm in 1925 and by the Conference on Faith and Order at Lausanne in 1927. At Amsterdam in 1948 a giant step was taken in the establishment of the World Council of Churches: a loose federation that now includes 201 Protestant and Orthodox bodies in some fifty countries, representing about three hundred million members.

A resonant sounding board of Protestant opinion, the

World Council of Churches, has sponsored extensive studies of the nature of Church unity and the means to attain it. At the Evanston assembly in 1954, the Committee on Faith and Order submitted a special report, "Our Oneness in Christ and Our Disunity as Churches."

The report stressed the following points: 1. The present evident reality among the Churches is disunity, which is an inevitable consequence of the depravity of human nature. 2. Nevertheless the Christian Churches may be said to have unity because their head, Christ, is one. This unity, though now invisible, will be made manifest by Christ at the time of His second coming. 3. Repentance and submission to the guidance of the Holy Spirit through sacred Scripture were urged upon the Churches in their pursuit of visible unity.

The report made by the Faith and Order Conference at Oberlin three years later presented no definite concept of the nature of Christian unity. It declared, however, that Protestant unity of spirit is seeking organizational expression in a fellowship of good works and intercommunion rather than in unity of belief, worship, and structure.

What then are the net results of Protestant ecumenical efforts from the first meeting at Edinburgh in 1910 to the Third Assembly of the World Council of Churches in New Delhi in 1961? They may be summarized as follows: 1. On the basis of such common denominators as belief in sacred Scripture, the rites of baptism and the Lord's Supper, the operations of the ministry and the fellowship of good works, some progress in mutual relations has been achieved. 2. Ecumenical efforts have led to the establishment of the World Council of Churches, other councils in different countries, and a number of agencies (more than twenty in the U.S.A.) having ecumenical connections, purposes, and activities. 3. They have achieved the merger of some Christian bodies, encouraged practices of intercommunion, and have secured some cooperation among various denominations but no essential unity.

Eager to get things done and to see tangible results, Americans are apt to think that the ecumenical efforts have yielded rather meager results. It must be remembered, however, that some of these differences in doctrine and in polity stem from shortly after the Reformation, and others are also of long standing. Nevertheless, the last few decades have witnessed the merger of about a score of denominations in this country, and other still larger mergers are now pending. The proponents of such mergers point out that the present wasteful duplication of Church structures and organizational machinery and personnel mean that the Church expenditures are multiplied about tenfold.

Indeed, the leaders of American Protestantism are virtually unanimous in decrying the mushrooming of denominational Churches in areas where one or two would amply suffice. Dr. Martin E. Marty, associate editor of the *Christian Century*, expresses the prevailing viewpoint when he says: "In competitive denominationalism there is little that is legitimate: by its nature self-serving and self-seeking, the approach to Church life which models itself on a 'free enterprise' business motif necessarily amounts to 'presenting ourselves' and not Jesus Christ."

Speaking of the folly and the tragedy of denominational overlapping in evangelical Protestantism in North America, Charles Clayton Morrison, former editor of the *Christian Century*, said: "The way to end Protestant sectarianism is for denominations to *cease being Churches*. It is their absurd and arrogant assumption of the ecclesiastical character and functions of the One Holy Catholic Apostolic Church that is the locus [occasion] of our sectarianism and the sin of our disunity which the ecumenical spirit deplores and with which it cannot live."

Missionary Efforts Frustrated by Disunity

Another powerful factor which has stimulated the efforts of Protestants to achieve unity is the magnitude of the problems confronting their missionaries in foreign lands. The natives are often bewildered and confused at the spectacle of missionaries all claiming to preach the religion of Christ while they differ so widely as to what its doctrines are.

The divided and conflicting character of such Christianity is so apparent even to the primitive peoples of New Guinea that they recently requested its competing emissaries to stay out. "The ex-cannibals of the world," commented British Congregational minister Cecil Northcott, "are teaching us a Christian lesson: can we not cease to be *cannibals* among ourselves? Instead of eating together at the common table we tend to eat one another in a kind of blasphemous competition."

Catholics Begin Unity Movement

The movement for unity among Protestants thus arose from the efforts to heal their numerous divisions and developed for several decades outside the mainstream of Catholic interest. In this vast communion embracing members in all the countries of the world, there is unity in faith, in worship, and in the acknowledgment of the same supreme spiritual authority. Nevertheless, Catholic leaders could not look out at a divided Christendom without realizing that this is contrary to God's plan and to the express wish of Christ for unity among all his followers. Here is the cause of the gnawing pain in the Mystical Body of Christ.

During World War II Catholic priests and Lutheran ministers, sharing the same cells in Nazi prisons and concentration camps, found themselves praying to the same Lord and finding in Him their comfort and strength. They were reading the same Scriptures and frequently saying the same prayers.

In the ordeal of war, imprisonment, and suffering they came to realize how much they have in common and the stark tragedy of the circumstances that divide them.

A new friendliness and warmth marked their relations after the war. The *Una Sancta* movement fostered that friendship and promoted a dialogue, through which they have found increasing ways to cooperate and to grow in mutual respect and esteem. The dynamism of the movement is confidence in the power of Christ, Who transformed water into wine at the wedding feast of Cana in Galilee, to transform many into one. With the warm approval of Pius XII, headquarters for a similar movement, *Unitas*, were established in Rome under the leadership of Father Charles Boyer, S.J., an ecumenical scholar of international reputation. In Belgium, Holland, Switzerland, and France, discussions between Protestant and Catholic scholars concerning possibilities of unity are taking place with increasing frequency.

Since 1916 the Octave for Christian Unity from January 18 to 25, which originated in the United States in 1908, was extended to the universal Church. During that time Catholics are encouraged to pray earnestly for the unity of all the followers of Christ. The acknowledgment of their guilt in hindering such unity by their worldliness, disedifying example, pride, and lack of charity are mirrored in the following words of the litany recited during that octave, especially in the churches of Europe.

"For controversies marked by irony, suspicion and exaggeration, for lack of understanding, for unfeeling judgment concerning our non-Catholic brethren. Forgive us, O Lord. For the acts of violence and the injustices we have tolerated in the course of history against our Protestant brethren. Forgive us, O Lord. For proud complacent attitudes shown in times past towards our Orthodox brethren, and for our present indifference to them. Forgive us, O Lord."

Gets Movement Off the Launching Pad

It was not until 1959, however, that the movement for the unity of all Christians took on new stature, importance, and meaning. On January 25 of that year a seventy-seven-year-old Pope, who had been elected less than three months before—many thought as merely an interim Pontiff—astonished the world by announcing that he would convoke an Ecumenical Council, one of whose chief purposes would be the advancement of Christian unity. The Pope implemented his announcement by setting up a Secretariat for Promoting Christian Unity, and inviting Protestant and Orthodox officials as observers.

This caught the imagination of the world. After almost four years of careful preparation, Vatican Council II opened on October 11, 1962. More than half a million people packed St. Peter's Square to watch over twenty-five hundred prelates from all countries march into St. Peter's Basilica for the inaugural session. Two days later, at a special audience for the delegate-observers and guests, representing seventeen Orthodox and Protestant Churches, Pope John said: "There burns in my heart the intention of working and suffering to hasten the hour when for all men the prayer of Jesus at the Last Supper (for unity) will have reached its fulfillment."

The Pope's unfailing kindness, gentleness, humility, warmth, and spontaneity won the hearts of all. The most privileged of all attending the Council, the non-Roman Catholic delegates and guests were given choice seats and provided with all the documents used in the discussions. They alone were provided with interpreters, who translated into their respective languages the talks of the Council Fathers. They mingled freely at the coffee bar with the bishops, cardinals, and the theological and Scriptural consultants, with all of whom they discussed the matters treated in the Council.

Their opinions were not only welcomed but also solicited,

so that they quite rightly felt that they were not mere passive onlookers but actual, though indirect, participants in the deliberations. The Council Fathers took cognizance of their presence and not a few in their talks saluted them as *carissimi observatores*—dearest observers. As the observers point out in their articles, they all felt that their opinions and views were being considered by the Council Fathers and were not without influence in affecting the decisions.

Pope John and his Unity Council, as it has come to be called, were thus the factors which galvanized the ecumenical movement into new life and vigor. They lifted the movement off the launching pad, held it before the eyes of the world, and then got it clicking in practically every country. Pope Paul VI has continued the same policy and program as his predecessor. Indeed, his trip to the Holy Land, where he met some of the Orthodox leaders and discussed in a warm and friendly manner the possibility of further steps to Christian unity, has added a new dimension of depth to the movement. Not only all Christians but all men and women who esteem peace and concord saw in it the harbinger of better things to come.

Albert Cardinal Meyer

Albert Cardinal Meyer, Archbishop of Chicago, the largest archdiocese in the U.S.A. with more than two million Catholics, is one
of the outstanding scholars in the American hierarchy and a leader
in the ecumenical movement. Born in Milwaukee, Wisconsin, on
March 9, 1903, Albert Meyer studied at St. Francis Seminary in
Milwaukee and at the North American College in Rome, where he
was ordained in 1926. After ordination, he continued his studies in
Rome, receiving the doctorate in sacred theology, and three years
later the licentiate in Sacred Scripture from the Pontifical Biblical
Institute.

After his return to this country, the young priest spent a year in
pastoral work in Waukesha, Wisconsin, and then was assigned to
teach Biblical archaeology and dogmatic theology at St. Francis
Seminary, where he himself had studied for the priesthood. In 1937
he was appointed rector. In 1938 he was made a domestic prelate
and eight years later was appointed Bishop of Superior, Wisconsin.
His administrative ability as well as his scholarly attainments were
recognized by Pope Pius XII, who appointed him Archbishop of
Milwaukee in 1953.

While there he was elected the president general of the National
Catholic Educational Association. Commenting upon his regime in
Milwaukee, the New York *Times* said: "He has not dealt with
every administration detail personally, but when a crisis has arisen
and a decision needed to be made, the archbishop has made it and
remained calm and good tempered." Besides being an able administrator, Archbishop Meyer was widely acclaimed by the people of
Milwaukee as "a most fatherly bishop to his people and his priests."

In September 1958 he was appointed Archbishop of Chicago, and
in the following year was elevated by Pope John XXIII to membership in the Sacred College of Cardinals. While in Chicago the archbishop has become a leader in the struggle for civil rights and,
largely under his initiative, there was held the First National Conference on Religion and Race in January 1963, which has proved
so influential in directing the energy and influence of all the

Churches in support of civil and human rights. The cardinal's forth-right stand on race relations caused *America* to cite it as "shining proof that the mantle of leadership has indeed fallen on resolute shoulders." Testifying before the President's Commission on Civil Rights when it visited Chicago in May 1958, the archbishop said: "Gradualism would be merely a cloak for inaction if we do not turn our immediate attention to the legitimate claims of middle class Negroes who wish to leave the ghetto."

He is convinced that religion must be translated into one's daily life. "Religion cannot be separated from life," he said. "The Christian Gospel applies to politics, business, social and domestic life." The cardinal's uncompromising stand against racial inequality in housing has been widely acclaimed by citizens of all faiths, races, and colors.

Tall, slender, and kindly, Cardinal Meyer is scholarly and ascetic in appearance. The habits of prayer, meditation, and study, formed during his long years in the seminary, have continued into his busy life as the administrator of his large archdiocese, which comprises the largest Catholic school system in the world. During the sessions of Vatican Council II, Cardinal Meyer was one of the leading spokesmen for the American hierarchy and his calm, temperate, and scholarly views exercised a great influence upon the thinking of the Council, while his addresses and pastoral letters have been of great influence in shaping the direction of the Catholic ecumenical move-ment in the United States.

THE SCANDAL OF
A DIVIDED CHRISTENDOM

From the earliest times, tendencies toward disunion have existed among Christ's followers. In the year A.D. 50, the Apostles under the leadership of Peter assembled in Jerusalem to refute the opinion of those who claimed that Christians were bound to observe the law of circumcision. St. Paul, to whom we owe the sublime hymn of charity in Chapter 13 of his First Letter to the Corinthians, found it necessary at times to speak with strong and even harsh words. In this same letter he said: "What is your wish? Shall I come to you with a rod, or in love and in the spirit of meekness?"

Both in the words of our Lord and of St. Paul we see the spirit of a severe attitude toward those who cause these scandals. The reason for this severity is ultimately none other than love, a jealous love, above all, for the purity of doctrine. The Apostles were made authorized witnesses, responsible for the preservation and the faithful transmission of that to which they were to testify; not only were they to transmit faithfully, but also to control what they have transmitted, that it may be preserved without alterations.

To this very grave obligation imposed on the Apostles and heads of the Church to be faithful in the preservation and transmission of doctrine, which is an obligation intended to preserve the unity of faith, there corresponds on the part of their subjects, the faithful, the obligation of following the masters, accepting their doctrine and submitting themselves to the orders they promulgate. It is the jealous love of the unity in faith, therefore, together with the responsibility of protecting the faithful against error in faith, that made the Apostle Paul say and write such strong words: "And if anyone does not obey our word by this letter, note that man and do not associate with him, that he may be put to shame." This same spirit of love of truth, love of unity, love of faithful souls, and love also of erring souls has constantly animated the authority of the Church to be vigilant concerning the purity of doctrine in order to protect the faithful from every dangerous influence.

This is why the Church has always insisted that the faithful should take care not to offend against revealed doctrine and the norms of the Church even in discussions and collaboration between Catholics and non-Catholics. Throughout the entire work for union one must take diligent care, therefore, of the soundness of one's own faith, and of the integrity of Catholic dogma, aspiring always to the sublime goal proposed to us by St. Paul that all may attain "to the unity of the faith and of the deep knowledge of the Son of God, to perfect manhood, to the mature measure of the fullness of Christ."

When we speak of the scandal of a divided Christendom, we must be careful to remember that severity toward error must be rooted in love for those who are in error. The severe texts of the New Testament, previously mentioned, concern those who personally and consciously detached themselves from the real faith and from obedience to the Church of Christ. The scandal of a divided Christendom of today represents the heritage transmitted through long centuries of division. In the same way that it is no credit of ours to have been born and educated in a family belonging to the Catholic Church, neither is it to the discredit of others that they are sons of parents separated from the Church.

That is why the late Pope John XXIII could say in his very first address: "With fervent fatherly love, we embrace the Universal Church, the Eastern and the Western alike. And we open heart and arms to all who are separated from this Apostolic See, where Peter himself lives in his successors, even to the consummation of the world, fulfilling the command of Jesus Christ to bind and loose upon earth and to feed the Lord's entire flock. . . . We pray therefore that all may come willingly and gladly. . . . No strange house will they find but their own."

Again, when we speak of the scandal of a divided Christendom, we must also remember the great patrimony which we share in common. While we deplore that which still divides us, we must not fail to recognize more and more that which already unites us. Among Eastern Rite Christians, for example, we find a regular Apostolic succession of their bishops, and with this, valid sacraments, particularly the Holy Eucharist and the Mass, which should be the great bond of unity. In their doctrine they preserve the ancient and patristic tradition. The veneration of the Most Blessed Virgin Mary is also dear to them. Among our Protestant brothers we find an ardent attachment to Jesus as Lord and Saviour, a great veneration of the Word of God, and the serious effort to observe the commandments of God in their daily life, which often put many of us to shame.

Most important of all, when we speak of the fact of a divided Christendom, we cannot simply quote the words of our Lord, "for it must needs be that scandals come," and complacently decide that nothing can be done about it. In the most solemn moment of His life, Jesus Christ prayed that His followers might be one, as He and His Father are one, with a most intimate religious unity.

When we see Christians still deeply divided after so many centuries, we begin to realize that, although we may be accustomed to these divisions and even complacent about them, Christ is deeply concerned, and at the judgment we shall have to answer Him for our complacency. We must take a warning from the barren fig tree which produced many green leaves, but no fruit, and which received Christ's curse.

If, therefore, the Lord himself confers grace on our separated brethren who are in good faith, and if the Church admonishes us to help them with fervent prayers, we also must embrace them with true and supernatural charity, of which the late Pope John and our present Holy Father, Pope Paul, have given us such magnificent examples. From this charity there will spring above all a real and ardent zeal for union and the fervent prayer for it, the understanding of this unity which is so very necessary, the conquest of resentment and false prejudices, a reciprocal, sincere esteem. The only caution that we must follow is this: our charity must remain in every way authentic, that is to say, absolutely faithful to the whole truth of Christ, and of His spouse the Church, according to the words of St. Paul: "For we can do nothing against the truth, but only for the truth."

Following, therefore, the teaching of the Church, we can never fail to take an interest in our separated brothers. The unity of the Church, willed by her divine Founder himself, is like the other marks of the Church—sanctity, catholicity, and apostolicity—an essential trait. But in its positive reality, unity is not yet complete, not perfect, but needs our work to make it ever more full, to overcome victoriously all obstacles and difficulties.

The life of the Church in the past fifty years has been characterized in a special way by three great movements: the eucharistic-liturgical movement, that of Catholic Action, and that of the missions. Together with them, the movement which is now commonly called "ecumenical" has developed ever more strongly, today assuming truly great proportions. It is important for all of us that we understand this movement accurately, and according to our ability and position in the Church also participate in it.

What Is Ecumenism?

What will help to heal these wounds of Christian division so that Christ's prayer for unity in His Church may be fulfilled? Under the inspiration and gentle urging of the Holy Spirit, there is growing in the Church today a great movement toward reunion. It is expressed by the word *ecumenism*.

This word is derived from the Greek word which is practically equivalent to the word *catholic*, and both of them carry the meaning of *universal* or *worldwide*. Vatican Council II is an outstanding manifestation of this universality.

We call the present Council "ecumenical" because, through the bishops, all parts of the worldwide Catholic Church are represented. The Catholic Church is truly an "ecumenical" Church, that is, unified in faith, sacraments, and authority throughout the world. In this sense, the Council of bishops is truly and essentially ecumenical and represents Christ's ecumenical, or catholic, Church. Yet it lacks the perfection of ecumenicity which would be present if all those who wish to acknowledge the supremacy of God and who wish to follow Christ were united in it as one single witness.

The Council is truly and essentially ecumenical because it consists of the bishops of the ecumenical Church, yet it strives for a more perfect ecumenicity in which all who seek God and Christ may be united. Pope Paul VI says: "The Council aims at complete and universal ecumenicity." It opens the door and calls to men of good will, to all who seek closer union in Christ.

Ecumenism, as defined by Father George Tavard, is "the movement of thought and action which is concerned with the reunion of Christians." Since Christians are grouped in communities, or "Churches," one level of communication will be between the Churches themselves, and of this level Father Gustave Weigel, S.J., remarked: "The ecumenical movement is not an arena for the triumph of one Church over another. It is a fraternal confrontation of divided but brother Christians. . . . It is not the purpose of the ecumenical dialogue to make conversions. It is an effort of Christian love to give and receive witness to the Gospel." In this spirit, non-Catholic observers were invited to attend the sessions of the Vatican Council in order that they might find out the teachings and the opinions of the Church's bishops.

The Dutch theologian, Father Edward Schillebeeckx, O.P.,

defined ecumenism of the individual level: "In my opinion the word 'ecumenical' should describe an attitude of mind attuned in faith to a visible unity, not only of love and hope but also of faith, among all people who confess Christ as Lord, and in fact more generally among all people who acknowledge religious values in human life." Not only is ecumenism a general movement in the Church, it is also an attitude of mind and heart on the part of each Catholic and Christian, an attitude which should express itself in a resolve to act.

To attain this attitude of mind and heart we must listen to Christ's prayer for unity uttered at the Last Supper as a prayer coming from the depths of His Sacred Heart, a prayer that He said aloud because He wishes His Apostles and all His future followers to take it to their own hearts and so make His prayer their own desire and prayer: "that they may be one in us." We who accept Our Divine Lord's teachings through the gift of faith also accept His prayer for unity through that same gift of faith.

If the unity of Christians seems humanly impossible, this should not discourage us. "What is impossible to man's power is possible to God." We know through faith that to fulfill the desire of Christ's heart we must pray and work for Christian unity. "For everyone who asks receives; and he who seeks finds." To this prayer and work of ours Christ will add the divine power of His grace, so that the unity of Christians will be effected in God's good time.

This Christian unity we seek is not just any kind of unity, not the unity of a crowd watching a basketball game, nor of students listening to a lecture, nor of workers under the same factory roof. We seek the religious unity which Christ prayed for, which he compared to the mysterious unity existing between Himself and His Father, "that they may be one in us."

This is a visible unity of men with each other, yet is not a mere human organization such as a business corporation or a political alliance between nations, for these are produced by mere human organizing ability. Although it is visible, it is not merely a unity of brotherhood and friendliness, such as a fraternal lodge; nor like many organizations for religious tolerance and cooperation, although these are praiseworthy. Nor is it merely a spiritual union in which Christians are united in a genuine love of Christ and hope for mutual salvation and nothing more.

We seek a genuine unity in divine faith in Christ, since only on this firm foundation can divine hope and charity abide in permanence. This unity of faith, accepting the fullness of God's revelation in Christ, allows great diversity in other matters. Those who attend Mass in one of the Catholic Eastern rites will recognize many differences in its liturgy when compared to Mass in the Latin rite, yet the same sacrifice is offered, and the worshipers acknowledge the same spiritual authority of the Vicar of Christ on earth.

"This unity, at once hidden and visible," says Pope Paul VI, "cannot be realized save in the identity of faith, participation in the same sacraments and the proper harmony of a single ecclesiastical direction, even though this allows for a great variety of verbal expressions, sacred rites and ancient customs, lawful institutions and ways of life." The marvelous unity of worship amid the splendor of various liturgical rites celebrated by Holy Mother Church strikingly illustrates the Pope's words.

Ecumenism is an attitude of mind and heart which moves us to look toward our separated Christian brethren with respect, understanding, and hope: with respect, because we recognize them as brothers in Christ and regard them as friends rather than opponents; with understanding, because we seek to find the divine truths we share in common, as well as recognize honestly the differences in faith that lie between us; with hope, that we may grow together in a more perfect knowledge and love of God and Christ. We seek the truth in charity, not in a spirit of rival sectarianism. We seek dialogue, not debate.

This ecumenical spirit should not restrict itself to our separated brothers, but should look beyond them to "all people who acknowledge religious values." It should look to the Jews, with whom we have a common bond in our spiritual father, Abraham; we who are spiritual Semites have a common heritage with the sons of Abraham who follow the law of Moses. This spirit also directs our attention toward the followers of Mohammed, who believe in the same God and share many of the same prophets as do we.

It looks even farther, to all the Oriental religions which bear witness to the claims of the absolute Being upon Whom we depend. Finally, it looks to those who are repelled by organized religion but who nevertheless acknowledge God as the Supreme Being, explicitly or even implicitly by their respect for the true dignity of man. The true ecumenical spirit seeks whatever religious values and truths we may have in common with other men.

Practical Application

To know about ecumenism is not enough, unless we also have the resolve to put our knowledge into daily practice. Again Pope Paul gives valuable advice: "If we are in any way to blame for that separation, we humbly beg God's forgiveness, and ask pardon too from our brethren who feel themselves to have been injured by us. For our part, we willingly forgive the injuries which the Catholic Church has suffered, and forget the grief endured during the long series of dissensions and separations. May the heavenly Father deign to hear our prayers and grant us true brotherly peace."

Many of our own sins may have prolonged the separation of Christians, or even aggravated it: sins of indifference, contempt, self-righteousness, arrogance, prejudice, false-witness, scandal, by which we may have offended others and held them away from unity in the Church. Perhaps we have been indifferent to the welfare of other Christians in our neighborhood or community, perhaps we have held those outside our Church in contempt, wrapping ourselves in our own self-righteousness. Prejudice may have closed our eyes to the religious goodness in our neighbor; perhaps our deceitfulness or failure to live up to our Catholic obligations has scandalized those who are outside the Church and has held them aloof. This is a time for serious examination of conscience.

For a good examination of conscience we ought to know what actions to do and what to avoid, as well as to learn what we have in common with our Christian brothers. Reading and study about the historical divisions of Christianity are valuable aids to this. In all study and discussion it is essential to remember that ecumenism is best served not by compromising the principles of our Catholic faith, but by explaining "the reasons for the hope that is in you," and by respecting, without agreeing in all aspects, with the faith of our Christian brother.

Good works must accompany knowledge, for knowledge in the mind is sterile unless the heart puts it into practice. Pope Paul himself has given the example by his pilgrimage to Jerusalem, a journey undertaken as a good work to implore God's blessing upon the cause of Christian unity. To attain this understanding of our separated brethren and to work effectively toward Christian unity, we need prayer above all else. Christian unity is only possible through the help of God's grace, and God's grace is given through prayer, especially through the united prayer of the members of His Mystical Body, the Church.

Our Lord at the Last Supper repeated to His Apostles: "Whatsoever you ask the Father in my name, he will give it to you." No better prayer is possible than our united prayer as a community in the Sacrifice of the Eucharist as we attend Mass on Sundays or during the week, for then Christ in a most perfect way fulfills His promise, "Where two or three are gathered together in my name, there am I in the midst of them." In this sacrifice, we join in Christ's own prayer for unity, an intention beautifully expressed by the prayer in the votive Mass for the Unity of the Church:

"O God, who leads back to the true path those who have wandered, and who gathers those who have dispersed, and keeps together those whom you have gathered: we pray thee, mercifully pour out on thy Christian people the grace of union, that having put away all division and being converted to the true Shepherd of thy Church, they may serve thee worthily, through Christ our Lord."

Franklin H. Littell

Dr. Franklin H. Littell, professor of Church History at Chicago Theological Seminary, has long been active in the ecumenical movement. Born on June 20, 1917, in Syracuse, New York, he studied at Cornell College and at Union Theological Seminary and received his Ph.D. from Yale University and his doctorate in theology from the University of Marburg. He served as minister of youth at the Central Methodist Church in Detroit and subsequently became director of Lane Hall at the University of Michigan.

Later he spent nearly a decade in Germany as religious affairs and educational officer for the U. S. Government and an educational foundation. At one time he was chief Protestant adviser on the staff of the U. S. High Commissioner for Germany. He is a consultant on religion and higher education to the National Conference of Christians and Jews.

A Methodist, Dr. Littell has represented his own Church in the dialogue and in ecumenical affairs for many years. He was a delegate to the World Conference of Christian Youth in Amsterdam in 1939, and an observer at the third session at Vatican Council II. He is a member of the Notre Dame Colloquium and on the editoral board of a number of magazines, including *The Journal of Ecumenical Studies* and *The Journal of Bible and Religion*.

A Church historian, Dr. Littell has taught on several faculties before coming to Chicago. He has given important lectures at Texas Christian University, Michigan State University, Bethany Theological Seminary, and Baylor University. He was a featured speaker at the National Institute on Religious Freedom and Public Affairs held in Washington in 1962, at the National Conference on Religion and Race held in Chicago in 1963, at the Biennial Assembly of the Union of American Hebrew Congregations in Chicago, and at the plenary session of the Quadrennial Convention of the National Council of Churches in Philadelphia.

He has also addressed the clerical faculty of the University of Notre Dame. A specialist in Church History, he has written many articles for scholarly journals and is the author of numerous books.

Chief among these are *The Anabaptist View of the Church*, which received the Brewer Award of the American Society of Church History in 1952, *From State Church to Pluralism*, and *The Free Church*, and he is the co-editor of *Weltkirchenlexikon Handbuch der Ockumena*, a handbook on world Christian affairs. In 1939 he married Harriet D. Lewis, and they are the parents of four children.

A NEW LOOK AT
THE SIXTEENTH CENTURY

From Johannes Cochlaeus and his *Commentaries on the Action and Writings of Martin Luther* in 1549 to Josef Lortz and his *Reformation in Germany* in 1939, Catholic interpretation of the Reformation has shifted from outraged polemic to critical but perceptive irenic. The Luther who less than a century ago was still a "false prophet," "a liar and deceiver," a man of "sin-laden life," is now recognized as an *homo religiosus*, even "a great Christian man of prayer."

In the change of climate, most notable since the accession of Pope John XXIII of blessed memory, it seems only appropriate that the efforts of Catholic colleagues to understand the Reformers as something other than instigators of world calamity should be met by an equal openness of face. Very little attempt has been made so far to deal with the realities of our common and separate histories in a way responsive to the new mutualities in Biblical studies, liturgies, and social ethics, including the encounter with totalitarianism. In the final analysis, our growing rapprochement will be doomed to shatter perhaps mysteriously, perhaps for reasons which escape even the perception of scholars, unless we gain an understanding of Church History quite different from those presently obtaining.

Did Protestants split off from Roman Catholicism? Do St. Francis and St. Thomas belong to our common heritage? Or did Christendom become so corrupt that continuity of doctrine and order was utterly lost, and the "True Church" could only be recovered from the "Fall" by "restitution"— by grafting new shoots upon the stump of the apostolic age? Or are both our confusions, Protestant and Catholic, plunging so rapidly into a "world come of age" that only the "non-religion of the future" can provide the idiom for a "post-Christian era?"

It should be evident, I think, that only a "new Church History" with a new periodization can, when finally accepted by Catholic and Protestant scholars, seal for generations to come the fact that we have reached a new level of Christian fraternity and accept the common guilt and common grandeur of our past. And this new view is urgently needed, not only because of the challenge of the uprooted intellectuals but because of the demonic power of anti-Christian ideologies among the masses.

The Totalitarian Challenge

Both within the Churches and without, the twentieth century has become one of the most critical ages in the history of the Christian movement. Indeed, in the encounter with totalitarianism—Nazism and Communism—we have the most serious challenge to the faith since the rise of Islam over a millennium ago. At the same time, the Churches have slipped badly in Western Europe, for so long the geographical center of Christendom. In countries both Catholic and Protestant, where over 95 per cent of the population are baptized, only from 3.4 per cent to 16 per cent are practicing Christians. And even here the definition of "practicing" may be very minimal, signifying only the one confession and one communion a year required by the Fourth Lateran Council (A.D. 1215). Having neglected the proletariat and lost the intellectuals, the two most important elements in industrial society during the nineteenth century, the European Churches now find themselves in what their most sensitive interpreters call a "post-Christian era."

Modern totalitarianism is, as distinguished specialists like Gordon Zahn of Loyola, Carl Friedrich of Harvard, Arthur Cochrane of Dubuque, and the late Waldemar Gurian of Notre Dame have pointed out, qualitatively different from the older and more familiar tyrannies and despotisms. The totalitarian ideologies, whether Communist or Nazi or, for that matter, American Nativist, win their way by appeals to cloudy concepts like "positive Christianity," "progressive religion," "Christian America." And where they come to power, they win their way by the wholesale apostasy of the baptized.

Without the treason of the baptized, dialectical materialism would never have triumphed in the "Holy Russia" of Eastern Orthodoxy, Nazism would never have gained power in Germany and Europe. Neither would anti-Semites and professional anti-Catholics have such a following in the greatest intact Protestant area left in the world: the Deep South of the U.S.A. It is this fact which gives tragic dimension to the present crisis in Christendom, lends urgency to our efforts to uncover and expose the errors of the past and present, and makes imperative that we discover new ways of relating the commitments of faith to public policy.

The State-Church Pattern

It was the Peace of Augsburg (1555) and the Treaty of Westphalia (1648) which fastened upon the Western Churches that peculiar relationship of confessional and cultic conformity and governmental policy which subsequently grew demonic and led to wholesale betrayal of the Universal Lord of the Universal Church. We therefore turn to a discussion of the divisions of Latin Christendom in the sixteenth century, not as an interesting intellectual exercise but out of our dire necessity to learn who we are, and where we are, and what time it is in the unfolding of God's purpose for the peoples of the earth.

Without anticipating in too great detail the conclusions to be reached during this review, we may say that if we were to continue to draw our supplies exclusively through the long tunnels which lead back to the *Confession of Pope Pius IV*

(1564), the *Formula of Concord* (1577), and the *Canons of the Synod of Dort* (1619), our undertaking would be worse than useless and our dialogue would be silenced before it began. The three great patterns of Western establishment, Roman Catholic, Lutheran, and Calvinist, here stood fixed in mutual rejection. Each then claimed to represent exclusively the true style of Christian belief and practice, and each was officially tolerated or perhaps favored at law—the choice of preferred religion depending upon governmental policy and decision.

How then did this come about? How did governmental action, which had been conceived from the time of St. Augustine as an instrument to sustain the unity of Christendom, become decisive in accomplishing and enforcing its dividedness? What—to put the question in popular language—went wrong?

What Happened to Christendom?

There are two common misconceptions of the divisions of the sixteenth century, current among Protestants and Catholics alike, which serve to obscure our view of what really happened. In the first place, there is the view that during the Middle Ages the *Corpus Christianum* was unified and single-minded, and that this magnificent and apostolic unity was brought to an end in the sixteenth century. This view has been popularized by romantics and moralists, especially among liturgists and architects, who like to point backward to a Golden Age, as a teaching device for making their contemporaries ashamed of their degeneracy. The spirit of the Gothic revival has led us to detect our common heritage in the Latin Church: medieval studies are even coming back into Protestant seminary curriculum.

On the other hand, it has also produced a number of monstrosities such as a commercially built neo-Gothic cathedral housing a Methodist congregation in a wheat town on the Great Plains. Our common Protestant and Roman Catholic heritage in the Latin Church may well be emphasized, broadening the common basis beyond the era of the early Church and the age of the Church Fathers and ecumenical symbols. But before we plunge overboard in praise of medievalism, let us recall that in this time the ordinary communicant was expected to be silent, docile, and obedient.

As Professor Figgis has emphasized, during the Middle Ages the "Church" was for all practical purposes the professionals: the clergy and those in orders. And as Professor Thompson of Chicago put it, the life of the ordinary man was in the Middle Ages "nasty, brutish and short." For those of us who have reason to suspect that our own forefathers were hewers of wood and drawers of water, the bright colors of the primitivists' Golden Age of the medieval past tend to fade out on closer inspection.

Neither—and this is the important point—did the sixteenth century experience the division of a previously unified Christendom. If the Middle Ages were, as Professor von Ranke stressed, the time of the Christianization of the Germanic tribes, we can understand the extremely varied religious forms and practices which in fact characterized even the high Middle Ages. It is only necessary to recall that the number of the sacraments was fixed at seven as late as 1439 at the Council of Florence (1438–45), less than a hundred years before Luther's posting of the Ninety-five Theses (1517), to see the point. St. Augustine had listed formulae such as the Creed and the Lord's Prayer as "sacraments." Hugh of St. Victor (d. 1141) had enumerated as many as thirty, divided into three groups. Many of the saints had defined all Christian relationships as sacramental, a position to which the Quakers returned in the seventeenth century. As we study the forms of belief and practice in the 979 different political and ecclesiastical entities which obtained in central Europe in the Middle Ages, we are struck with their extreme variety, not with their uniformity.

Or, to consider another body of proof of variety, consider the use of the Crusades. The Crusades began as a peace movement, to turn the relentlessly warring princes toward the Muslim enemy at the gates of Europe and away from each other's throats. But they were also used in the attempt to achieve a greater uniformity in Christendom. It is difficult now to reconstruct the teachings and practices of movements such as the Bogomili or Albigenses, for we are dependent for evidence upon those who attacked and destroyed their churches and cultures.

We do learn, however, that over one hundred thousand of the Bogomili, dissident Christians in the old Bosnia and Herzegovina (now in Yugoslavia), went over to Islam rather than submit to centralization. And in the Provençal district, a crusade within Christendom reduced to a wasteland the most cultured and civilized section of France. The Middle Ages were not a period of Christian unity and uniformity. It may be true that, in a general way, most of the West was in communion with the Bishop of Rome. But most of the medieval Popes didn't work at it very much, and until the rapid development of cash economics following the discovery of America, the connection wasn't felt too keenly at the level of practical affairs.

With the reform movements before the Reformation, and in the Protestant and Catholic reformations themselves, we have an effort to achieve unity of faith and practice over wider areas than ever before. And at the end of that period, in spite of the tragic division into three major confessional blocs, there were more peoples and tribes over wider areas caught up in common confessions of faith and common cultic practices than had been previously the case. During the drive toward a general consensus of the Christians, and in collision with each other, each of these movements fell short of reforming and purifying the religious life of all western Europe. Yet we must be aware of the unitive thrust of their effort, and not merely of the painful separations which resulted and have endured to the present day.

The second misunderstanding—and here I expect less agreement than on the previous interpretation—is the widespread notion, among both Catholics and Protestants, that the Protestants split off from the Roman Catholic Church. What happened, it seems to me, was that during the intensified religious concerns of this period greater sections of Christendom were unified, but none succeeded in covering the whole of western Europe. The three forms which emerged, with Lutheranism granted legal standing in 1555 and Calvinism at the end of the Thirty Years' War (1648), represented simultaneously greater blocs of unity and more dramatic division.

The term "Protestant" first arose during the Diet of Augsburg (1530), and long after that the leaders of the reform movement claimed to represent the true tradition as given by the Scriptures and interpreted by the Early Fathers of the Church. What we Protestants call "Roman Catholicism" was established at the Council of Trent (1545–63) and defined by the canons and decrees which emerged therefrom. The theological and disciplinary conclusions reached there represented a new level of agreement, even though some Catholic governments refused to implement all of the disciplinary decrees. But it was a consensus from which the Lutherans and Calvinists, both of whom also claimed to represent the ancient and classical tradition, were excluded.

They, on their part, went on to achieve the hard and unyielding formulations of doctrine and discipline which we find in the *Formula of Concord* and *Canons of the Synod of Dort*. They too claimed to have settled for time and eternity the form of words and style of life by which Christians must be governed. What happened was that charity failed on all sides, the princes and powers interfered directly in the religious disputes for their own ends, and three incomplete expressions of consensus, which did not really represent the best mind and spirit of Christendom, were fastened upon three sections of Christendom.

All three definitive sets of formulae reckoned without God's continuing and surprising work in history. Although the theologians and the princes seemed to have fastened permanent division upon Christendom, there were spiritual forces at work which were to lead our several sections of the Christian movement to the point where dialogue is again possible across the lines. And, if I mistake not, the basic thrust of that which lies back of the sequence which runs from Edinburgh (1910) to New Delhi (1960), and has thus far informed the spirit of Vatican II, is the recovery of that truly catholic and universal tradition which forms our common heritage before the sixteenth-century fixed positions.

Post-Reformation Developments

Sustaining this recovery is the awareness of several truths which tended to be neglected during the acrimonious debates which resulted in the formal division of Western Christendom. For one thing, we have today come to be aware of the danger to sound religion of a situation where governments use or misuse confessional conformity for political purposes. Even in the sixteenth century, with the emergence of modern nationalism, the policy of such Christian princes as Philip of Hesse, Maurice of Saxony, Henry VIII of England, Francis of France, Philip II of Spain, not to mention the emperors Charles V and Ferdinand II, often involved the sacrifice of true religion to the exigencies of dynastic ambition. The principle *curius regio eius religio* meant the triumph of a certain type of toleration; but it also fastened an unhealthy, particularistic network of alliances upon the Churches which eventually corrupted the universality of the Church.

In more recent times we have seen the open heathenism of established cults, serving governments rather than the Lord of the Church, anointing the high places like low-grade

Canaanite religion rather than obeying the disciplines of the covenant, perverting religion to nationalistic or even racial purposes. The Roman Catholic Church perceived the mortal danger earlier than the Protestant state-Churches, and after the experience with the Law of Associations during the French Revolution, set out to restore the image and authority of a genuinely international communion. The subjection of Protestant establishments continued longer: it was only after World War II, for instance, that leading Lutherans like Church President Martin Niemöller and Bishop Berggrav of Norway began to challenge the control of Churches by temporal governments.

Religious Liberty

The true goal, we are coming to see, is not tolerance, which is only astute, but religious liberty, which is noble. Many Christians, of many confessions of faith and communions, are coming to understand that only that service is pleasing to God which is voluntary and uncoerced. As that awareness grows —and the principle of religious voluntaryism has more than justified itself where it has been tried—the magnificent conviction of the Great Bill of Religious Freedom of Virginia (1784) will be spread throughout the Christian world. "What is not the religion of a man's choice," said William Penn, "is the religion of him that imposes it, so that liberty of conscience is the first step to have a religion."

There were those who perceived this truth even amidst the harsh controversies and heretic-hunting of the sixteenth century, and we should by now be able to pay them the tribute due the pioneers of religious liberty. They were those to whom the key concept was *restitutio*—restitution of the Early Church—rather than *reformatio:* the so-called "Left Wing of the Reformation." Remember Caspar Schwenckfeld, who consistently urged that the cause of Christianity be advanced by the sword of the spirit which is the Word of

God rather than by the physical sword of law and political coercion.

In a letter of 1549 to Jakob Sturm at Strassburg, he wrote that "civil authority has no jurisdiction over the Kingdom of God; that government was divinely ordained for the sole purpose of maintaining an orderly life in human society, but has not right either to influence or to interfere with religious convictions; the individual is accountable to Jesus Christ as the head of the Kingdom of God." Or recall Pilgrim Marpeck, lay leader among the South German Brethren, who argued against all coercion of faith by government and all pride of party name. Unity had been one of the marks of the Early Church, and in the restitution of the True Church there were to be no "sectarian" names, only "Christian" and "brother."

To Schwenckfeld, type of the individual spiritualizers, and Marpeck, type of the Biblical Anabaptists, might be added the Catholic reformer Georg Witzel. Witzel saw in a return to the Early Church a program for Christian reform. At first he associated with the Left Wing, urging a root and branch program to be carried out along the model provided, he thought, in the Acts of the Apostles. Later, when he returned to obedience to Rome, he wrote over twenty books arguing that the common platform on which the Churches might be reunited and purified should be the ancient liturgy of the old Catholic faith.

All of the restitutionist groups were agreed that a "fall of the Church" had occurred at the time of Constantine, when Church and state were united and the suffering Christians became themselves persecutors. Periodizing history in this way, the restitutionists were articulate in insisting that the government, although necessary to punish the evil and protect the good, should not interfere at all in matters of faith.

In this respect the mainline Anabaptists anticipated the modern understanding of religious liberty, whereas those who kept to the old line of intensive cooperation between Church and state, whether Catholic, Lutheran, Calvinist, or Anglican, developed new arguments for and new methods of persecution. In this situation, the prudential policies of toleration adopted when wars of religion proved coerced conformity impossible of attainment represented some gain in decent human relations. But toleration was a long way from the religious liberty and voluntary commitment which make interreligious dialogue possible and meaningful, and of which we are the heirs in America.

Modern Missions

Second, even before the demonic misuse of religion by the modern nation-states, another important force was at work which was to help to disengage the Churches from particularistic political controls and to lift up again the vision of a truly Universal Church. This force was the rise of the modern missionary movement, which has come to full tide only in our own century. During the sixteenth and seventeenth centuries, the Catholic witness through missions, particularly in the sacrificial efforts of Jesuits and Franciscans, was far more significant than anything done by way of the Protestant state Churches. Indeed, as late as 1651 the theological faculty at Wittenberg was still condemning missions and arguing that the Great Commission was exhausted at the time of the Twelve and the Seventy.

Of course, the conquistadores of Spain and the gentlemen adventurers of England all went forth with the Christianization of the natives as a stated purpose. In practice, however, with the exception of devoted Christians such as Bartolomé de las Casas or John Eliot, even the clergy of the colonizers understood "Christianization" to mean "Europeanization." And "Europeanization" meant, at that time, fitting into the white men's plans for exploiting the fields and forests and mines by means of slave labor.

Most of the Christian work with the natives in Spain and New England, and later in Asia and Africa, was simply an extension of European culture-religion and of the politically supported and manipulated ecclesiastical offices. Even more than in the now-divided Christendom of western Europe, this use or misuse of religion hindered the development of a genuinely affirmed and indigenous Christianity.

It was the rise of the modern missionary movement which opened the way for a new appreciation of the meaning of the Universal Church. It forced the distinction between European Christendom and the claims of a Universal Church. The defensive mechanisms with which the European establishments surrounded the old settlements denied that truth. Vatican I and the Eisenach Conventions of the Evangelical Church in Germany, to mention two examples, carried on the defensive traditions of the Council of Trent and the Formula of Concord. But a Spirit was at work, drawing all men to Himself, Who was to break into the open in the ecumenical synods of the twentieth century.

Even while the ethnocentrism was working which was to end in the apostasy of millions of the baptized, and in the demonic misuse of hyphenated religion by the totalitarian ideologies of the modern age, faithful missionaries were at work in the distant corners of Africa, Asia, and the islands of the sea. And their work was carried increasingly by the free Churches. Today three-fourths of all the Protestant missionaries at work around the world are supported from America, and American Catholicism too has become the strongest single center of the Catholic world communion.

It is no longer possible for any but the most backward of Catholic or Protestant leadership to deal with present problems as though the traditional style of European state-Churches were still normative for the Christian movement. For western Europe is no longer the center of world Christianity: that center has shifted to the younger Churches, including the younger Churches of North America. And these Churches are closer to the Churches to which St. Paul wrote his epistles than they are to Constantine or Charlemagne or

Charles V, or to the wars of religion which separated the Latin Church into its present traditional sections.

We are brought to the most important single fact about our situation: the uniqueness of the American experiment in religious liberty and the shift of the American Churches, Catholic and Protestant, from identity with the European establishments to identity with the younger Churches of the mission fields. The bright morning star of the "Great Century of Christian Missions" (K. S. Latourette) has been the success of the missions, Catholic and Protestant, in North America. At the end of a century and a half of home missions, we have in America more practicing Church members, better attendance, and more general giving for Christian causes, than ever before at any time or place in two thousand years of Church History.

The Ministry of the Laity

Third, this whole development, with its many expressions in Christian service, education, and direct influence on public policy, has been marked by an activation of the frozen assets of the Churches: the enormous potential for good of an aroused and devoted laity. It is no accident, but an appropriate spiritual progression, that the ecumenical movements which began in reaction against European culture-religion, and gained courage through the impact of world missions, should today be expressed in an awareness of the tremendous power of the apostolate of the laity.

Here too we have passed beyond the point where the sixteenth-century Fathers stopped short. Luther, to be sure, spoke at times of the priesthood of all believers. But the reference was deliberately omitted in the Augustana Confession of 1530, and lacking appropriate structures, the emphasis atrophied and died. The Protestant scholastics of the second and third generation after the Reformation had neither use nor patience for lay initiative, except in princes or town councilors.

The Catholic communion had long known what to do with aroused laymen: they were channeled into the orders, there to work out their Christian service without requiring any basic changes in the Church's traditional way of doing things. With the exception, again, of tiny restitutionist movements like the Mennonites or Quakers, both Catholic and Protestant Church bodies have only recently come to give attention to the real role of the laity, as the whole believing people of God, witnessing at work in the world.

As this understanding of the nature of the Church comes to the fore, new in articulation but old in New Testament substance, those who are alert to the lay apostolate reach fraternal hands across the walls which have for four centuries divided Catholics and Protestants. They are alert to the calling of all Christians by reason of the ordination of their baptism. They read Congar's *Lay People in the Church*, Kraemer's *The Theology of the Laity*, and Neill and Weber's *The Layman in Christian History* with equal zeal. They study the publications of the Department on the Laity of the World Council of Churches and paragraphs 82–103 and 223 of *Mater et Magistra* with like enthusiasm.

In the spiritual warfare of the Christian faith with false orders of being, and in the battle for men's souls across the whole world map, the energies and commitments of the great multitude of lay people are no longer an option or a program augmentation: with them rests the whole possibility of a successful translation and implementation of the Gospel. It has pleased God in the fullness of time to raise up a whole new people out of many kindreds and tribes, created not by blood but by baptism, no longer content to be commanded as silent, docile, and obedient serfs, but rather themselves the carriers, the protagonists, of the faith. The business of those of us who are ordained to the special ministry is very simply this: to train and equip them that they may run well and faithfully the race in which their feet are set.

In none of these most important forces shaping our lives and decisions in the way of positive Christian service did either Catholic reformation or Protestant reformation make a significant contribution. Religious liberty and voluntaryism, world missions and lay apostolate, are all post-sixteenth-century developments, even though there were scattered individuals and groups who had already caught a glimpse of things to come.

The Recovery of Dialogue

Today we can perceive the real accomplishments of the sixteenth-century Fathers, even as we regret the lack of charity between parties and the confusion of political and religious concerns which fastened division upon Christendom. To have creative dialogue, to attain a renewed *consensus fidelium*, men must listen as well as talk. At a certain point in the disputes of the sixteenth century, and in spite of desperate attempts at unity at Hagenau and Worms and Regensburg (1540–41), our Fathers ceased to hear each other out. The debate was ended too soon. And then they used the coercive power of government relentlessly to enforce the imperfect and incomplete consensus for which they had severally settled.

But now, our thinking ennobled by a brighter Christian undertaking of the rights of persons and the sacredness of conscience, our vision lifted by the witness of the missions to the universality of the Church, our anticipation heightened by new evidences of lay devotion and discipline, we can press on together toward that Christian future which God has surely prepared for His people. We know that He is the One who keeps His promises, and that His plans may be fulfilled in ways most surprising even to the faithful.

As we live and work in hope, we need each other. And

we can speak openly with each other, and even serve the Least Brother together, as in the great common effort launched in January 1963 by the National Conference on Religion and Race in Chicago. Because God has given us names and faces and the spirit of liberty, we can move beyond the impasse of the sixteenth-century reformations to complete the discussions then broken off. It is of fundamental importance that most of the basic issues before Vatican II have been precisely those on which Protestants once took a position: the place and authority and use of the Bible, the meaning of lay vocations, the use of the vernacular in the liturgy. Catholic writing and discussion of these matters recently has helped some forgetful Protestants to recall their own heritage, and if it becomes a common heritage in the process, all the better. But most important of all are those factors which are post-Reformation, as already mentioned.

Of these the chief is religious liberty, and it is here that our common experience as Americans, Catholic and Protestant alike, draws us closer together in learning to witness to the values of high-level, non-manipulated religion to our co-religionists who have not yet broken cleanly from an earlier and self-defeating relationship of Church and state. Established Churches not only lack the values of voluntaryism and weaken the true base of Christian missions, they also breed militant unbelief of a kind of anti-Christian atmosphere among intellectuals which has a hard time getting a footing where affiliation is purely voluntary and bears no weight in reference to the rights of citizens at law.

"Every human being," wrote Pope John XXIII in *Pacem in Terris*, "has the right to honor God according to the dictates of an upright conscience, and therefore the right to worship God privately and publicly." True dialogue is only possible in such an area of liberty, and the most important thing about it is that it opens the way to unintimidated affirmation of the truth. There are civil benefits from religious liberty, to be sure, but these are derivative. The true

case for religious liberty is theological, deriving from a respect for the integrity of persons. And related to this is the
fact that there are some things to be discovered in open
dialogue which can be discovered and declared in no other
way.

Let us therefore press forward in growing together, in
confidence that He Who has begun to bring us out of the
sixteenth-century impasse will not abandon us now, if we
earnestly seek to know and do His truth.

Robert McAfee Brown

Few names in the ecumenical movement in the United States are better known than that of Robert McAfee Brown, Professor of Religion at Stanford University, Stanford, California. Born May 28, 1920, at Carthage, Illinois, he studied at Amherst College, Union Theological Seminary, and Columbia University, where he received his Ph.D. degree. He has done post-doctoral work at Mansfield College, Oxford, and at St. Mary's College, St. Andrews University, Scotland.

Dr. Brown served as a chaplain with the U. S. Navy and later as assistant chaplain at Amherst College. In 1951 he became Professor of Religion at Macalester College, and two years later became Auburn Professor of Systematic Theology at Union Theological Seminary. Since 1962 he has been Professor of Religion at Stanford University, and was an observer at the second session of the Vatican Council. A member of Phi Beta Kappa, the American Theological Society, and the Society for Theological Discussion, Dr. Brown serves on the editorial boards of *Christianity and Life* and *Presbyterian Life* and is a member of the Committee for Revision of the Book of Common Worship of the United Presbyterian Church of the U.S.A.

He is the author of *Observer in Rome, Prophet for Today, The Bible Speaks to You, The Significance of the Church, An American Dialogue* (with Gustave Weigel, s.j.), *The Spirit of Protestantism*, and is the translator of de Dietrich's *God's Unfolding Purpose* and Casalis's *Portrait of Karl Barth*. He is the general editor of Layman's Theological Library (twelve volumes) and is presently contributing an article each month for *The Commonweal*. He was married in 1944 to Sydney Thomson, and they are the parents of four children. A baseball fan and an amateur carpenter, Dr. Brown has become increasingly involved in the Protestant-Catholic dialogue and has played a leading role in the ecumenical movement in this country.

In 1960 he formulated "Rules for the Dialogue" which was published simultaneously in the *Christian Century* and *The Commonweal*, and later featured in *Time*. Ever since, these rules have served as the guidelines for discussions between Protestant and Catholic scholars, and they are still valid today. The rules are: 1. Each partner must believe that the other is speaking in good faith. 2. Each partner must have a clear understanding of his own faith. 3. Each partner must strive for a clear understanding of the faith of the other. 4. Each partner must accept responsibility in humility and penitence for what his group has done, and is doing, to foster and perpetuate division. 5. Each partner must forthrightly face the issues which cause separation, as well as those which create unity. 6. Each partner must recognize that all that can be done with the dialogue is to offer it up to God.

NINE STEPS TO UNITY

On a certain Monday morning in October I was in the coffee bar at St. Peter's talking with an American bishop. We were both attending the Second Vatican Council, though in somewhat different capacities; he was there as one of the Council Fathers, while I was there as one of the Protestant observers. After some discussion of the collegiality of bishops, he asked me where I taught. When I replied, "Stanford University," his response was instantaneous: "Stanford, eh? Listen, last Saturday your football team clobbered Notre Dame. What kind of an ecumenical gesture is that?"

This may prove only that it is sometimes easier for Catholics and Protestants to develop rapport in a theological discussion than in a football stadium, for his remark was something of a conversation-stopper until we got back to an exchange of opinions on Karl Rahner's interpretation of Vatican I. But I would insist that ecumenical rapport must develop simultaneously in the areas of theological understanding and practical day-to-day relations, and that a breakthrough in either area affects the other area as well. If a Protestant gets to know the faith of his Catholic neighbor better, the two of them can work more effectively on the common civic concerns they already share; while, conversely, if a Protestant works on common civic concerns with his Catholic neighbor, he has a greater chance of learning what the latter's inmost religious convictions really are.

I shall try to illustrate a number of ways in which traffic can proceed up and down this two-way street, drawing my examples as much as possible out of the still-fresh experience of being present at the second session of Vatican II during the fall of 1963.

1. Our concerns about Christian unity must be steeped in the life of prayer, which is always the "next step" toward greater unity. This almost sounds platitudinous, but I stress it because I am discovering that prayer *for* one another can gradually, by the power of the Holy Spirit, be transformed into prayer *with* one another. Twice a week all fall during Vatican II the Protestant observers met in a Methodist Church near St. Peter's to pray *for* the Council. Every morning, however, we were also present at Mass in St. Peter's, and we found ourselves more and more engaged in praying *with* the Council.

There were many portions of the Mass in which we felt we could participate without doing violence to our own faith or appearing to trivialize the faith of our Catholic brethren, portions that have been part of our own Protestant liturgical heritage as well—the *Kyrie*, the *Gloria*, the *Credo*, the *Sanctus*, the *Pater Noster*, the *Agnus Dei*. I think that I have been brought closer to an understanding of the real meaning of Roman Catholic faith by attending Mass five times a week for ten weeks and praying with the Council fathers, than by all the many books of Catholic theology it has been my responsibility to read in the past five years.

During the discussion of the schema on ecumenism, a number of bishops quite independently of one another called attention to the difficulty we experience in sharing common worship. As a result, bishops from missionary areas, bishops from Eastern rite Churches, and bishops from Europe, asked for relaxations in the regulations forbidding Catholics to participate in common worship with non-Catholics. This is particularly vexing on family occasions such as baptisms, weddings, and funerals, but it is also vexing when it obstructs our learning how to join together in the simplest acts of common prayer.

Some of these barriers are in process of being overcome during that period each January when Catholics are celebrating the Christian Unity Octave, and Protestants are celebrating the Week of Prayer for Christian Unity. And I am persuaded, not only for theological reasons but out of my experience last fall in Rome as well, that we must proceed to more, rather than less, common worship together, actively sharing in those prayers and responses that are part of our common heritage as Christians, and at least observing in respectful silence those portions of the worship of one another that we cannot, as yet, share.

On the night of President Kennedy's death I was at the Canadian Theological College in Rome—the lone American and the lone Protestant in the building. But as we all said together the *Pater Noster*, upon learning of the President's assassination, I knew that I was in the midst of fellow Christians, with whom it was possible to join in a common act of prayer to a common Father, and in my time of personal bereavement I was sustained by that fact.

2. A second "step to Christian unity" is a common acknowledgment of our guilt for the events that separated us in the past. It has often been difficult for Catholics to feel that they should acknowledge responsibility for the rifts that now divide Christendom. Since the Second Vatican Council, however, it should no longer be difficult, for the Pope himself set forth mutual confession and mutual pardon as the conditions of ecumenical advance. Speaking of the separation of Christians one from the other, Pope Paul said in his opening allocution on September 29, "If we are in any way to blame for that separation, we humbly beg God's forgiveness and ask pardon too of our brethren who feel themselves to have been injured by us. For our part, we willingly forgive the injuries which the Catholic Church has suffered, and forget the grief endured during the long series of dissentions and separations."

Again and again during the Council sessions this statement was quoted, as bishop after bishop reiterated the conviction that only as sin is acknowledged can forgiveness be granted. When both sides engage in mutual confession, both sides can engage in mutual pardon, and when such an attitude is present there are literally no limits that can be built around what the Holy Spirit can do with such a basis for genuine reconciliation.

3. Another step toward unity, and one that is perhaps even harder than to acknowledge one's fault, is the attempt to engage in inner renewal. Protestantism's best gift to the ecumenical future will be a purged and purified Protestantism. Catholicism's best gift will be a purged and purified Catholicism. Our task is not to point out the faults so obviously and glaringly present in the other's life, but rather to work to remove the faults so insidiously present in our own life.

This need for inner renewal was vividly illustrated by the speeches made in the Council. South American bishops inveighed against the Church's identification with the rich and its lack of concern for the poor. A German cardinal insisted that the Church purge itself of every trace of anti-Semitism. A Mexican bishop urged a more charitable attitude toward the sect groups. A French bishop wanted more concern for those in need, whether Catholic, Protestant, Jewish, or non-believer. An American bishop reminded the Fathers that they must give the layman more to do than "obey, pray and pay." Over and over again the theme was: the Church as it now is, is a far cry from the Church as it ought to be. Many of the Fathers put the ecumenical overtones of this point as follows: The Church cannot simply "wait" for people to return to it; the Church must engage in the inner renewal which removes the legitimate reasons people have had for being unwilling to relate themselves to it.

4. Before we can take active steps toward unity, we must be clear about the nature of the unity we do and do not share. The phrase so commonly used nowadays is a good symbol of what our true situation is. That phrase is the phrase "separated brethren." The basic word, of course, is the noun. We are brethren. Why are we brethren? Not sim-

ply because we share a common humanity, but because we share a common baptism. As Catholic ecumenical thinkers have been pointing out with increasing vigor, this fact of our common baptism underlies the whole ecumenical venture. By virtue of baptism, we are all, in some sense, united with Christ; we are all, in some sense, within the Church. The Catholic may feel that the Protestant shares this membership within the Church very imperfectly, but baptism is nevertheless the basis of a real and indelible bond between us, on which we can build.

We are not only brethren, we are also separated brethren. No satisfaction at our underlying brotherhood can be allowed to make us complacent about the fact of our separation; but no despair over our separation can be allowed to make us forgetful of the fact that we are brothers. Here, then, is both the glory and the agony of our situation. We can never act as though the other did not exist, and we can never accept our separation from the other as a satisfactory situation. We are already bound to one another in deeper ways than we usually acknowledge, and only as we see one another in these terms—as brothers, albeit as separated brothers —can we get to the heart of our problem. Any "steps to Christian unity" that do not proceed from this fundamental assurance are likely to be steps in the wrong direction.

5. Since we are brothers, albeit separated brothers, who must enter into union with one another, one of our basic tasks is to become better acquainted. This means exploration, at all levels, both of those things we share and of those things that divide us. Theologians must engage in this enterprise in theological discussion groups. Catholic seminarians must pursue deeper acquaintance with Protestant seminarians, and vice versa. And laymen in local parishes must seek ways to reach out and come to know their counterparts in neighboring parishes.

The Vatican Council itself furnishes a good basis for beginning such attempts at acquaintance on the latter level.

Any Catholic parish that invites neighboring Protestants to an evening of discussion about the Vatican Council can be assured of a good response, and one hopes that the reverse would be true also. Catholics willing to discuss a book like Hans Küng's *The Council, Reform and Reunion* will find Protestants amazed, delighted, and rejoicing in what they find therein. Such local study groups, beginning with a discussion of the Council, could then move into other areas: the place of Scripture, the message of the prophets, the significance of baptism, and out of such exchange not only become acquainted with one another's convictions, but also become acquainted with one another as persons.

As such acquaintance deepens it is more and more possible to discuss differences as well as similarities, and to do so without self-consciousness or rancor. I discovered during the second session of the Vatican Council that the longer I was there, the more free and unstrained were the conversations I could have with Roman Catholics at the coffee bar. Catholics did not just want to hear polite praise from me; they wanted to know what I "really thought," and before long an atmosphere of enough trust and confidence had been established so that I could tell them what I "really thought" —that I really thought the liturgy schema was a stunner, and that I really thought the communications schema was a disaster. Both things. Not just the first, and not just the second. For if carping criticism is no help, neither is routine praise.

I also discovered, by virtue of the privilege of being in attendance at all the Council sessions, that some things that bother Protestants very much about the Catholic-Protestant situation bother Catholics equally. For years, Protestants have chafed over the rules and regulations surrounding "mixed marriages," and have felt that these make geniune ecumenical encounter on the local level next to impossible. But I discovered at the Council that this matter bothers many of the bishops as well.

66

Since there was no mention of this problem in any of the *schemata* under discussion, it was all the more impressive to discover how many bishops from different parts of the world raised the matter of mixed marriage regulations as one of the thorniest of the problems with which *they* had to cope, and recommended changes in Catholic legislation on the matter. I had previously thought that most Catholics lived in bland indifference to the fact that there was a "problem" here. Perhaps now that we both acknowledge that there is a problem, we can begin to talk together about ways of coping with the problem—ways that will not compromise the convictions of either side, but can help to make religion a creative rather than a destructive factor in a mixed marriage, once the latter has taken place.

It is one of the signs of maturity to be able both to give and to receive criticism in a spirit of charity. If the criticism is surrounded by bonds of mutual concern and love, it need not be destructive but can actually be creative. When we have reached this point in our relationship with one another we have taken a gigantic "step to Christian unity."

6. Sometimes it is this awareness of the issues that divide us at present that can force us to a reassessment of the past. Both Protestants and Catholics need to restudy their own past history. The conventional Catholic polemic against the Reformers is beginning to change—I heard one bishop on the Council floor say that Catholics must recognize that the Reformers' *intention* was a recovery of the Gospel and not a disruption of the Church. And the conventional Protestant polemic against Catholic liturgy ("magic . . .") is beginning to be replaced by a more responsible attempt to understand why the Mass is so central to Catholic faith—and somehow the charge of "magic" just doesn't fill the bill any more, if it ever did.

A look at the past—an attempt to understand where we *are* by examining where we *came from*—may be one of the most important things we can do together. And to the degree that we can do this without emotional polemics, we may both be able to grow in the process, and to grow toward one another.

A good example of this "step to Christian unity" is the treatment accorded the Mariological material at the Vatican Council. By a narrow magin, but nevertheless by a sufficient margin, the Council Fathers voted not to have a separate *schema* on Mary, but to incorporate material on Mary into the *schema* on the Church. Part of the reason for this decision was their feeling that separate treatments of Mary tend to encourage Mariological devotion in isolation from the rest of Catholic faith. Another part of the reason was their recognition that ecumenical relations would be helped rather than hindered by the relocation, particularly if the material were recast in predominantly Biblical terms.

Such an action has all sorts of creative ecumenical possibilities. If the new material on Mary, to be presented at the next session of the Council, does have a predominantly Biblical orientation, then this fact will place a real obligation on the shoulders of Protestants. It will force us to re-examine in a new way the Biblical materials about Mary. Protestants have not really done this before, due to emotional biases engendered by a feeling that Mariology has gotten out of hand by straying so far from the Biblical materials. But the Council's recent action creates at least the possibility than an issue which has been ecumenically divisive in the past could become ecumenically creative.

Our examination of our differences, then, must include a willingness to re-examine past reasons for those differences, in the hope that we can gradually overcome at least some of them.

7. This suggests another "step to Christian unity" that can be taken promptly. One of the French Protestant observers at the Council told me that there are over two hundred joint Protestant-Catholic Bible study groups in France today. In America we have scarcely begun to explore the beneficial

possibilities of such an endeavor. Catholics and Protestants have the good fortune to share substantially the same Scriptures. (The Catholic canon is a little longer than the Protestant, but with sixty-six books still shared in common we have enough to keep us busy for the forseeable future.) We agree, furthermore, that in a unique way God has spoken to men through the Scriptures. We agree that the Scriptures are the fountainhead of our faith and that within them we find the Bread of Life. If we want to know about the heritage we share, as brethren in Jesus Christ, it is to the Scriptures that we must go.

What could be more obvious, therefore, than that we should go to them together? It is a commonplace that Catholic and Protestant Biblical scholars have shared one another's research and findings for close to three decades now, and there are resources of Biblical interpretation that both Catholics and Protestants can use together. If two neighboring parishes, one Catholic and one Protestant, want to come together to renew their understanding of the Christian faith, there could be no better place to embark upon this quest than through common Bible study. With a priest and a minister available as resource people, such groups can genuinely ask themselves, "What is this Book trying to say to us today in the midst of our divisions, and in the midst of our solidarity despite our divisions?"

Every morning at the Council, before the work of the day began, there was the ceremony of The Enthronement of the Gospel. An early illuminated manuscript was brought forward and placed on the altar for the duration of the session, as a reminder to the Fathers that their proper work was the elucidation of that Gospel, and the presence of the book upon the altar served as a useful reminder of that proper work, whenever anyone began to stray away from the content or the spirit of the Gospel.

The Bible is the basic resource of the faith we share. Consequently, as we share our study of the Bible, we will share yet more of the faith we share.

8. In the midst of the above activities, and in the midst of cultivating the above attitudes, there is another thing we can do specifically and tangibly. We can join forces in the sharing of our common civic responsibilities. We do not need to agree about the Dogma of the Assumption to agree that all men are of equal worth to God and that the color of one's skin is an irrelevance to God and to those who call themselves God's children. Even while we explore our doctrinal divisions, we can experience our civic unity. No true Catholic and no true Protestant can accept the notion that restrictive housing covenants are right, or that a member of a minority group should be denied the privilege of eating in a restaurant.

Where civic injustice exists, in other words, Catholics and Protestants can already make common cause. Not only that, they *must* make common cause. It is a cheap evasion to say that we cannot share civic responsibility together at the city planner's table because we cannot yet share bread and wine together at the Lord's Table. If we cannot demonstrate our solidarity in Christ by our united action against racial and economic injustice, we have little cause to believe that the world will take much notice of what we say or do elsewhere.

As was suggested earlier, it is often the case that as we work together on "getting out the vote," or mobilizing opinion for a bill in the state legislature, we really come to know one another for the first time. If Catholics and Protestants are discussing a fair housing bill together, they will finally find themselves discussing the doctrine of man together—which is what a fair housing bill is all about in the first place.

The solidarity that is gained by these common forays into the body politic is a most sustaining experience. Anyone who participated in the March on Washington will understand this feeling. There were many Protestant and Catholic clergy-men present on that occasion. Since most of them, whether Protestant or Catholic, wore clerical collars that day, it was hard to tell one from the other. And the important thing is that *on that day it didn't particularly matter*. What mattered was that the Church of Jesus Christ was finally beginning to involve itself in the racial struggle, and that at the point of involvement in the racial struggle there was neither Jew nor Greek, bond nor free, black nor white, Catholic nor Protestant. On that day, making even that minimum social protest, Catholics and Protestants were brought close to one another. If it is true that "the world is too strong for a divided church," it is also true that a divided world needs a strong church. The whole cause of Christ is strengthened at those points where, without compromising our own basic convictions, we can still work together.

9. The final "step to Christian unity" must be put as a caution and a warning, as well as the sounding of a hope. Many people thrust themselves into "Catholic-Protestant relations" with fervent zeal and enthusiasm, discovering that all sorts of barriers due to misunderstanding can be demolished. But then they get to the hard-core differences that still remain, despite all the good will, and when they discover that unity is not just around the corner, they lose hope. If they are Protestants they mutter about Catholic intransigence (*"Why* must they stick to their belief in the infallibility of the Pope?"). If they are Catholics they mutter about Protestant stubbornness (*"Why* can't they see that Christ intended to found one Church, and that the Church he founded is the Roman Catholic Church?"). Some Protestants go as far as to decide that Catholic ecumenism is only a "trick"—a kind of soft-sell to make it easier for non-Catholics to submit to Rome.

There are indeed awesome barriers that stand in the way of full unity, and it is paradoxically a "step to Christian unity" to recognize the apparently discouraging fact of those barriers. Nothing but disillusionment will come of a naïve hope that unity can be achieved by just a little more talking. The differences that will remain when all the talking has been done are still monumental differences. It is admittedly hard to see what ultimate good can come of all the talk, and even of all the action, if the end product is still Catholic insistence that the Catholic Church is the only true Church, coupled with Protestant insistence that reunion can come only as Catholicism renounces its claim to be the only true Church.

This sounds like an ultimate impasse if there ever was one. It would be an ultimate impasse were it not for the Holy Spirit. And the only condition under which Protestants and Catholics can take genuine "steps to Christian unity" is at some kind of real risk. The risk is that what will emerge at the end of the road will not simply be the Catholic Church as it now is, with all Protestants absorbed into it, nor will it be the Protestant Church as it now is, with all Catholics absorbed into it. What will emerge is something we do not yet really see. Unity will not come if either group simply waits for the other to move toward it. Unity will come only as both groups move out *toward* one another, recognizing that after their confrontation with one another, neither will be quite the same as it was before the encounter took place.

This means, as the first chapter of Vatican II's proposed *schema* on the Church insists, that we have to do, at the heart of our faith, with a mystery. We cannot totally and definitely outline or blueprint the structure of the Church. Its boundaries are known only to God, and cannot be exhaustively stated in any formulae, however inspired. This means that both Catholics and Protestants must be open to insights about the nature of the Church that may thus far have been denied to both of them, and it also means that neither group can be content to be quite as static as it has been in the past.

If such talk sounds strange to Catholic ears, I can only insist that both Pope Paul, in his talk to the Protestant observers, and Cardinal Léger, in a speech to the Council Fathers, inveighed against what they called "theological immobilism," the notion that God's truth has been captured in some kind of final form by man's doctrinal statements. We must always believe that the Spirit can lead us to a *new* grasp of "the faith once delivered to the saints."

We can believe, for example, that it is the will of Christ "that all may be one," without being absolutely sure how that oneness is to be achieved. But if we do believe that Christ wills his children to be one, we must do all within our power to destroy whatever barriers we can that are still keeping his children divided. This will not destroy all the barriers, but it will destroy some of them, and will thereby create a new situation. And that, indeed, is the main "step to Christian unity" that must be taken in our day—the creation of a new situation. We do not know what will emerge out of the new situation. But God does. And that is sufficient.

Hans Küng

(Interviewed by Tanneguy de Quénétain)

Professor of Fundamental Theology at the University of Tübingen and a leading Catholic ecumenist, Hans Küng was born on March 19, 1928, in Sursee, Switzerland. He studied at the Pontifical German College in Rome and the Gregorian University in Rome, where he received the licentiate in both philosophy and theology. Ordained in 1954, Küng attended the Institut Catholique at the Sorbonne in Paris where he obtained his doctorate in theology in 1957, after submitting his thesis, *Justification: The Doctrine of Karl Barth with a Catholic Reflection.*

In it, Küng concluded that there is a substantial agreement between the views of Karl Barth and those of the Catholic Church in regard to the doctrine of justification. This pioneering study has been widely acclaimed by leading Catholic and Protestant theologians, including Barth himself, who considers it as a striking evidence of the growing reconciliation within the ranks of Christianity. Barth wrote the preface.

After serving in a parish at Lucerne for two years, Küng joined the theological faculty of the University of Münster in Westphalia, Germany, and since 1960 has been Professor of Fundamental Theology at the University of Tübingen in the Federal Republic of Germany. His book, *The Council, Reform and Reunion,* has been translated into French, Dutch, Spanish, and English and has been widely acclaimed by Protestants and Catholics alike.

Its basic thesis is that both Catholicism and Protestantism must undergo extensive reform from within before unification can be achieved. The author calls attention to the successful reforms within the Church dating back to the tenth century, as well as those accomplished since the Reformation. He advocates granting broader powers to bishops and limiting the authority of the conservative, Italian-dominated Roman Curia; liturgical reforms that would authorize bishops to adapt the rites to the needs of their people, including the use of the vernacular in the Mass; and the reform or abolition of the

Index of Prohibited Books. Dr. Küng proposes a re-examination of clerical celibacy and the laws concerning mixed marriages. "If Catholics carry out Catholic reform," he says, "and Protestants carry out Protestant reform, both according to the Gospel, then because the Gospel of Christ is but one, reunion need not remain a Utopian dream. Reunion will then be neither a Protestant return nor a Catholic capitulation, but a brotherly approach from both sides."

Reviewing the book in *The Saturday Review*, Henry Pitney Van Dusen, former president of Union Theological Seminary, said: "It combines in an amazing degree fully informed and authoritative scholarship, fearless and utter fidelity to truth, grace of presentation which can proceed only from uncommon beauty of spirit, and a devoutness so intrinsic, so authentic, that it dares to expose all that outrages and negates that genuine piety."

In the spring of 1963 Küng came to the United States for a two-month lecture tour and spoke to overflow audiences in cities and at universities from coast to coast, and everywhere he received standing ovations. In his lectures he advocated abolition of the Index and of the star-chamber techniques used in dealing with questions of heresy. He pleaded for a greater role of individual conscience and responsibility in making decisions and proposed a public declaration by the Church that all men have the right of freedom of worship and of conscience. "It is urgently necessary for the Church," he said, "to repudiate all of the methods of totalitarian states and to abandon forever any attempt at coercing conscience or compelling belief."

He was appointed by Pope John XXIII as an official theologian for the Council. Küng is a prolific contributor to many theological journals. Some of his other books are: *That the World May Believe, Structures of the Church, The Council in Action, Christ in the World,* and *The Christology of Hegel.*

A BROTHERLY APPROACH
FROM BOTH SIDES

In convoking Vatican Council II, John XXIII hoped to bring about a renewal of the Church in such a way as to make possible a reconciliation with the Protestant and Orthodox Churches. But has not this now become a rather secondary problem? Isn't today's essential problem the question of how to reconcile the Church with the modern world?

In several respects these two problems are very closely linked to one another. First of all we must remember that the function of the Church is to proclaim the Gospel to the world. But the essential difficulty, in Asia, in Africa, and even in Europe, is the terrible dissension among those whose mission it is to do so. If those very people who set out to preach Christian faith and charity are divided in their own faith and do not act with charity toward one another, how can they hope to persuade the unconverted? How can they declare that their own religion is the best of all?

Then there is the problem of how to reform the liturgy in such a way that it will be comprehensible to contemporary man. What we need is a simpler and more sober liturgy which would be comprehensible in all respects: language, gestures, and symbols. And it is important that all the faithful should be able to take part in it, because partaking of the Eucharist is essentially a communal act. Now these requirements are precisely those that were formulated by the men of the Reformation, four hundred years ago. Therefore an adaptation of the liturgy to the needs of contemporary man would also satisfy the legitimate demands of the Protestant reformers.

Finally, the theological basis for a discussion with the Protestants is excellent. Because Protestant theology has developed more freely than our own, and has kept in touch with current philosophical ideas, it has much to teach us.

But in that case, why have the Protestants not been more effective, not only in Europe, but elsewhere? Why has not Christianity, through the Protestants, made much more progress in the world?

I have no wish to stress the weaknesses of others. I have come to the conclusion that at this point in history it is the duty of theologians in either camp to discover what is worthwhile in the other camp and what is wrong in their own camp. Having said that, and since you have confronted me with the question, I would say that what the Protestants have lacked is a truly ecclesiastical conscience.

The Church, after Christ, has two poles: the community of the faithful and the sacred ministry. The Protestants have laid new emphasis on the first pole—and with reason; but they have greatly neglected the second. In exalting, rightly, the invisible body of the Church, they have dissolved, mistakenly, many of the visible structures as they were already outlined in the New Testament. The Protestants' depreciation of the sacred ministry and of its authority has seriously weakened the Church's influence. Because Protestant missionary societies have organized themselves, by and large, in an autonomous way, apart from the Churches, they are a great deal weaker than the Catholic missions. In the same way, the division of religious thought, illustrated particularly in the phenomenon of the sects, is also a consequence of the depreciation of priestly authority.

As far as the Catholic Church is concerned, is it not a fact that the most serious problem is that its theology is still Aristotelian and is expressed in the language of St. Thomas Aquinas, whereas our contemporaries are more receptive to the arguments of Darwin, Marx, Freud, or Einstein? The Church and the modern world do not speak the same lan-

guage, so how can they be expected to understand one another?

In the case of St. Thomas, it is the spirit rather than the letter that one ought to retain. St. Thomas himself is infinitely preferable to Thomism. It is indeed useless to repeat formulas and theses in the sort of language that does not effectively communicate the Gospel to modern man. A reformed theology ought to concentrate on Scripture, and at the same time take into account people's preoccupations at the present time. That was precisely St. Thomas's problem in the Middle Ages.

Furthermore, the simultaneous coexistence of several Catholic theologies should be encouraged. One should not confuse unity of faith with uniformity of thought. St. Thomas never thought of himself, or of anyone but Christ, as "the Way, the Truth and the Life." The notion that all Christian thought ought to be made subordinate to one sole official theology is very recent. It dates from the nineteenth century. At the Council of Trent, the Fathers divided themselves into Thomists and Scotists (disciples of Duns Scotus). In St. Thomas's time there was a strong Augustinian school, and a Franciscan school led by St. Bonaventure. In the Church of the first millennium there was a Greek theology that was quite different from the Latin. And, finally, we ought not to forget that the Gospel of Jesus has been communicated to us not by one evangelist, but by four, who have presented Christ to us from quite different angles.

One of the serious problems of the Church in its missionary effort is to bring the Gospel to various countries whose traditional ways of thinking elude all classification in terms of Western categories. If the Church is really to take roots in Africa or in Asia, it is essential to allow for the development of a regional theology. This undertaking is delicate and full of hazards, but it is indispensable, and is one of the major questions confronting the Church as of now.

But does not such a freedom of theological research imply

a complete recasting of the Holy Office whose inquisitorial tendency you have denounced?

Yes, in the opinion of many bishops, the Holy Office wields an influence which is too exclusively repressive and negative. The research of the students of exegesis and of dogmatic theologians has been interrupted again and again by too-hasty interventions which cut short necessary discussions, as well as by methods which leave the accused no opportunity to defend or correct himself. The case of Galileo is not the only one in which there was a too-hasty condemnation of propositions which had later to be recognized as valid.

Many bishops would like to see the Holy Office transformed into a theological commission more representative of the various trends inside the Church. The purpose of such a commission, composed of experts of international status and repute, and organized along the lines of the pontifical Biblical Commission or the Secretariat for Unity, would be to help theologians in their research instead of obstructing their initiative.

During the first session of the Council, did the bishops take sides in the theological controversies?

I am very glad to say that they did not. The Council does not have the Holy Ghost at its disposal to solve in a matter of days the problems which have been troubling theologians for centuries. Besides, a theological definition has never been a solution for all problems. As St. Paul reminds us in the First Epistle to the Corinthians, "We know in part, and we prophesy in part. . . . We see through a glass, darkly"; and it is only at the end of the time that we shall come to see the truth "face to face."

Do you think that the seminaries, under their present form of organization, are training priests to encounter the modern world in an appropriate way?

No; by and large seminary students live in a world that is intellectually and materially too closed. To be capable of proclaiming the Gospel to the world they ought to remain in touch with the world throughout their training. That is, in fact, what happens here at Tübingen. The seminarians who have ordinary civilian status until they attain their sub-diaconate, go to the same university as all the other students, since there are no separate theological faculties in Germany. Moreover they are allowed to go and work for six months or a year in some other university of their own choosing. In that case, they live with a family.

And supposing the seminarian takes a fancy to his hostess' daughter?

If he's liable to do that, it's better that he should do so before he enters Holy Orders rather than afterwards. In any case, experience has proved that our system is at least as good as the more restrictive systems.

There is one problem which seems to be much on the minds of German clergy: the question of mixed marriages between Catholics and Protestants. What does this amount to?

It is a serious problem which, especially in Germany, is not in the least theoretical but very practical. At Tübingen, where there are both Protestants and Catholics, 47 per cent of all marriages are not valid in the eyes of the Church because a Catholic has married a Protestant without subscribing to the conditions laid down by Canon Law. We are thus in a situation which makes pastoral work exceedingly difficult, for while we accept as valid a marriage between two Protestants, or even two heathens, a mixed marriage is considered invalid, unless two conditions are fulfilled. The ceremony has to be performed by a Catholic priest, and the Catholic partner must promise both to bring up the children as Catholics and to work for the conversion of the non-Catholic partner. Before the canon of 1918, a Catholic who married a Protestant outside the Church in Germanic countries was considered to have made an illicit marriage—but a valid one. The canon of 1918 unfortunately put an end to this tolerance.

What solution do you advocate?

I am of the opinion that the present canon should be modified along the following lines: firstly, mixed marriages in which the ceremony is not performed by a Catholic priest should be recognized as valid, and a procedure acceptable to both parties to the marriage should be sought. Secondly, the promise to work for the conversion of the non-Catholic partner should be replaced by some such formula as the following: the two partners undertake to respect and mutually to enhance their Christian faith. And thirdly, the question of the education of the children and of their baptism should be discussed with a view to finding a solution that would satisfy the Christian conscience of both parties.

In the course of your lecture tour in America, you took a stand in favor of freedom of conscience. And the Secretariat for Unity is presenting to the second session of the Council a plan which favors religious liberty. Why is the Church changing its traditional attitude?

The reasons, thank God, have nothing to do with opportunism. One cannot found a valid theory of religious liberty on the basis of a promise not to persecute Protestants in a Catholic country, in exchange for compensatory provisos in some Protestant country. For the Christian, the foundation of religious liberty is the dignity of the individual as a human being. Only the individual human being can be judged. So, according to Catholic morality, the right—and indeed the duty—of the individual is to follow the dictates of his fully informed conscience. Subjective conscience holds priority over any objective standard.

Which are the most important positive results to have emerged from the first session of the Council?

I think one can name five main points. First, the Council has given to all Christians and to the world at large an image of the free and lively community that the Church ought to be. Second, the presence of Protestant observers and the welcome which they received demonstrated that the Catholic

Church in its entirety is turning its attention to ecumenical problems. Third, the Council's concentration on problems of a practical and pastoral nature showed that the Church wishes to leave the doors open, avoiding doctrinal definitions of a kind that might widen the gulf separating Catholics from other Christians. Fourth, the decision to reorganize the Council's working methods was a guarantee of better preparation for the second session. Last, it is a good and important thing, from the ecumenical point of view, that the first decisions of the Council concerned liturgical reform.

One of the principal claims made by the Protestants is that the Mass no longer has anything in common with the Last Supper. The Council of Trent put an end to certain shocking abuses, but maintained the medieval Mass at which the high altar replaced the table altar, and the Mass lost the essential character of the Eucharistic repast: the participation of the faithful was restricted—and the priest communicated alone, uttering the essential prayers in an undertone, and in Latin, which is no longer understood by the people.

What did the Council decide about this? And, in your opinion, is it enough?

The Fathers insisted that Mass ought to be simple and intelligible, and that the vernacular should find more place in it; they demanded that the liturgy be adapted to the mentality of the various peoples; and they insisted on the reading of the Scripture during the liturgy, and on the active participation of all the faithful.

To what extent do you feel Latin should still be used?

Personally, I am in favor of the whole Mass being said in the language of the country in which the Mass is being celebrated. Latin is not the mother tongue of the Church. Jesus spoke Aramaic; and our Mother Church, the Church of Jerusalem, said prayers in Aramaic. Then the Greek tongue was adopted, because it was the most universal language at the time of the Roman Empire. In the middle of the third century, Latin supplanted Greek in the Roman liturgy because it had become the language most commonly used in the western part of the Empire. But, at the same time, adapting itself to local conditions, the liturgy was translated into Syrian, Coptic, and Armenian. In order to spread the Gospel throughout the Balkans, the monks Cyril and Methodius used Slavonic—with the full agreement of Rome.

It is often argued in favor of Latin that it bears witness to the unity of the Church and that, thanks to its use, "everyone feels at home everywhere."

That could be another way of saying that abroad as at home no one really understands what the priest is saying at the altar. If people are to take part in the offices they need a translation. Otherwise all that remains is a vague religious feeling which has nothing in common with that prayer "in spirit and in truth" for which Christ asked. As for the unity of the Church, the use of Greek or Syrian in Catholic churches in the East indicates that it is not affected by the use of more than one language.

Finally, Latin has been disastrous for our missionary effort in countries outside Europe. As Cardinal Costantini said, "It is not the Great Wall of China so much as the wall of Latin that has hindered our efforts to convert the Chinese."

What other reforms do you deem necessary for Mass?

The Eucharistic prayer should no longer be murmured in an undertone by the priest, but should be spoken in a loud and intelligible voice. It should be accompanied by a recital of the Last Supper, as was the practice of the Church during the first millennium. The Mementoes could well be replaced by prayers of intercession at the Offertory. In the sermon a much greater emphasis on the Scriptures is needed. There should also be less genuflexion and burning of incense, suppression of the Last Gospel, and the prayers at the foot of the altar. Finally, and above all, we should lay greater stress upon the Eucharistic repast, and try to re-establish for the faithful the two sorts of Communion. Apropos of this, the

Protestants have grounds for reminding us of the words of Christ when he proffered the chalice: "Drink ye, all, of this." We should no longer have to explain Mass; the liturgy ought to explain our faith for us as it did in the past.

There is another serious problem that everyone is talking about these days: the decentralization of the Church. What principles ought to govern this?

The "subsidiary" principle, as it was advocated by Pius XI in his encyclical *Quadragesimo Anno*. The community should never undertake something which the individual is capable of doing for himself. The higher echelon should never take on something that can be done by the lower echelon. We need as much freedom as possible, and only such bonds as are necessary. This principle is exceedingly important, for decentralization can only become a reality if it is applied to all the degrees of the hierarchy, from the Pope and the bishops to the priests and their congregations.

But such a decentralization implies a recasting of the Curia. In your opinion, what sort of relations ought to be established between the bishops and the Curia?

What is more important is the question of relations between the bishops and the Pope. The power of the Curia stems from human law, whereas the power of the bishops, like that of the Pope, stems from divine law. The Curia should be no more than an executive arm. Some bishops have proposed that a central commission, representing the various Episcopal synods, and endowed with legislative power, should meet twice a year in Rome. The commission's decisions would have to be approved by the Pope, then put into execution by the Curia. Finally, in virtue of the "subsidiary" principle, the bishops would be endowed with a wider range of initiative in all matters. And then it would be necessary to internationalize the Curia so that it became truly representative of the different cultural groups that make up the Church. Is it not distressing that the Secretariat of the United Nations should be more "catholic" in its composition than the central organ of the Church? Such an internationalization, by reconciling unity with diversity, would restore its catholicism to the Church.

Karl Barth

(Interviewed by Tanneguy de Quénétain)

Among the most distinguished names among Protestant theologians is that of Dr. Karl Barth, who is regarded by many as the founder of a distinctive school of Protestant theological thought. Born on May 10, 1886, in Basel, Switzerland, he is the son of a New Testament scholar of the Swiss Reformed Church who gave up his pastorate to teach theology at a seminary in Basel. Barth studied at the Universities of Bern, Tübingen, Berlin, and Marburg, having among his teachers two of the outstanding exponents of liberal Protestant theology, Adolf von Harnack at Berlin and Wilhelm Herrmann at Marburg.

After being ordained by his father in 1908 in the Reformed Church in Bern, Barth served for some years in pastoral work. In 1919 he published his book, *Römerbrief*, a commentary on Paul's Epistle to the Romans, in which he rejected the liberal theology of his former teachers. In his book Barth restored to theology the view of God as supreme, transcendent, and divine. He also emphasized the sinfulness of man, which he felt liberals had neglected in overemphasizing the goodness and dignity of man.

The book attracted wide attention both from his critics and from his advocates and disciples. In 1921 Barth become Professor of Reformed Theology at the University of Göttingen, and in 1925 took the chair of theology at the University of Münster. His great work, *Church Dogmatics,* consisting of twelve large volumes, has been widely heralded as the Protestant counterpart of the *Summa Theologica* of St. Thomas Aquinas. A vehement opponent of Nazism, Barth was dismissed in 1935 from his post at Bonn and accepted a professorship of theology created especially for him at the University of Basel.

He remained in this position until his retirement in the spring of 1962. In April of that year, Barth made his first visit to the United States and gave a series of lectures at the University of Chicago and at Princeton Theological Seminary. He received a D.D. degree from the University of Chicago, and the citation accompanying it states: "Barth's concern was to reassert the centrality of God over and against the centrality of man in the method and message of theology. He has devoted a lifetime of research, writing and teaching to this concern." His lectures at both institutions were attended by thousands of people, many of whom traveled considerable distances to hear him.

A short, blue-eyed, gray-haired man, Barth is genial, sympathetic, patient, and has a nice sense of humor. He married Nelly Hoffman, a violinist, and they are the parents of four children. For many years he has been interested in the ecumenical movement, and that interest is vividly reflected in his interview, marked by both warmth and candor.

PROSPECTS FOR CHRISTIAN UNITY

In your opinion, is the problem of bringing the Churches together the paramount problem of Christians today?

It is certainly one of the great problems which we ought to face squarely, and it is also something of a scandal. The division of the Church is one of those scandals which a Christian cannot brook, like war, for instance. One cannot resign oneself to war, even though one is aware that there have always been wars up to now, and there may be others. But, having said that, the fact remains that the unity of the Church does exist, but on an invisible and spiritual plane.

All those who have faith in Christ, who hearken to the Word of God as it has been handed down to us in the Scriptures, are members of this invisible Church. And my own aim has always been to teach an ecumenical theology, which refuses to be confined within the narrow compartments of a particular faith. I am, of course, of the Reformed tradition. But I believe, as did Calvin, that there is only one sole master of the Church and of the world. Consequently it is not Calvin whom I strive to obey, but Christ.

It is, of course, true that the Church's invisible unity ought not to be contradicted by visible divisions. So all our efforts ought to be directed toward facilitating the realization of a visible unity. I do not know when this will be achieved. But I know for a certainty that it will be achieved, since, at the end of time, Christ will return again; and in him the Church will find her visible unity.

Do you think that any step backward in this ecumenical movement could in present circumstances, when much of the world is busy building an atheistic civilization, deal a terrible blow to the Christian cause?

Of course not. Every epoch believes itself to be crucial to

the destiny of humanity. As for the question of atheism, I am by no means convinced that this age of ours is any worse than those periods that are officially labeled Christian. In the Middle Ages, for instance, it was above all the outer forms of civilization which conveyed an impression of being Christian.

Christianity at that time was an official institution. But one had only to look behind the façade at the way the kings and nobles and priests were living, and the grotesque superstitions to which the common people were a prey, in order to realize that the essence of the message of the Gospels was understood and obeyed by very few. There are two sorts of atheism: practicing atheism and doctrinal atheism (Nietzsche's kind or Sartre's).

On balance, I find the first kind a great deal more pernicious than the second, in that it can be masked by an official Christianity. Look at the German Christian-Democratic Party. What real relation can there be between Adenauer's politics and Christianity? Doctrinal atheism at least has the advantage of being the sincere expression of the practicing atheism of a lot of people who call themselves "Christians." It is, in fact, a superior phenomenon insofar as it testifies to a heart-searching, authentic metaphysical anguish; it also obliges us who are Christians to take the Word of God more seriously.

It has been said that Protestantism is better adapted to the world of today than Catholicism. Calvin showed himself to be more indulgent about things like interest-bearing loans and the possession of worldly goods than St. Thomas Aquinas, and in so doing prepared the ground for the rise of capitalism and an industrial civilization. How do you feel about this?

That is certainly not the aspect of Calvin that I like best, because that side of things leads to confusing the interests of the banker with those of the Christian, and putting one's soul in a safe.

In the same way, the parallel between Protestantism and

democracy has several times been pointed out: a parallel arising from the fact that, in comparison to the Catholic Church, we enjoy greater freedom of thought, and that the organization of our Churches has a much more democratic approach. This parallel has its validity, but only up to a certain point; and that point is crucial.

In fact, Western democracy is much less the offspring of the Gospel than of Jean-Jacques Rousseau. It is founded on a natural philosophy, according to which it is Nature that has created all men equal; and it is in order to pay respect to Nature that this equality has to be respected in our social contract. But from the Christian point of view, the equality of men is not a fact of Nature but a free gift from God, a grace which enables them to become equals in Jesus Christ. The two points of view are not at all alike.

In your view, what is the greatest obstacle to reconciliation between the Reformed Churches all over the world and the Catholic Church?

I think the greatest obstacle could well be a very small word which the Roman Church tacks on to the end of every one of our propositions. This very small word "and." When we say Jesus, the Catholics say Jesus *and* Mary. We seek to obey only our sole Lord—Christ. The Catholics obey Christ *and* his earthly vicar, that is to say the Pope. We believe that the Christian is saved by the merits of Jesus Christ; but the Catholics add: *and* by his own merits, that is to say, his good works. We think that the only source of Revelation is the Scriptures; the Catholics add: *and* Tradition. We say that knowledge of God comes from faith in his word, as it is expressed in Scripture. The Catholics add: *and* from Reason.

Here, in fact, one finds oneself in the midst of the fundamental problem of the relationship between grace and freedom, as far as man's salvation is concerned. In this respect, it seems to us that the Roman Church puts too much emphasis on the possibilities open to the sinner and not enough on the omnipotence of God. There is something about the Catholic conception of free will which seems to us to diminish the majesty of God and the gift of grace which He makes to us in order that we may attain our salvation.

It is clear that this great problem is at the root of our theological preoccupations. But from the point of view of the faithful as a whole the most visible demarcation line between the two Churches is undoubtedly the worship of the Virgin. If a Catholic child happens to go into a Protestant church he is immediately struck by the absence of a statue of the Madonna. We are extremely sensitive about this question, and have come to the conclusion that the exultation of the Virgin, that is to say of a person, has been taken much too far by Rome. We dread the thought that the Catholic Church may one day elevate to a dogma its conception of Mary as Co-redemptress.

And then, too, the forms of worship are very, very different. When I attend a Catholic High Mass I ask myself: why all this pomp? Just imagine St. Paul coming back among us and taking part in a pontifical ceremony in St. Peter's. What would he make of it? I myself prefer a simpler and more concentrated form of worship. A Catholic Mass rather puts me in mind of a play staged in a foreign tongue.

Of course, in all this there is an element of personal taste. I have listened to some Catholic preachers who gave excellent sermons. Then again, I have heard others who confined themselves to questions of public morals. . . . This sort of thing happens just as often in our own Church. And, when a Protestant pastor's sermon is bad, then the result is even more disastrous because, for us, it is the preaching of the Word of God which constitutes the very center of worship, whereas in the case of the Catholics it is the sacrament of the Eucharist.

Which of these two forms of worship do you think approximates most closely to the form of worship practiced by the primitive Church?

Neither of them. Catholic worship is too flowery, too

overdone, whereas ours, because it has tried to purify itself, now smacks of the synagogue. One might say that the great temptation for Protestantism is Judaism, whereas the great temptation for the Catholic Church would be paganism.

Recently I met a Catholic priest in Bavaria who had had his church reconstructed along novel and extraordinarily interesting lines (with the approval of his bishop, of course). The altar is, naturally, in the middle, but is shaped like a large table. It does not carry the tabernacle, which is placed upon a smaller altar to the right of the high altar, and it faces the pulpit, which is placed on the right side of the high altar.

On the pulpit there is inscribed a quotation from the Epistle to the Corinthians, which reminds the faithful that "the foundation of the Church is the Word of God." Thus a new balance has been established, in visual terms, between the role of preaching and the role of the sacrament. Besides, the faithful communicate at the same table as the priest. So the communal aspect of worship, an essential part of Christian belief, is thus considerably stressed. Naturally the priest says Mass facing his flock.

I would be happy to see the Council encourage the general adoption of this pattern. In the traditional Mass, in which the priest turns his back on his flock, one is rather too apt to feel that he is a sort of privileged delegate, whose function is to pray to God in the name of the community, whereas he should be praying to God in company with the community. I have no idea what decisions the Fathers of the Council will take in liturgical matters, but I do hope that they will decide on a greater use of everyday language during the service—to do away with the impression of being "a play staged in a foreign tongue."

Finally, I feel it would be a good thing if one could reestablish Communion as something for everyone, instead of simply reserving it for the priest. Why should the priest alone have the right to Communion in both kinds, that is, wine and bread? There is something there that has a taste of ecclesiastical privilege, and I find it disagreeable.

The so-called "Roman intolerance" has often been severely condemned. Do you find the charge still justified after all these centuries?

Things have certainly improved since the sixteenth century. But one has to recognize that there is still a natural tendency toward intolerance in the Roman Catholic Church. When the latter is in a weak or minority position in any given country, then she advocates tolerance. But when she is in the majority, she does not set nearly so much store by it. Although a law against it is at present in the making, there is a small Protestant community in Spain which is subjected to all sorts of vexatious persecution.

They are not allowed to have a bell-tower on their churches; when a Spanish Protestant does his military service he is forced to march off to Mass every Sunday with his Catholic comrades; if he fails to genuflect at the same time as the others, he is punished. That is intolerance in its most naked form. Even if we admit that it is we who are the heretics, and that it is up to the Roman Church to combat this error, all the same, it is not by using police methods that one should seek to overthrow the devil, but by appealing to the Holy Spirit.

Which do you think are the most hopeful avenues of approach to the ultimate reconciliation of the Churches? One often has the impression from the outside that all this is a vast and vain quarrel about mere words.

It may be a quarrel about words, but those words are important because they define certain basic choices in our conception of Christianity. I do not see how one can ever evade the theological issues. One cannot just exclaim, "Come on! Let's all march forward together!" if one does not know where one is going or how to get there.

The whole problem resides in knowing how far it may be possible for both sides to reach agreement as to the sense and meaning which should be given to that little word "and," of which I was talking earlier. For the moment we are not in agreement, but I do not deny the possibility of agreement. For, after all, the Reformed Churches, even if they do put Scripture above Tradition, do not deny the importance of Tradition as an aid to the interpretation of Scripture. They do not deny the responsibility of man himself for the accomplishment of his own salvation. They do not deny the benefit that sacraments confer as signs of grace. But they do not value these things as highly as the Catholic Church does.

However, many things may change. The Catholic Church itself admits of change, not only as far as the forms of worship are concerned—they have undergone considerable changes over the centuries—but also on the theological plane. At the same time, no Catholic theologian can admit that all the forms are fit subjects for change—dogma, for example. This concept of the magistracy of the Church reaches its culminating point in the doctrine of papal infallibility, which, in its existing form, is unacceptable to Protestants.

But happily the Catholic Church, even if it is unable to go into reverse on a question of dogma, is nevertheless able to modify the interpretation of a dogma. And this is a sphere in which Catholic theologians are extraordinarily able. Here is an example: only ten years ago I was convinced that, between the Protestant and Catholic views on justification by faith (and by good works, for the Catholics), an impenetrable wall was in process of building. Then one of my Catholic friends, the eminent theologian Hans Küng, wrote a work in which he affirmed that, on the problem of justification, there was no conflict between the theories of the Protestant Karl Barth and the decisions of the Council of Trent.

It is true that, in my conception of faith, I insist on the necessity for an active faith, which has a direct effect upon works. But I believe that I have remained faithful to the true conception of the Reformed Churches, to which, in my view, the Fathers of the Council of Trent were rigidly opposed. Well anyhow, it seems that I was mistaken, and that, without my realizing it, we are really in agreement. Hans Küng certainly understood my own thesis perfectly, and I dare to think—though I am not too sure—that he also understands perfectly the thesis of the Fathers of Trent.

Do you consider that Catholics and Protestants are closer to or farther away from each other than they were a century ago?

Infinitely closer; there is no comparison. And this in spite of the proclamation of the dogma of the Assumption, which made such a bad impression in our Church. For nowadays both sides are getting to know each other and look upon each other as being on the same level, whereas in the old days we hardly knew each other at all. At the start of this century, when I was a theological student, there was no question of my reading a book by a contemporary Catholic. To read such works was, for Protestants, simply unthinkable. And in the same way, Catholics who for the most part knew us only from reading works refuting our beliefs, received a very strange image of the Reformed Churches.

Today, however, the "iron curtain" has been raised, and I find myself quite at home when I am working with certain Catholic theologians. I even wrote a preface to Hans Küng's book, and the book received the *imprimatur*. I embarked on that book rather as Noah embarked on the Ark, with a dove in my hand, and I awaited the deluge. But, so far, there has been none. In other words, reconciliation depends essentially on knowing. The more we learn to know each other, the better we shall understand that though there is only one Christian faith, there are several different and quite valid ways of expressing it.

In the event of the Churches being reconciled, what would be Catholicism's most valuable contribution to Protestantism, and vice versa?

The great trump card held by the Roman Catholic Church

is the overwhelming impression of solidity and continuity that she gives—even if that continuity may be open to question. With us, there is an invisible continuity, but it is one that makes much less impact, owing to the fact that Protestantism is divided into many different confessions; and also because, with us, few questions are ever completely closed. The majority of Protestants who have gone over to Catholicism have been in search of rest and of that intellectual and spiritual security than can be provided by a Church which is solidly organized and has a strong hierarchy. On the other hand, Protestantism attracts people who are hungry for movement and freedom.

In truth, both conceptions are necessary because they are complementary to each other. There can be no movement except in relation to stability, and vice versa. But I am opposed to conversions, to moves from one Church to another. In the first place, converts tend to become insufferable zealots; they either become ultra-Catholics or ultra-Protestants. And then these conversions constitute a denial of the invisible unity of the Church, a denial which is very much to be deplored. I believe myself that everyone should stay where he is, and attempt to probe more deeply the message of the Gospels. It is only in such a way that a true reconciliation will eventually take place.

Do you feel that the decisions of the Council are necessarily encouraging to the idea of the reconciliation of the Churches?

It is obviously impossible to give any clear-cut answer to that. I am not the Pope, and the Pope has not asked my opinion. The organization and the conduct of this Council are closely linked to the personality of John XXIII, and he alone knows what he wishes to do. Still, having said that, I must say that I do not believe that Vatican Council II has, like Vatican Council I, put more distance than before between Catholics and Protestants. I doubt whether there will be any spectacular move toward reconciliation, but at least there will be certain reforms in matters of detail which will head in the direction of reconciliation.

Moreover, the way in which Protestant observers have been taking part in the Council is a very remarkable thing in itself, for a start. They attend all the sessions, not only of the plenary assemblies, but also of the working commissions. And after each session they are invited to give their views to the Secretariat for Promoting Christian Unity. Through this oblique approach, they become involved, in a certain sense, in indirect discussion with the Fathers of the Council.

The Pope has just added the name of St. Joseph to the prayers of the Canon of the Mass. Does this decision not run the risk of greatly annoying Protestants?

It does not annoy me. Since Rome admits the intercession of the saints, why should St. Joseph be kept to one side? Personally, I like St. Joseph very much. I was talking about this recently to an American Jesuit. I am just as much in favor of the development of "Josephology" as I am opposed to the development of "Mariology." For Joseph, in my view, has played in relation to Christ just the kind of supporting role which the Church ought to be playing.

The Roman Church, I know, prefers to compare its own role to the more glorious role of Mary. The Church brings to the world the message of the Gospels in the same sort of way that Mary gave us Christ. But the comparison is not a true one. The Church is incapable of giving birth to the Redeemer, but she can and should serve him with a humble and unobtrusive zeal. This, precisely, was the role of Joseph, who was always very discreet and left all the glory to Jesus.

97

Yves Congar

One of the most articulate ecumenical voices in France is that of Yves Marie Joseph Congar, O.P., a consultant for the Theological Commission of Vatican Council II and a prolific and brilliant writer. Born on April 13, 1904, at Sedan, Ardennes, France, he studied at the Institut Catholique in Paris and the Dominican House of Philosophy and Theology at Le Saulchoir and was ordained on July 25, 1930. He served as professor at the Dominican House of Studies at Le Saulchoir from 1931 to 1954, except for the war years, and taught fundamental theology and ecclesiology.

Father Congar was mobilized during World War II and was taken prisoner. Aside from his professorial activities he has been active in writing for many magazines, dictionaries, and encyclopedias and in conducting spiritual retreats and conferences. He assisted in the founding and directing of the collection of the *Unam Sanctam* and in directing the *Review for Philosophical and Theological Sciences*.

He is the author of many scholarly works which have profoundly influenced theological thought in Europe, and among his works are the following: *Disunited Christians, Principles for Catholic Ecumenism; Sketches of the Mystery of the Church; True and False Reform in the Church; Stages in a Theology for Lay People; Mystery of the Temple; The Ways of the Living God; Priest and Layman: Their Task of Evangelization and Civilization; the Holy Church; Tradition and Traditions; Tradition and the Life of the Church; Christ, Mary and the Church; Faith and Theology* and *Nine Hundred Years Afterwards* (notes on the Eastern Schism).

Father Yves Congar wrote the lengthy article on "Theology" in the *Dictionnaire de Theologie Catholique* and is a frequent contributor to many magazines, including *Vie Intellectuelle*. He is a member of the central commission for the *Semaines Sociales* of France and is a member of the committee for the establishment of a new magazine, *Concilium*, as well as a member of the academic council for the Institute for European History. His attendance at both sessions of the Council, where he served as an expert and a consultant for the Theological Commission, enabled him to secure an authentic insight into the thinking of the Council. He is a willing and able collaborator in the efforts of all scholars to promote better understanding and good will, and thus pave the way for the unity of all Christians.

CONQUERING OUR ENMITIES

All those who have had some experience of confrontations between Catholicism and Protestantism know what grave difficulties beset even the most sincere desire for mutual understanding. One is reminded of trench warfare in 1914–18 when, after long artillery preparation and at the cost of almost superhuman efforts, the infantry would take over the advanced lines, thinking they had broken through the front, only to find barbed-wire entanglements still intact on the other side. So it is with Christian unity: when, after patient and laborious efforts, the misunderstandings on the question of Justification or the *ex opere operato*[1] have been cleared away, we come up against the insuperable wall of papal infallibility or devotion to the Virgin Mary.

In addition to such dogmatic difficulties, the importance of other types of obstacle, called in the ecumenical movement, non-theological factors of division, has been better understood since the Edinburgh conference of 1937. By this are meant the reflex reactions linked up with our habits, the sociological group to which we belong, or inherited historical memories, which all help to project a formidable or contemptible image of "others," those opposite us.

Factors of opposition of this kind are not confined to divided Christendom, but are found in all types of human relationships. While C. H. Dodd, the likable Congregational theologian, was publishing a courageous and lucid article in the *Ecumenical Review*, "Concerning Unavowed Motives in Ecumenical Discussions," *The American Journal of Soci-*

[1] Editor's note. *Ex opere operato* is a Latin expression, meaning by virtue of the work done. It is used of a sacrament considered independently of the merits of the minister or the recipient. The contrasting Latin phrase is *ex opere operantis*, meaning by virtue of the work of the agent.

ology printed a most revealing study of "Misunderstandings in Human Relations" by M. G. Icheiser. The author analyzed the way in which we form false images or caricatures of others, which in turn make any friendly relationship with them impossible.

Current ideas are taken for facts and people may be convinced, for instance, that all North African Muslims are homosexuals. Events, groups, and people are unified in a convenient and simplistic representation though the reality is in fact far more diversified, so that through using inaccurate data false images are built up. We only notice what concerns us most directly or what strikes our imaginations vividly; our classifications are stereotyped and finally untrue.

If each of my readers were to apply the results of this analysis to himself and, in particular, notice how malformations of this kind condition the way he judges members of other religious groups, I am convinced that both his honesty and the "re-neighboring" of disunited Christians, of which Pope John XXIII spoke, would gain by his self-examination. Let us try and take the analysis of the psychological and moral sources of this most harmful attitude a step further.

In his extraordinary *Legend of the Grand Inquisitor*, Dostoyevsky shows that men are obsessed by a need for security, finding expression in the need for bread, for social cohesion, and the need to refer oneself to an undeniable authority. For reassurance and the absence of worry men will barter even their freedom. This same need for security, aided and abetted by a natural laziness, leads us to avoid being called into question and nourishes in us a fairly blind esprit de corps. We find stability and security in the social or religious group to which we belong. Anything which appears to attack or question it is seen as hostile, something against which we must defend ourselves.

The defensive reflex is further strengthened by the universal instinct to justify oneself. It has been said that self-justification is one of the strongest motives in history, and it doubtless explains why so many "great men" have caused so much suffering to others. Men prefer to persist in a given course rather than appear to have been in the wrong or retract what they may have said. A feeling of solidarity and the desire for self-justification together lead to the adoption of a suspicious attitude toward the other group and its members.

Distrust is one of the most deep-rooted feelings in man, together with the feeling of injustice. It can sterilize the most loyal and sincere efforts. The history of social conflicts is full of examples. Employers may make the most interesting offers. Yet if the workers are distrustful, not only will the offers be useless, but they will regard them as merely part of a scheme aimed at disarming and dividing them, satisfying them at small cost in order to avoid reaching a genuinely sincere and substantial agreement.

Here we may cite an example which is at the same time close to our subject. During the terrible famine of 1920–21 in Russia, the Holy See sent help and we personally know some of the men who took part in this humanitarian enterprise. Yet this action on the part of the Holy See was interpreted in certain Orthodox circles as a base political action, ignobly taking advantage of the misfortunes of Russia to further the cause of the Vatican. Thus it is that in the face of persisting suspicion even a friendly gesture will be interpreted unfavorably.

This will be even more marked where those who wish to intervene are powerful and present to outsiders an image of power. Father Pire, the founder and inspirer first of "Europe of the Heart," then of "The Heart Open to the World," winner of the Nobel Peace Prize, made at a recent conference the following significant observation: "If I go out to the unfortunate people of hungry lands wearing the label of some powerful collective association, I risk not really meeting them at all. They will probably accept what I bring because they need it, but I will not have created any link between them and me. I will not have furthered the growth of the little plant of peace which grows in no other soil than the hearts of men. Things will be quite different if I come simply as a *person* wishing to meet other *people*. It is the power of the social group whose agent I appear to be which hides us from each other."

The tenacious suspicion with which Catholic initiatives or even the mere presence of Catholics are met needs no other explanation. In his *Apologia*, Newman quotes a letter which he wrote on September 12, 1841—four years before his conversion—to an ardent Catholic.

"Suspicion and distrust," he wrote, "are the main causes at present of the separation between us, and the nearest approaches in doctrine will but increase the hostility, which, alas, our people feel towards yours. While these causes continue . . . I am sure that, while you suffer, we suffer too from the separation; *but we cannot remove the obstacles*. It is with you to do so. You do not fear us; we fear you. Till we cease to fear you, we cannot love you."

We believe that Newman put his finger here on the essence of the "anti-Roman complex." We could quote examples of this complex not only in the past (Lord Clarendon in 1660 said of the Scots that their religion consisted entirely of a horror of the papacy), but also in the present; taken not from distant lands but at home in our own. One need only consult R. A. Billington, *The Protestant Crusade (1800–1860)*, or the works of Paul Blanshard or, in England, of G. G. Coulton or C. J. Cadoux, to find examples by the dozen. The important thing for us is to take thought and to try and understand the meaning of an attitude which is still so widespread.

The fundamental explanation of the anti-Roman complex is that the Catholic Church is seen on the one hand as an authoritarian body, with a teaching function which she allows no one to belittle, and on the other hand as a well-organized and often effective power. Men defend themselves and protest against authority and power.

It is especially the power aspect of the Church, the historical forms of which, it must be confessed, have often owed little to the Gospel, which gives rise to distrust and hence to aversion and self-defensive reactions. All attempts at explanation are ruined in advance. St. Vincent de Paul's comment is as significant as it is profound: "One must first show men love and kindness, otherwise they will neither listen to us nor believe us: the devil is very intelligent and yet we do not believe him for he is not kind."

If Pope John XXIII gained the hearts and hearing of men to such a remarkable degree, it was without doubt through his kindness, understanding, and sympathy. Thus did he illustrate the truth of Dr. Albert Schweitzer's words: "The finest work for peace is to fight against the prejudice of distrust." In fact, Pope John himself said: "We try unceasingly to be a man of peace in the widest sense of the term. Deviations grieve us and we prefer to emphasize those things which *unite* men, accompanying each on his road as far as we may without sacrificing the exigencies of justice and the rights of truth."

Bishop Fred Pierce Corson, the President of the World Council of Methodist Churches, touched perhaps on an even deeper aspect of the secret of the immense hearing obtained by Pope John and of his action in the world. Speaking to the World Assembly of the Methodist Churches in San Francisco, he said of the Pope shortly after the publication of the encyclical *Pacem in Terris*, "He is a Pope who loves *men* more than *power*." This remark brings us back to Father Pire's comments on the conditions necessary for a true meeting between men and for a wholly peaceful victory over the complexes of distrust, self-defense, and opposition, which make barren all our efforts at explanation, even on questions of doctrine. The nature of these conditions deserves more attention.

This is illustrated in the life, thought, and work of Mahatma Gandhi. "It is not a question of gaining a victory over the enemy," he said, "but of conquering enmity and gaining peace." He spent his time not in leading a struggle against adversaries but in leading them toward the truth. There were not only Hindus and the English: within the Indian people there was the division between Hindus and Muslims. At the age of seventy-seven, Gandhi undertook a harassing tour from village to village in a land full of murders and violence, in a land crying out for vengeance. He set himself on purpose to stay with Muslims, to appeal for Muslim organizations, to such an extent that Hindus accused him of betraying the Hindu cause and in the end he was in fact shot by one of these Hindus.

When asked why he went to so much trouble and exposed himself to such great dangers, he would reply: "Throughout this tour I wish to assure the villagers, as well as I can, that I feel not the slightest hostility towards any of them. I can only prove it if I live and move among those who mistrust me." In order to conquer mistrust, Gandhi saw no other means than to enlist himself without counting the cost in an action inspired by love and generating an atmosphere of confidence. And indeed there is no other means.

Let us take another example, nearer to our subject: Christian ecumenism. Professor Peter Meinhold of Kiel himself relates the following anecdote in his book, *Der evangelische Christ und das Konzil* (Freiburg 1961). A Lutheran theologian, he had been invited to speak on the Vatican Radio and had been very impressed by the fact that not only had he been able to speak without restriction, but he had not been asked either to submit his text in advance or even to give details of his subject. The point is slight but significant. If similar examples of greater importance became more frequent, the atmosphere would soon be changed from distrust to confidence and a true dialogue would be possible. But why speak in the conditional or the optative voice? Has not my wish already been fulfilled? We have already witnessed that extremely important event: the presence of observers at the Vatican Council.

I have myself heard from the lips of many of them, including Professor Meinhold, the moving account of their experience. They came and were welcomed. Nothing was hidden from them. They had evidence of this not from fine-sounding declarations (there were none), but from the facts. They received the same texts as the bishops and the theological experts. They were present at all the general sessions. They heard speeches in which bishops expressed their opinions and, on occasion, criticized the positions of other bishops with a freedom of speech surprising to many. A Calvinist observer said to me after one such debate: "For the first time in history the Catholic Church is washing its dirty linen before witnesses."

The observers were very deeply moved by the opening ceremonies of the sessions. First there was a celebration of the Eucharist at which their presence was not of course required, though many came and prayed. Then came the solemn enthroning of the Gospels. For me this was the most moving moment. From the far end of the immense basilica a bishop with a candle-bearer on either side came forward, holding a large book of the Gospels, open and aloft. In the meanwhile the bishops sang either the Creed or the hymn, *Christus Vincit, Christus Regnat, Christus Imperat!* The Gospel book, still open, was placed upon the altar. This book presided over the Council.

Only then were those who were not permitted to be present at the discussions asked to withdraw. The Secretary-General of the Council, Archbishop Pericles Felici, would call out in a loud voice, "*Exeant omnes!* Let everyone withdraw! *Remanere possunt Patres conciliares, periti, officiales, observatores!* The Council Fathers, the theological experts, the official personnel, and the observers remain!" Thus the observers were not merely admitted with the rights we have just mentioned but they had their place in the regulations of the Council and were thus an integral part of it.

It is well to mention that the Secretariat for Christian Unity facilitated the work of the observers in myriad ways. They were received by the Holy Father who that day did not receive them seated upon his throne as is customary, so that it would be clear that he was not claiming authority over Christians who were recognized as such, but who were not in communion with the See of Rome. These were only little actions, but they created a new climate of confidence. This does not signify that we have reached a doctrinal entente, but it does mark a prelude.

In the innumerable attempts at reunion which have succeeded each other ever since the initial rupture, such preludes and psychological preparation had unfortunately been disregarded. More than one attempt led to nothing for this reason, and even those which appeared to succeed were short-lived. This was the case in particular of the Union between the Greek Orthodox and Rome, proclaimed at the Second Council of Lyons in 1274, and even of the Union proclaimed at the Council of Florence (1438–43), though the preliminary theological discussion had been much more serious. We have learned better nowadays and we know that the complex of distrust must be eliminated, the conditions of a true exchange of ideas must be established, and both sides must come to regard each other as brothers, before any substantial rapprochement in doctrinal fields can be reached.

What has been said does not in any way diminish either the objectivity or the importance of the realm of ideas. I am a man devoted to the study and teaching of doctrine and I think it would take a lot of torture to make me admit anything against the objectivity or the supremacy of doctrinal truth. It is a simple admission of the facts. The act of intelligence giving honor to the truth is no different. But before apprehending truth and being, the mind must be open to both, ready to welcome them. One may consult on this subject the works of that genuine Thomist, Professor A. Forest of Montpellier. Before an explanation can really be accepted, its acceptance must be psychologically and therefore morally possible. Let us not forget the observation of St. Vincent de Paul: "We do not believe the devil because we do not love him, and he has never been able to make himself loved."

Thus the facts once again speak clearly for themselves. It is a fact that things have been and are possible in the ecumenical atmosphere of today which have been impossible during four centuries of polemics and hot and cold war. Works such as those by the Rev. Max Thurian in France, tackling difficult subjects which have been closed to discussion for several centuries—the Eucharist, the Virgin Mary, monasticism—are only possible in this ecumenical atmosphere. It is not without significance that their author is a Brother of the Community of Taizé, a man of prayer. Prayer, and as far as it is allowed, prayer in common, is one of the principal conditions of the ecumenical climate.

Only after eating together, praying and talking together, can the discussion of certain questions be approached in such a way that the other side is both heard and understood. Only then is there any real possibility of rapprochement. Pope John defined the laws governing this rapprochement when he spoke of the different stages: 1. Before union he envisaged a period of meetings and dialogue, which might be fairly long. 2. Before any formal discussion, he saw a period of "re-neighboring," a time in which to become good neighbors, in which both sides became aware of what they had in common in spite of their dissensions. 3. The need to live together on good terms (Letter to the Clergy of Venice, April 24, 1959).

Working together whenever possible is certainly an invaluable aid. I did not sufficiently recognize this element of truth in the program of practical Christianity (life and work) in my book published in 1937 (*Chrétiens désunis;* English translation, *Divided Christians*). This article of the program has, moreover, been entirely revised by the Ecumenical

Council of Churches in an atmosphere no longer tainted with the Liberalism which was still perceptible in Stockholm in 1925. Professor Heuss, shortly before withdrawing from the presidency of the Federal Republic of Germany, told the Protestant Kirchentag in Munich on August 17, 1959 how much he had gained from his collaboration throughout his career with Catholic men and expressed the wish that all his fellow countrymen and fellow Protestants might share his experience. The United States of America is certainly one of the places where this experience could be renewed.

Such an experience must, of course, be undertaken in a positive spirit: in a spirit free of rancor, distrust, prejudice, and narrow-mindedness, unworthy of a Christian who brings to the feast the bread of sincerity and truth. We would like to conclude this appeal to "conquer our enmities" with a story drawn from the life of St. Nicholas of Flue, the patron saint of Switzerland.

Nicholas had been a judge and had brought up many children—ten, if we are not mistaken. He then withdrew to lead a solitary life near the Lake of Lucerne. There in his solitude men were accustomed to come and ask his advice. This happened in particular at a moment when the Swiss Confederates, in disagreement over various important points, threatened to enter into conflict with each other.

A group of delegates came to find him and explained the subject of dispute. Nicholas took off his girdle, tied a knot in it, and handed it to the delegates saying, "Will you untie this knot?" They did so easily. "Thus," said Nicholas, "must men's difficulties also be unfastened." But as his questioner, Im Grund, protested that it was not so easy, Nicholas said to him, "You could not untie this knot either if we all pulled at the ends of the cord, and that is what men always want to do."

Bernard C. Pawley

Bernard C. Pawley, Canon and Treasurer of Ely Cathedral, is a leader in the ecumenical movement in England. Born on January 24, 1911, at Portsmouth, England, he studied at Wadham College, Oxford, and at Wells Theological College, and was ordained at Lichfield in 1936. After curacies at Stoke-on-Trent and Leeds he served as an Army chaplain from 1939–45, seeing service in East and North Africa, Italy and Germany. He was a prisoner of war from 1940–42.

He has paid numerous visits to European churches of all kinds, particularly Roman Catholic ones, in the interests of further unity and has studied the development of the liturgical and Biblical movements in considerable detail. He was sent on a visit in 1956 to Milan, then the archdiocese of the now Pope Paul VI, whose acquaintance and friendship he has enjoyed since.

When the Archbishop of Canterbury, Dr. Geoffrey Fisher, called on Pope John XXIII and Cardinal Bea on his historic visit in 1960, it was arranged that the Anglican Communion should be represented in Rome by a delegate who would study the preparation for Vatican Council II and report on it.

Since the spring of 1961 Canon Pawley has occupied this position, and from October 1962 he has also been an observer at the Council, being the special guest of the Secretariat for Promoting Christian Unity and the representative of the Archbishops of Canterbury and York. He is therefore in an advantageous position for assessing the recent developments in the Roman Catholic Church and of discussing their value for the future of the ecumenical movement.

He is the author of *An Anglican View of the Vatican Council*. It is worth noting that his name was suggested to the editor as the ideal person to express the views of the Church of England by Archbishop Michael Ramsey of Canterbury and by Bishop John P. Treacy of La Crosse, Wisconsin, who had several discussions with him during the Council.

AN ANGLICAN VIEWS THE COUNCIL

In attempting to assess the position of the Second Vatican Council at the end of its second session, your essayists all appear to be attempting a dangerous venture. They are trying to estimate the size, direction, and strength of something which is very much on the move. But fortunately the situation is not fully described by this simile. The observers at the Council have naturally been asked almost daily whether they are optimistic or pessimistic about the eventual effectiveness of the Council.

In self-defense I have worked out as an answer a set piece, which consists invariably in saying that, of course, optimism and pessimism in this sense are not Christian concepts, and that a sufficient evaluation of the present situation can be made by a realistic comparison of it with the circumstances which obtained so recently as five years ago, or even with the condition of the Roman Catholic Church at the beginning of the present Council.

When Pope John XXIII, of blessed memory, announced the Vatican Council in 1959, there is no doubt that the whole effective government of the Church was opposed to it, and indeed immediately set about to see that, if it did happen, it should bring about as little change as possible. And there must have been those who hoped that if they played out time long enough the elderly Pope might die before the Council got going, and that they would immediately be able to elect a successor who would be wiser than to repeat this error.

This extremely conservative point of view, which was that of those who were then in power, was based on the beliefs that, to begin with, the Church stood in no need of doctrinal reform, doctrine being permanent and immutable; that there was no practical question of sufficient importance in the air to warrant the calling of a Council (this being an extraordinary instrument of government, whereas all day-to-day administration reforms could and were being made by the ordinary government of the Church); and that, the decrees of the First Vatican Council being what they were, the calling of another Council might endanger the uniqueness, the sovereignty, and the infallibility of the papacy.

To remember those days now is like taking a look back into the Middle Ages, so much has happened since. Two sessions of the Council have taken place, and the bishops can confidently say, "*Nous avons changé tout cela.*" ("We have changed all that.") This change has not yet been worked out in detail or been given permanent administrative form, but of its reality there can be no doubt. It constitutes perhaps one of the most important single events in the Church history of the twentieth century.

What it amounts to is this, that the bishops of the Roman Catholic Church throughout the world, meeting for the first time for a century (and a century ago, of course, the world was a different place) have decided that they want to take upon themselves, under the headship of the Pope, the government of the Church of which they are by consecration the chief ministers. It was widely known before the Council began that there was much dissatisfaction in the air. France, Belgium, Holland, and parts of Germany were known to be seething with desire for wide reforms, though it was supposed that this was once again a case of "*le Gallicisme*" (a term used in Roman European ecclesiastical circles to mean some scatter-brained French enthusiasm), and, that once the Church got together in its international might, it would soon put an end to efforts for reform.

From the point of view of an Englishman, for example, who was quite intimately acquainted with ecclesiastical developments on the continent of Europe, but who also knew at first hand the conservative mentality of the Anglo-Irish hierarchy in Britain, the prospects were, to say the least, doubtful. Furthermore, the whole Latin and Latin-American world was supposed, by those who only knew it from outside, to be predominantly conservative.

There were known to be rebellious spirits in the U.S.A., but we in Britain again tended to assume that because of the large Irish element in the U.S. hierarchy, there must be a majority who would have strong prejudices against change of any kind. How wrong we were! And to those whom we thus misjudged, herewith our generous apology.

Pope John had given three main directions to the Council. It was to be an *aggiornamento* (a bringing-up-to-date) of the whole life of the Roman Catholic Church in whatever departments it appeared to need it. The urgent pastoral needs of the Church in all parts of the world were to be made to prevail over all other considerations. Moreover, was to have in the forefront of its concern also the tragic disunion of Christendom. That did not mean to say that the Council was exhorted to negotiate or initiate any actual schemes for union, but that, to put it from the other direction, nothing should be discussed, planned, or decided in any of the Council's sessions without real, deep consideration not only of the existence, but also of the beliefs, hopes, fears, and needs of what was now the "other half" of Christendom, the "separated brethren."

These three aims were solemnly and clearly enunciated by the Pope. Readers can therefore imagine the surprise and the indignation of many of the Fathers of the Council who, on receipt of the prepared agenda, found that no noticeable attempt had been made by the preparatory Commissions to implement any of these intentions. As to *aggiornamento*, this seemed to some to mean little more than to acknowledge the fact that the radio had been invented, and seeing to it that good conservative-minded Catholics were always appointed by the bishops to speak on it.

Modern knowledge? Restatement of the faith in modern terms? Not on your life! The "Catholic faith" had always been the same from the first, and to suppose that it could be adapted to suit the passing whims of successive ages was the well-known heresy of "modernism." What was needed was a firmer, wider, louder statement to the world of the one, true, immutable faith.

As for Union, or "Ecumenism," as the practise of it is called, that also appeared on the agenda material in a strange shape, certainly not in a way which could be said to encourage those outside the Roman Catholic Church to understand. The pattern of it was the same as perhaps it had been in official teaching for a long time. There was one Church, having one earthly head, from whom all others had separated themselves (this applied even to the Orthodox Patriarchates of the East!).

The way of ecumenism was simple. It involved a return as soon as possible of the wanderers to the one fold. All that ecumenism could mean for the Council was the explanation of some of the "difficult" doctrines, to remove what were only misunderstandings and prejudices. That done, the return of the separated brethren, Orthodox, Anglicans, Protestants, and all others could be expected quite quickly.

These papers, prepared largely under the direction of prelates whose main responsibilities and experience were in Rome, were to prove very unacceptable, both in tone and in content, to most of the bishops of the Council, though before they assembled face to face (which they had never done before) none of them could have realised how strong the objections would be, and how a majority would support them. To some the whole situation appeared to be a deep and deliberate conspiracy to defeat the express intentions of the Holy Father.

The history of the first session of the Council, largely due to the relentless thrust of American journalists, is now widely known. It can be briefly summed up as being a determined and successful effort of the bishops of the Council to wrest the power in the Church out of the hands of the Roman

Curia (that is, the Church's departmental organisation in Rome itself) and to put it firmly back where it belonged, and always should have been, in the corporate authority of the world-wide episcopate acting in conjunction with its head, the Pope. This had nevertheless not been a sordid struggle of ambitious persons seeking power, but the reasonable action of reformers removing an abuse of power.

It has seemed necessary to make this lengthy reference to the situation at the beginning of the Council in order to enable readers to perceive the amount of progress which has been made. The history of the Council has shown unbroken progress in the reform of the government of the Roman Catholic Church. The two main practical consequences of this have been: First, the actual taking over from the Roman Curia by the bishops in Council of the *magisterium*—the teaching authority—which, under the Pope, has really always been theirs. Secondly, a determination to see that in between Councils the Pope's chief body of advisers shall not be a number of clerics who live most of their lives in Rome, but a "senate," as it were, of the bishops themselves, drawn from every quarter of the earth and representing every kind of interest and opinion in the Church. To this move, the bishops had the most immediate and generous response from Pope Paul VI who, in the interval between the first and second sessions of the Council, expressed his intention of bringing about a reform of the Curia.

This whole development has been of immense consequence for the Roman Catholic Church, for Christendom, and for the prospects of eventual reunion. It has broken down a stronghold which appeared to many Roman Catholics, and to all Christendom outside the Roman Communion, as impenetrable. Moreover, it has thus enabled new ideas, in theology, in liturgy, in biblical scholarship, in sociology, and in many other fields, which otherwise might have been extinguished at birth, to come flooding into the field of discussion.

Ideas, methods of research, practical proposals for reform, and even individuals, who under the old regime were restrained, inhibited, and even in some cases persecuted, have suddenly had their restrictions removed and have felt able to speak freely. This does not mean, of course, that everybody is able to speak as he pleases in the Church's name, for the Church (which now means the bishops acting with their head, the Pope) still retains the right to distinguish authoritatively between divergent opinions.

In the Council, at least, there has been the greatest freedom of discussion. As is widely known, the Fathers have shown themselves to be engaged in what every free assembly is, a tussle between "conservatives" and "progressives," with a less articulate, but in the long run more powerful majority, sitting patiently in the centre waiting to adjudicate on the merits of the two contending wings. It is the working out of this great drama, under the guidance of the Holy Spirit, which has been the great spectacle of the Council. It represents a Roman Catholic Church which is essentially different, and better than the one we knew five years ago. That very state of affairs will probably be the main single achievement of the Council.

The first session had been a trial run. The bishops had never met before. But the theme of it was uniform and single. They intended to implement the directives of Pope John, to whom they were deeply attached, and they would stand no interference from anybody to defeat them. By these simple criteria they judged the drafts which were submitted to them.

The Liturgy, with which they started, was probably the best draft yet submitted to the Council, though even that suffered considerable amendment. It had a pastoral tone. It did what the great pastoral heart of Pope John yearned for. It took the brakes off. It enabled the faithful in distant lands to hear the Mass in their own language. It enabled regional conferences of bishops to decide questions which otherwise would have had to be submitted to Rome. And so it passed through into law, and has now been promulged by Pope John's successor, to the satisfaction of all, the actual first fruits of the Council's labours.

The other drafts, on the "Two Sources of Revelation" and part of the draft on "Ecumenism," were rejected for the very reason that they did not breathe the spirit of the great Pope's intentions. In the meanwhile, between the sessions, they were to be rewritten with those intentions in mind. The new redistribution of power, the new decentralisation, was a fact. It had come to stay.

When, to the dismay of all, Pope John died in the interim, there were prophets of gloom who said that the College of Cardinals would certainly elect a successor who would put a stop to the "liberalism" which had run riot at the Council. Here again, however, they proved to be wrong, for in the election of Pope Paul VI the cardinals gave the Church the leader it needed, the most qualified (if the choice had to be confined to an Italian) to follow the "Roncalli line."

Thus the tone and trend of the discussions in the first session, the decisiveness of its voting, and the rejection of the original agendas, all showed that great things could be expected of the second. To speak only of the Anglican observers (who consisted of one Englishman, one American, and a Ceylonese, the writer being also present as a "guest of the Secretariate for Unity"), they had reported home most favourably.

They were not totally unprepared for the changes which had happened, because Anglicans perhaps keep in closer touch with Roman Catholic affairs than do the Protestant Churches, but even to the Anglicans the strength of the newly apparent "progressives" was a surprise. The question for them, as for all the observers, now was whether the Council, which had established itself so firmly in the position of the Pope's advisory committee in the government of the

Church, would undertake the radical work of revision and restatement.

The draft agendas which had been rejected at the first session were not billed to reappear at the second. But the two most important items of all, at least for the observers, were to be the main subjects for discussion at the second session —the Church, and Unity. The debate on the Church was found to be central.

It had been felt in Roman Catholic circles that the theology of the Church needed further defining and clarification. The teaching of Pope Pius XII on the Church as the Mystical Body of Christ had left some questions unanswered. The First Vatican Council had defined in vacuo the infallibility of the Pope, without setting it adequately in the context of the episcopate. The hoped-for shuffle of the source of authority in the Church also presupposed some hard thinking on the nature of the office of a bishop. The fact that the laity of the Church were now literate surely called for some adjustment of the classical distinction between the *ecclesia docens* and the *ecclesia discens*. (That is a distinction which casts the hierarchy in the role of teachers and the laity in the role of mere learners in the Church.)

Those whose interests were chiefly concerned with the prospects of Christian Union were naturally anxious to see what the Council would make of their particular questions. Who is in fact a member of the Church? If, as is the case in Roman theology, a child is made a member of Christ by baptism, what then is the status of one baptised outside the Roman Church? And what was to be the status, as Churches, of those Christian bodies which bore the marks of Churches and were not in communion with the Bishop of Rome?

Rome had never ceased to speak of the Eastern patriarchates as Churches, even after the separation. How could they very well speak otherwise of, e.g., the Patriarch of Jerusalem and his people? Some of these latter questions naturally fell into the province of the draft on ecumenism, but they were not without their importance in the debate on the Church as well.

There is no point in disguising that the draft on the Church, as presented, was a disappointment. It is not easy to explain the attitude of observers to these things, for the attitude of one group of observers would perhaps differ from that of another. But that of the Anglicans can be taken to be *a priori* (from first principles, so to speak) one of the most sympathetic. None of us were so naïve as to suppose that the new currents of thinking would have carried the Council preparatory commissions so far as to make a doctrine of the Church which would please us.

Incidentally, we hope all readers realise that the Anglican Church believes itself, with the Orthodox, to have retained the Catholic doctrine of the Church, to which the Roman Church has added things which were not believed "*semper, ubique, ab omnibus*" ("always, everywhere, by all")—the memorable phrase used by St. Vincent of Lérins (died about 450).

What we did hope was that the draft would fulfill the Pope's intentions by taking account of, showing knowledge of, and if they were wrong, answering, non-Roman difficulties about Roman ecclesiology. This unfortunately the draft totally fails to do. As some of the bishops complained, it just hands out, at catechism level, the old school-room stuff about the Church, ill-adapted for the modern age.

To take a case in point, the papacy: infallibility, primacy, universal jurisdiction, and so forth. Under this head the draft repeats dogmatically and uncritically the conciliar teaching about the papacy, quoting familiar biblical texts, whose interpretation is everywhere questioned, and papal teachings of recent date. What was difficult for the observers was the total lack of reference under this head to the huge corpus of writings which now exist, questioning and claiming to disprove, first of all, the biblical arguments on which the papal

claims are alleged to be based and then the reasons subsequently given for the extension of them.

It is perhaps better, in memory of Pope John, that these
things should not have been argued out in the draft. That
is not the place for controversies. But if there were to be
footnotes, and if there were to be "explanations," it would
have been better if they had shown some elementary knowledge at least of the existence of other schools of thought,
and of other interpretations of Holy Scripture.

Cardinal Bea had expressed the hope, which he no doubt
still entertains, that there would be somewhere in the drafts
"explanations of the dogmas which have been obstacles between us." The only "explanation" that can be said to find a
place in any of the drafts of this session was a feeble reminder that the Pope's infallibility was not personal to him
as an individual, but applied to him only in his official capacity, and even then only under the most careful, defined circumstances—as if there were any observer or knowledgeable
non-Catholic who was not already aware of this.

It seemed ironical that there should be sitting in the observers' box, day by day, Dr. Oscar Culmann of the University of Basle, who has perhaps done more, by his Petrine
studies, to shake the biblical foundations on which the doctrines of the papacy are made to rest than any other man in
the world, yet there is no reference, in text or notes, to his
work. The draft evaded, rather than answered, the question
of baptism and Church membership by saying that Christians baptised outside the Roman Catholic Church were "in
a certain way" attached to the one Church, though they were
not in full receipt of the benefits of membership.

Furthermore, the question of the nature of bodies outside
the Roman Church, it left largely to the draft on ecumenism.
It did go so far as to say, however, that the Holy Spirit
worked in them, that in so far as some of them had valid
orders and valid sacraments they had marks of "the true
Church." But the whole draft assumed without argument

that when the Creed spoke of "the Catholic Church" it meant "the Roman Catholic Church" as now understood, and none other. On these slender foundations it was hoped to rebuild the dilapidated and divided Church of God.

The discussion, however, was of a higher order than the agenda paper, because it was free and open to all the bishops and did not allow itself to be dominated, as presumably the preparatory commissions had been, by the theologians of the Holy Office. The main feature of the debate was the bringing out and setting up as a signpost for the whole Council the principle of the "collegiality" of the bishops. The principle, which was not put out for dogmatic definition, was laid down clearly by the fathers by a heavy majority. It seemed to many to contain the seeds of immense future progress. Here might be the beginnings of a solution of the problems of the papacy.

The conservative theologians immediately attacked it as being a threat to the papacy and as being theologically untenable, though the theological commission was reminded that its job was not to tell the Council that its decisions were theologically untenable, but to formulate them in intelligible theological language. The outcome of all this debate was for the observers a most hopeful part of the Council. The picture of the Roman Catholic Church, which emerged from it, was a different one from that to which the world was accustomed.

If all this discussion was finally formulated in practice there would be a Pope having at his call a permanent "senate" or sub-committee of the bishops, totally international in character, having the Roman Curia as its administrative service; then national or regional "conferences" of bishops deciding matters which belonged to their local knowledge; and then the whole "college" of the bishops "with Peter" rather than "under Peter," feeling themselves jointly and individually heirs of the trusts, responsibilities, and privileges which Christ had bequeathed to the Apostles. With this picture of the apostolic college and succession, the Anglican delegates, naturally, felt themselves very much at home.

The other main interest, for the observer, in the draft on the Church was in the question raised concerning the inclusion of material concerning the Blessed Virgin Mary as a chapter within it. What is believed outside the Roman Catholic Church to be excessive, non-scriptural, and non-Catholic devotion to Mary is, of course, one of the chief dogmatic obstacles to union. One of the great interests in the Council, therefore, was to see which party would prevail: the "High Church" party, which wanted even further dogmas about Our Lady to be defined, or the "Low Church" party which, like Pope John, wanted no further dogmatic definitions and moreover wanted such doctrines, as there already were, stated and "explained" as far as possible from their scriptural and patristic origins.

The way in which the issue was decided was most interesting and most satisfactory to the observers—and for several reasons. First, by bringing Our Lady within the scope of the Church Militant, it saved her blessed name and figure from the impious hands of those who seem ever determined to make a semi-celestial personage of her. Secondly, because it showed up whither Mariology and Mariolatry were drifting. Was it not said in the Council that Mary was better understood in the context of Christology and Soteriology (the doctrines of Christ's nature and of how He saved us) than in the context of the Church? One of the Council wits stated that they who said such things were guilty of trying to excommunicate Our Lady! And thirdly, because it represented a real attempt to bring devotion to Our Lady within a compass, in which many others would be prepared to recognise a common heritage.

The draft on the Church now stands awaiting amendment and a certain amount of rewriting in the light of the debate. As far as the Anglican observers are concerned it represents an immense advance on what it would have been only a few years ago, for which they are most grateful. We sincerely hope that in its amended form it will show the following improvements, all of which have been mentioned in the course of the debate.

First, that its biblical references, especially those which concern the foundation and commissioning of the Church by Christ, the position of Peter among the Apostles, and his relationship to the subsequent bishops of Rome, will be "gone over" by the best available Catholic biblical and patristic scholars, of whom now the Church has a considerable number. Second, that any observations on these subjects will at least show acquaintance with, and the courtesy of reference to, the work of non-Roman scholars when and where it is relevant.

Third, that the consequences for ecclesiology of the existence as Churches outside the Roman Communion of the Eastern patriarchates will be squarely faced here, so that the case doesn't have to be argued all over again in the discussion on Ecumenism, and that the conclusions of this reasoning will then be applied *mutatis mutandis* [with the necessary changes having been made] to the consideration of the existence of the other Churches. Fourth, that more adequate consideration will be given to the place of the Holy Spirit in the Church, and of the preaching of the Divine Word as an essential activity of it. It often seems to outsiders that Roman Catholics judge others only by the criterion of whether they have a "valid" ministry or sacraments, as if it mattered not at all whether God's word was truly preached among them.

Fifth, and this might well be first, we could wish that the notion of the Church as a fellowship of sinners under judgement, yet rejoicing in God's gracious redemption, could find more room, one might almost say *some* room, in the draft. Although that truth shone most luminously through the opening discourse of Paul VI to the second session, it is most lamentably absent from the draft. The Church's majesty and glory, its privileges, its eternity, its power, were often exalted in the Council by the Cardinal Archbishops of Palermo and Genoa, in whose dioceses it should not be difficult to remember that the Church on its earthly side is fallible, sinful, and under judgement.

The Council next considered the draft on Bishops and the Government of Dioceses. Much of this discussion was naturally consequent upon the decisions of the draft on the Church, and some of its issues have been adumbrated under that heading. The "new" status of the bishop (which is, of course, only the restoration to him of his old rights) makes it natural for him to exercise many of his powers on his own initiative, subject as always to the general agreement of his peers in the national conference and to the sovereign responsibilities of the Pope.

One of the points in which Anglican observers were particularly interested was the proposal to reconsider the rightness of consecrating men to episcopal orders merely for the purpose of doing an administrative job. This, in Anglican eyes, would not amount to doing "what the Church has always done"; and the removal of this abuse (as it is believed to be) would clarify the "image" of the Roman Catholic conception of the episcopate.

The centerpiece of the whole session for the non-Roman observers was, of course, the debate on ecumenism. This draft had been rewritten in the interval, and now contained an over-all theology of ecumenism and guidance on the general principles of its application. The introductory oration assured the assembly that it would be followed up by a Directory or book of rules giving detailed instructions on how the new field of activity was to be carried out at the local level.

This is again too small a compass in which to give a detailed study of the draft. We can begin again by saying that it represents an immense improvement even on its immediate predecessor, the abortive *"Ut Omnes Unum Sint"* ("That All May Be One") debated, and handsomely rejected, last fall. As it represents the beginnings of the participation of the Roman Catholic Church in the world ecumenical movement, we can be truly thankful. We can now talk together (officially) without being spied upon by the agents of a Roman bureacracy. We shall perhaps be able even to say the Lord's Prayer, and a few others, together in public without being accused of "indifferentism." The whole draft is animated by a spirit of charity which amply reflects the love which burnt in the heart of Pope John, and which must carry all before it in the long run.

There were for the Anglican observer, however, many defects in the draft, most of which have been pointed out by the bishops themselves in the debate. The first, of course, is the (to us) naïve ecclesiology of it. Turn the scheme upside down, shuffle the pages, read the thing backwards, the conclusion is still the same, and ecumenism means only one thing: There is only one Church, and all the rest of us are separate from it (the Roman Catholic Church) and the sooner we all get back into it (Patriarchs of Jerusalem, Antioch, Alexandria, and all) the better. In fact, there is no such thing as ecumenism as commonly understood at all!

Those who know the Roman Catholic Church well are aware that there are many of her own reliable teachers who deplore this narrow view as much as we do. The draft itself compromises the view by its own frank and friendly attitude to the Oriental Churches. It is disappointing, however, that as yet, as in the draft on the Church, no real beginning is made in the resolution of this problem. The Eastern Churches themselves, by the way, will not have been pleased by the fact that no distinction was drawn between "orthodox" and other Eastern Churches. The Anglican Communion was disappointed to find no mention of itself in the list, for it could not have itself described as a "community which arose in the sixteenth century."

Here, as in the draft on the Church, we feel that the Roman Catholic Church, as its contribution to ecumenism, must resolutely face up to the facts of the present ecclesiastical scene. Unfortunately for its own theory of itself as the only Church and the only true means of grace from God to man, the hard fact is that God Himself calls, baptises, anoints, endows with His Holy Spirit, enlivens with His Word, feeds with the Holy Eucharist—in fact wholly redeems and sanctifies—countless men and women outside the borders of the Church of Rome. And where these things happen, there Christ is and there the Church is.

One is tempted to think of one of Our Lord's many rebukes to St. Peter in his formative period: "What God hath cleansed, that call not thou common." (Acts 10:15). There is in the text of the draft itself much welcome exhortation to Roman Catholics throughout the world to do more in the way of recognition and respect to those outside their communion, which will no doubt be readily obeyed. But the text hedges about the main question and only says that the "separated brethren" are *in a certain sense* members of the Church, and in a certain sense *in a kind of* communion with members of the Roman obedience, etc.

Although it is obviously not yet possible, nor would it be right, for the Roman Catholic Church to make any general declaration of ecclesiastical communion with the multitudinous sects outside her, it is to be hoped that in the course of the third session, or in the reconstruction which is going on in the meanwhile, she will show herself ready to recognise the Church status (because of the presence of God in them) of certain bodies she now only describes as "communities" and to adopt some positive attitude towards them. There have been speakers who have advocated this.

The general tone of the debate on ecumenism was encouraging, especially as the Church showed herself, in almost every country except Italy, anxious to enter into dialogue. And there, of course, there are almost no "separated brethren" to be loved, poor things; for, as one American bishop said, they've nearly all been persecuted out of existence. And that dialogue will undoubtedly take place. There are many intriguing differences of opinion as to where that dialogue might most profitably start. To be effective it must take place at every level and concern every activity of Church life.

There are in the ecumenical field already far too many people who look upon the problem entirely as a dogmatic one. Their Churches are represented in the observers' tribunal entirely by professors of academic theology. They wait anxiously to see if Rome is going to relax its dogmatic formularies and are disappointed when she does not, though they themselves remain entrenched behind their reformation bulwarks. This kind of academic confrontation must indeed take place, but within its proper proportions.

The most important task of ecumenism is to arrange an interchange of experience between congregations. The Protestant congregation, whose form of service consists mainly in listening to a monologue from a preacher, would do well to experience the congregational function of the Roman dialogue Liturgy. The Catholic congregation could profit from the experience of the Methodist "class," etc. The Anglican, standing in the middle of the road, can learn from everybody, and perhaps has something to give to all.

The Orthodox are surely meant to teach us the meaning of faith and how to recover its unity. They must lead the rest of us in learning how in our divided state we all have sinned against the truth, the Roman Catholic Church by adding to it and many of the rest of us by taking away from it. The whole exercise of recovery and renewal is a joyful prospect.

The debate on ecumenism came to an incomplete end. Some publicists, particularly from America, were hoping that the Council would make dramatic statements about the last two chapters of the draft, "On the Jews" and "On Religious Liberty"—or that the Pope would intervene and do so—and seemed to be disillusioned and disappointed when nothing happened. In this they were mistaken. Both subjects are of great complexity and need most careful treatment. In the view of many, both should be treated outside the subject of ecumenism altogether, lest it should be thought that Roman Catholic ecumenism amounts to nothing but general benevolence to all men of good will, no matter what they believe.

Americans, of all people, should understand the importance of precision with regard to religious liberty. Although the Council will undoubtedly vote in favour of it eventually, they will wish to avoid appearing to countenance, e.g., the action of wild fundamentalist sects who are ready to pour into backward countries, supported by American dollars, to impose upon simple people doctrines for which they can get little hearing in their own country.

So the great assize adjourned with its work uncompleted, but in the confidence that it had made much progress. The observers hoped that in the interim the new commissions would be able to carry that progress much farther, to the point of considering some of the remaining issues which have been mentioned above. Meanwhile, the whole Christian world rejoices in the new spirit of renewal which the Council represents, such as is enshrined in the following words from the draft on ecumenism: "Let all the faithful bear in mind that they will the better promote and even practise union among Christians, the purer and more evangelical life they strive to lead."

The whole measure of the Council can best be taken from the act of Pope Paul VI at the end of the second session, when he declared his intention to go in pilgrimage to the Holy Land. In doing so, he was not only acknowledging that all great ecclesiastical reforms must begin by a return of all to the renewal of basic Christian disciplines, but also illustrating the truth that ecumenism in its early stages will best be served not so much by intractable dogmatic confrontations as by imaginative personal contacts.

Max Thurian

When World War II broke out Roger Schutz, President of the Swiss Christian Student Movement, pedaled on his bicycle to the northern part of France and there, in the small, partly abandoned village of Taizé, founded a monastery. In January 1942, Max Thurian joined him and the two have worked closely together as Prior and Assistant Prior in the effort to introduce monastic life in the Protestant Churches. In 1949 the seven first brothers took their lifelong vows of celibacy, community of goods, and acceptance of the authority of the Prior, which correspond to the classical vows of chastity, poverty, and obedience.

Taizé is thus the first monastic community of men in the Reformed or Lutheran Churches. One of the chief objectives of the community is to work and pray for the unity of all Christians. Liturgy occupies a central place in the religious life of the community. In 1964 the community had grown to sixty, and to this little village in Burgundy come many visitors, Eastern Orthodox, Roman Catholics, and Protestants, from all parts of the world to join the community in virtually continuous prayer for the realization of that unity for which Christ prayed so ardently.

Frère Max Thurian works in the theological and liturgical fields and is the director of the review *Verbum Caro*. He serves as a research assistant for Faith and Order, the theological department of the World Council of Churches. Since 1949 he and Prior Schutz have visited each year prominent prelates and officials of the Roman Catholic Church in Rome. They were received by Pope Pius XII in two private audiences and had the unusual privilege of having four private audiences with Pope John XXIII.

Born August 16, 1927, in Geneva, Max Thurian studied theology at the University of Geneva until his ordination. He attended the World Conferences of Faith and Order at London in 1952 and at Montreal in 1963, and the World Conference of the Council of Churches at New Delhi in 1961. He is a prolific contributor to many liturgical and theological journals and is the author of *Confession, Marriage and Celibacy, Eucharistic Memorial, Confirmation, Eucha-*

rist at Taizé, The Virgin Mary, Visible Unity and Tradition, and *Modern Man and Spiritual Life.*

Along with Prior Schutz, Frère Thurian was an observer at the sessions of Vatican Council II, both being the special guests of the Secretariat for Promoting Christian Unity. Frère Max Thurian is probably the most articulate voice of the community at Taizé, and in his writings one catches an echo of the constant prayers of his brethren for the fulfillment of Christ's prayer for the unity of all His followers.

WALKING TOGETHER TO CHRIST

When Pope John XXIII announced the Council on the twenty-fifth of January 1959, the world understood that it was a question of a Council unifying separated Christians. This interpretation was, however, very quickly contradicted when it was shown that the Roman Catholic Church was in the first place to settle problems that concerned it alone before facing the problem of a unifying Council. After the first two sessions, however, it cannot be denied that the idea of Christian unity played a very large role in the discussions and in the published texts. We shall never sufficiently appreciate the importance of observers at the sessions of the Council. Even if they did not take an active part in the discussions, their presence was still a good sign and a constant appeal to the members of the Council.

Even when the members themselves were treating problems that concern only the Roman Catholic Church, and *a fortiori*[1] when they faced the question of Christian unity, they could not help but try to include all baptized people, all Christians. Many of the speakers adoped the habit of directing their remarks not only to the *eminentissimi ac reverendissimi Patres*,[2] but also to the *carissimi observatores*[3] (and, in the last session, to the lay audience). This was not merely a formula of politeness, but we felt very distinctly that they were concerned about being understood by Christians who are not Roman Catholics.

And so the Council, at first understood to be a Council preparing for unity, actually turned out to be, in spite of all denials to the contrary, such as it had been interpreted by

[1] With greater reason.
[2] Most eminent and Reverend Fathers.
[3] Dearest observers.

people throughout the world, and certainly such as the idea of it had come from the heart of good Pope John. It is at any rate a Council preparing for the visible unity of Christians. In what respect is it precisely that and how does it realize this objective? What are the problems that it sees in this reconstruction of Christian unity? What are the tentative solutions that it proposes? What are the obstacles that it brings to light on the road to unity?

I. THE REFORMATION OF THE CHURCH

The Roman Catholic Church Proceeds to Reform Itself

Ten years ago it would have been rash to speak or write about reforming the Church. Pope John XXIII launched with the Council the idea of the *aggiornamento* of the Church. This notion implies literally a bringing up to date. That means on the one hand that the Church feels itself grown old in some of its institutions and forms, and desires to be rejuvenated by the power of the Spirit; its message no longer appeals to the man of today and it must readjust and bring up to date its pastoral side. One of the aims of the Council is pastoral. That is to say, the Church wishes to find in eternal truth a new and a fresh expression which will correspond to the expectations and to the language of modern man.

On the other hand, *aggiornamento* also means that the Church wishes to renew its message by going back to the *sources* of faith. The simple pastoral *aggiornamento*, adapted to the man of today, leads the Church to a theological *aggiornamento* adapted to the will of God for today. Dogma and pastoral practice are very closely connected, and one can't modernize the one without the other. The Roman Catholic Church has, of course, no intention of changing its dogmas in the Vatican Council.

Dogmas are, however, susceptible of interpretation and, if

the Church in its pastoral effort wishes to be better understood by modern man, it is forced in its theological efforts to rethink the expression of its dogmas so that they may inspire a pastoral practice which will guide the man of today to confess Christian truth in his whole life. For the Church, rethinking the expression of its dogmas means revivifying its thought and its language at the very sources of faith: Scripture, apostolic tradition, the living liturgy, and the charity of Christ Himself.

All this is actually a reformation of the Church. It is not a change in the fundamental dogmas of faith, but only an effort on the part of the Church to make a new adaptation of its message to the sources of faith and to the man of today. This effort at reform cannot help but be favorable to the visible unity of Christians. As a matter of fact, schisms have often come about because of the refusal of the Church to adopt a necessary reform or the delay in applying such a reform. We can very well say today that if the reforms effected by the Council of Trent had taken place at the *beginning* of the sixteenth century, there probably would not have been any Protestant Reformation. Then the Catholic Reformation would not have had to be accomplished in an atmosphere of opposition to a schism.

Of course, we cannot remake history. We know that there were wrongs on both sides, that schism is never desirable nor happy. We can be happy, however, over the fact that the Church is today courageously facing a reform whose consequences can be considerable. It is to be hoped that the non-Catholic Churches also accept this effort at reform, because they themselves are only too often rigidly set in their own ways. It is only by means of this reformation of the whole of Christianity that we will find the road to the visible unity of Christians in a single Church.

The Church Wishes to Be a Servant and to Be Poor

The Council has seen the rebirth of the desire for poverty in the conscience of the Church. Much has been said about the Church of the poor. There is here, to be sure, an improper use of terms, because the Church is everybody's Church and not only the Church of the poor. Little by little, the idea has become clarified, and we see that the intention of many bishops is to re-emphasize poverty within the Church and its status as a servant.

The Church and particularly the hierarchy have often been defined juridically in terms of rights and powers. Today everybody feels the need of finding more Biblical and humble language for defining the Church and its ministry. Without totally abandoning the juridical aspect of the Church, we would prefer to see the idea of right replaced by the idea of *charism* (gift of the Holy Ghost) and the idea of power replaced by the idea of service (serving the people of God). These two Biblical notions of gift and service imply the virtue of poverty.

The Church knows that it is nothing without the power of Christ and the gifts of the Holy Ghost. It has its hands open to receive all things from the Father. What it has received in its poverty, it cannot keep for itself, for its own glory and well-being. It must rid itself of everything and hand it on to the whole world, giving it to everybody because it is everybody's servant. At the time of the first session many Fathers denounced the triumphalism of the Church, the zest for combat, victory, and glory, which is a perennial temptation for the Church. The vision of a Church, poor and serving the people, reveals the positive aspect of the criticism of triumphalism, which in itself is a negative thing.

The discussions over the schema treating of the Blessed Virgin had the same implications and symbolized to a certain degree the thoughts of the Council on the Church. There was a period during which the Roman Catholic Church thought it its duty to underline the grandeur of the vocation of Mary. Perhaps the time has finally come for it to lay greater stress on her poverty, humility, and service in relation to Christ. Not of course to diminish her grandeur, but to show that her greatness in the eyes of God consists not so much in a royalty and a power conceived in human fashion, but rather in the poverty of humble folk who are totally dedicated to the service of God. And so the greatness of Mary, such as we see her in the *Magnificat*, is the greatness of the blessed one, full of grace, seen in her poverty as the *servant* of the Lord.

The fact that the section on the Virgin Mary has become the sixth chapter of the dogmatic constitution on the Church brings out the point that, if the Church is a servant and poor, it is because Mary is that too: she is the first Christian and the figure of the Church.

This new consciousness of the Church of being a servant and poor prepares it in a way totally new for the ecumenical dialogue. When this consciousness is translated into action, non-Catholics will no longer fear to find themselves facing a Catholic Church seeking to conquer its enemies, but they will rediscover fraternal confidence in an effort of mutual service and in a real attitude of poverty and humility. To refind their visible unity, Christians must realize that they do not possess the truth, but that they are possessed by it; and if they wish to enlighten one another like brothers, they can only do it in the spirit of service and poverty of those who have received everything to share it with everybody else.

The Church Asks Pardon and Grants Pardon

Faith in the holiness of the Church has in the course of history justified a feeling of personal holiness in the serious-minded people of the various Churches. Because the Church is holy in its faith and its sacraments and an instrument of salvation, is no reason why it cannot be familiar with the stains of sin in its laity, clergy, and hierarchy. How often might it not have happened that a humble and repentant attitude would have prevented divisions and reconciled those who were separated? We must try to recover the lost virtue of admitting our mistakes and also the virtue of a sincere repentance and a generous compassion in order to recover our lost Christian unity.

Everybody knows how many doors the humility of Pope John XXIII has managed to throw open, doors that everybody thought closed for a long time to come. On September 29, 1963, when Pope Paul VI opened the second session of the Council and expressed words of regret for the divisions, and publicly asked pardon for the wrongs that might have been done to non-Catholics—sentiments he repeated on the occasion of the audience granted to the observers—everybody sensed that a new period was inaugurated in the ecumenical dialogue. Today more than ever is it necessary for the Church's welfare that the members of the hierarchy be really humble people and that they know how to admit sincerely their wrongs and their errors, that they ask pardon for them, and that they pardon everybody. The holiness of the Church, the body of Christ, will be all the more manifest.

The Church Sees the Possibility of a Church Outside Itself

A certain identification of the Roman Catholic Church with the complete body of Christ or even with the Kingdom of God has pushed outside the Church all baptized people who do not belong explicitly to the Church. The Council has realized that outside the Roman Catholic Church there is the possibility of a Church; not only of individual Christians who might be saved by reason of their ignorance and good faith, but real Church-like communities (Churches even, in so far as orthodoxy is concerned) which, even if separated from the see of Rome, can be instruments of salvation by reason of the faith they profess, the baptism they administer, the rites they celebrate, their love of holy Scripture, and their practice of charity.

The schema on ecumenism endeavors to make the most of the elements of churchness, which are to be found in the ecclesiastical communities separated from Rome. Prayer in common for unity is strongly encouraged, and bishops should stimulate the ecumenical movement in their dioceses. This is a totally new attitude, a positive and a generous one in regard to non-Catholics who are baptized and to the communities to which they belong.

If at other times the Roman Catholic Church might have appeared to other Christians to be in a state of rigid expectancy, waiting for them to come to her, without her having to walk toward them or with them, we have to admit today that the spirit of the Council—that is to say, the Holy Spirit who vivifies the Church—has modified the attitudes and impressions on both sides. It is no longer a question of the outsiders turning back or returning or coming home. All these terms are outmoded. It is a question of all of us *walking together* on the same road toward Christ, Who is the future of our unity. He is the one Who will accomplish this Christian unity.

Of course, the Roman Catholic Church believes the road is lined with the signs of the dogmas it believes in; we, of course, think that this trip together should be inspired by the Word of God as contained in the Sacred Scriptures. But both sides are convinced that the truth, so tied up with unity, cannot be proclaimed without serious concern about its being understood and comprehended by all baptized persons. Thanks to John XXIII, thanks to Paul VI, thanks to the tireless work of Cardinal Bea and his collaborators in the Secretariat for Unity, non-Catholic observer-delegates and observer-guests have been present at the Council, following the progress of the Council in which all the implications of the Church's traditional teaching have been coming to light.

Who would have thought five years ago that the dogmas of the First Vatican Council would be susceptible of receiving a new light from the teaching on the sacramental character and the collective aspect of the episcopacy, studied in an Ecumenical Council? The Roman Church is on the march, and we too are on the march toward a greater illumination, which will come from the visible unity of all baptized persons. In the dynamism of this forward march, under the inspiration of the Holy Ghost, we are freed from all fear: unity will not be the victory of one side and the defeat of the other, but the mutual recognition of the fact that no longer will anything essential separate us, once our dialogue has been perfected and once we have discovered together all the multiple ecumenical implications of the truth that urges us.

We are already united by baptism, by belief in the Trinity, and belief in Christ. Our road is one and the same because it starts with baptism and the fundamental faith expressed in the creed. We do not come from different origins; we all have one and the same origin. Pope Paul VI on the occasion of his consecration and on the occasion of the audience granted to the observers applied to the unity of Roman Catholics and other Christians the text of the letter of St. Paul to the Ephesians: "One Lord, one faith, one baptism."

Beginning now we can all rejoice over this fundamental unity which exists between both sides. By baptism we have been incorporated into the same body, the body of Christ: by reason of our fundamental faith as expressed in the Apostles' creed, by our faith in the Trinity, by our faith in Christ, we are all of one mind in glorifying the Father, the Son, and the Holy Ghost. We are all of one mind in regard to the mysteries of the Incarnation, the Redemption, the Holy Ghost, the Ascension, the Gifts of the Holy Ghost to the Church, the looking forward to Christ's second coming, and to the manifestation of the Kingdom of God.

Our progress toward a visible unity of Christians is solidly based on baptism and our fundamental faith, and consists in a mutual illumination in the dialogue in order to discover together the developments of dogma and to recognize one day the manifold richness of the one truth in charity. The Christian people have much to hope for in the *common prayer* for unity because, if the road is still a long one, our hearts are ready for the discoveries that the Holy Ghost wills to have us find out.

II. THE PROGRAM OF REFORM

The Church has begun by placing herself in the presence of her Lord and by reflecting on her prayer, her way of proclaiming the Gospel, and her role of a spouse contemplating her Lord. This was the essential work of the first session of the Council, which resulted in the practically unanimous vote of the second session on the magnificent constitution on the liturgy. Then in the second session the Church reflected on its nature and its structure in the important schema on the Church. The main points were the sacramental nature of the episcopacy, the collegiality of bishops, and the diversity of ministries: bishops, priests, and deacons. Finally, the Church reviewed its connections with all baptized persons in the schema on ecumenism. It is now ready to take up its relationship with the world in the texts on the Church and the world, on religious liberty, and on the Jews (schema 17).

The Liturgy

It is impossible to show here all the merits of the constitution on the liturgy. The application of this program of reform and the work of the commissions after the Council will bring to light, step by step, all the implications of this considerable reassessment of the liturgy.

This text shows a remarkable courage on the part of the Church which, without losing its respect for the traditions of the liturgy, is prepared to make the largest possible revision of the books used in the liturgy. In the future, all the liturgical texts will be subjected to a conscientious study and will be better adjusted to authentic sources and adapted to the needs of the man of today.

All the fruits of the liturgical movement of recent years are summed up in the insistence made by the constitution on the participation of everybody in liturgical functions. The liturgy is not a group of rites celebrated by the priests alone to insure the validity of the sacraments and the authenticity of the preaching of the Gospel. It is really something looked upon as the work of the people of God in the presence of its Lord in which each member, priests and lay people alike, participates in praising and praying according to the gifts and functions of each one.

After centuries of performing its rites in a purely liturgical language and one foreign to the majority of Catholics, the Roman Church has finally agreed to extend as far as possible the use of the language of the people into the liturgy. The consequences of this decision can be enormous.

The proclamation of the Word of God through readings from the Scriptures and through homilies has been restored to its place of honor, and thus the Bible assumes a position of great importance in liturgical functions. Provisions for a few cases of receiving Communion under two species knocks a breach in the wall, created by the Council of Trent when it was faced with the demands of the reformers of the sixteenth century. Obviously the doctrine has not been changed at all, but it is possible to foresee instances of Communion under two species multiplied in the future. And so it is that the Roman Church in the practical matter of receiving

Communion leaves itself open to satisfying the desires of Protestants and the Eastern Churches.

Finally, while dealing with matters characteristic of the liturgical reform, we ought to mention the matter of con-celebration. The possibility of several priests celebrating just one single Eucharistic sacrifice in particular cases of gatherings or meetings or pilgrimages or in convents, brings out the communal character of the priesthood and avoids the multiplication of Masses in one and the same place.

What we have mentioned about this fine liturgical reform contributes considerably to ecumenism. In all this the Church goes out to meet non-Catholics and in all fidelity to its dogmas prepares the way for a visible unity.

The Ministry

The most debated points in the constitution on the Church were the sacramental character of the episcopacy, the collegiality of bishops, and the diaconate. A significant vote showed that the majority opinion in the Council on these points was favorable. We cannot predict the final result of the voting in the third session, but we can foresee that these points will be definitely accepted, allowing for a few amendments.

The sacramental character of the episcopacy makes this office essentially distinct from the priesthood. The bishop is not just a priest above other priests, who has received added sacramental graces in order to confirm and ordain, and added powers in order to insure the integration and the unity of the parishes in his diocese. His office is proper and distinct; he receives it from a sacramental episcopal consecration. He receives special *charisms;* he is the head and father of a local church, his diocese; he is the successor of the Apostles; he has an office that is unique liturgically, theologically, and administratively.

Of course, this vision of the episcopacy will create new

problems in the dialogue with those Protestant Churches which have no episcopacy in the sacramental sense, or which do not have any bishops at all. As long as a bishop could be considered to be just a priest with more extensive jurisdiction and power, one could more easily imagine the restoration of the episcopacy in those Churches which do not have any. The sacramental character of the episcopacy creates a new difficulty in the ecumenical dialogue with Protestantism but not with the Anglican Church or the Eastern Churches. Just the opposite is the case here.

But even if new difficulties arise, we must bear in mind that the episcopacy appears in a new light and a more evangelical one; in this sense the sacramental character of the episcopacy should make the ecumenical dialogue easier. As a matter of fact, instead of being defined in terms of powers and rights, the episcopacy appears now much more of a *charism*, a gift of the Holy Ghost, an office and a service offered to the people of God. The episcopacy is a gift of God with a view to service. The bishop is given to the people of God in a local church, to serve it, to serve the clergy, to serve the lay people for the edification of everybody.

The idea of the collegiality of bishops has a very ecumenical aspect. The First Vatican Council ran the risk of making the Pope stand out in a sort of isolation. To say that the bishops are united to him collectively, as a group, responsible for the whole Catholic Church, amounts to removing to a great extent this impression of papal isolation. Of course, it remains to be defined how this group can operate, but the simple statement of the union of the bishops with the bishop of Rome, their head, concerned together about all the Churches, is already an act profoundly ecumenical.

The discussions about the diaconate revealed the desire to diversify the ministry with a view to the common good: bishop, priest, deacon, are all three given by God, invested with a *charism* intended to furnish a proper and distinct serv-

142

ice to the people of God. On the other hand, the diaconate brings out the pastoral concern of the Church. For instance, in some regions of Latin America priests are lacking, and the making of deacons out of married men, who have proven themselves as laymen to be servants of the Church, might be a big help to the Church there in the matter of preaching, spiritual direction, and administering certain sacraments, such as baptism, distribution of Holy Communion, perhaps even officiating at marriages. It belongs to the Church to define, in conformity with its great Christian tradition, the elements of this branch of the ministry for the good of all concerned in the spread of the Gospel.

Ecumenism

The schema on ecumenism, followed in all the discussions of the Council, each part of which, as we have already seen, has a certain ecumenical bearing, leads us to a conclusion which brings out very clearly one of the objectives of this bringing up to date of the Catholic Church: the preparation for a visible unity.

We should first of all single out the insistence on unity by baptism. In a certain sense all baptized people belong to the *Church*. Baptism is already in itself a sign of our visible unity, at least inchoatively: it is a solid and sure beginning of our future total unity. Although separated on important points, we do have a common fundamental faith which finds its expression in the Nicene Creed formulated by the First Council of Nice in 325 and reaffirmed by the First Council of Constantinople in 381, in the dogmas of the first four Ecumenical Councils, in the reception of the two major sacraments, baptism and the Eucharist (abstracting from the important question of the validity of the latter sacrament), and in the determination to preach the Gospel of Christ as contained in Holy Scripture. Finally we are deeply united in our common prayer for the visible unity of Christians, such as Christ wishes it, by the means that He wishes, and when He wishes it.

All these elements of unity fill us with great hopes for the ecumenical movement which now cannot help but make progress and become accelerated. The pilgrimage of the Pope to the Holy Land and his historic meeting with the patriarch of Constantinople afford new grounds for these great hopes. Some big problems still exist into which the ecumenical dialogue will have to dig more deeply. There already are indications, however, that we wish to pursue courageously the road to unity.

It has already been said many times that a declaration of religious liberty by the Roman Catholic Church would be a very important step forward. The text presented at the end of the second session is a very suitable one for making this gesture, so greatly desired by so many. It is to be hoped that it will be adopted in the third session after the necessary amendments have been made, but these must not weaken its character as an ecumenical event.

An important problem which comes up in the ecumenical dialogue, and which constitutes a sort of test for the future, is the problem of mixed marriages—marriages between Catholics and non-Catholics. Might it not be possible on the basis of our unity in baptism and in fundamental faith to find a broader canonical legislation according to the following perspectives?

It is very unsatisfactory to consider the problem from the single pastoral point of view, bringing up all sorts of dangers and demanding guarantees. The problem should be tackled by starting from a point of view properly ecclesiological and sacramental. Might it not be well to examine the following considerations and suggestions submitted with a view of deepening understanding, brotherhood, and love among Christians respectfully and thus further the movement for the fulfillment of Christ's prayer for unity among all His followers?

1. The marriage of two baptized people, that is to say, members of the body of Christ, even if they are divided from the point of view of belonging to different Churches, is a valid marriage, since the two baptized persons are the ministers of the sacrament.

2. If the marriage takes place in the Catholic Church, a second blessing by the non-Catholic minister should be allowed, for reasons of ecumenical charity and out of respect for the non-Catholic conscience.

3. If the marriage takes place in the Church of the non-Catholic, the Roman Catholic Church should have the right to demand in return that a blessing should likewise be given by a Catholic priest; he then becomes the official witness of the Catholic Church and the proof that the marriage is recognized by that Church.

4. A mixed pastoral program should be worked out by the Catholic priest and the minister together and this should help the mixed couple lead an ecumenical spiritual life and work out an ecumenical educational program for the children without any confusion or indifferentism.

5. For the sake of family unity it would seem preferable that the children be baptized and educated in the Church which was selected by the mixed couple for the celebration of their marriage.

6. The choice of the Church for the celebration of the marriage ought to be guided by consideration for: either the more faithful and practicing party or, if both parties are faithful and practicing, then the preference should be given to the woman who, since she is the mother, will have the more delicate responsibility for the children's religious education.

7. It is quite abnormal for the Catholic Church to recognize the marriage of two non-Christians and not to recog-

nize as valid the marriage of two baptized persons, separated by belonging to different Churches.[4]

8. The present position of the Catholic Church is not to its advantage: it is just the opposite, for statistics show that the rigorous position of the Church accounts for more mixed marriages in non-Catholic Churches; it should be clear that from a psychological point of view two people in love are irresistibly repulsed by a juridical rigorous regulation and accept a solution which appears to them more generous.

9. The practice of excommunicating Catholics married in a non-Catholic Church creates an enormous difficulty for many priests; the excommunicated Catholic party often tends either to join the non-Catholic Church or to fall into religious indifference.

In conclusion, the important task now incumbent on the ecumenical dialogue is a work of deep theological investigation into the doctrinal, liturgical, and sacramental values scattered throughout the different fragments of Christianity. The ecumenical discussions of the past have been too much dominated by the notions of power, validity, and legality. These notions are important, but they should be filled out by reflecting on the gifts of the Spirit Who breathes where He will, as well as on the transformation that these gifts bring about in human life. In all honesty these transformations must be recognized to exist in the different Churches, no matter what their canonical position.

For Catholic theologians this means a study of the doctrinal and sacramental values to be found outside the limits of the Roman Catholic Church. What significance is there, for example, in a Eucharistic ceremony outside the Apostolic succession, but which is performed with the sincere and firm desire to imitate the action of Christ in conformity with the primitive tradition of the Church?

[4] Editor's note: The Catholic Church recognizes both the sacramental character and the validity of the marriage of two baptized persons belonging to different Protestant denominations.

Unity can never be attained by the ecclesiastical and doctrinal victory of one side and the defeat of the other. We must, according to the words of good Pope John, *walk together*. In the course of this journey together we will get to know one another better. In knowing one another better, we come to realize still better that what unites us is always more important and stronger than what divides us. The day will come when we will be so intermingled that we will consider ourselves as being divided inside one and the same visible Church to which we all belong, and then we will pray to God to absorb these internal divisions without letting uniformity impoverish the necessary diversity in a refound unity.

Emile-Joseph De Smedt

Emile-Joseph De Smedt, Bishop of Bruges, Belgium, was one of the influential voices raised in behalf of the ecumenical movement at both the first and second sessions of Vatican Council II. Born at Opwijk in the archdiocese of Malines-Brussels, on October 30, 1909, he is the oldest in a family of nine. He studied at the Gregorian University in Rome, where he received the doctorate in philosophy and theology.

He was ordained on September 17, 1933, and served as the Director of the Seminary of St. Joseph and later of the Grand Seminaire at Malines. On June 29, 1950, he was consecrated a bishop and served as the vicar general and auxiliary bishop to His Eminence Joseph Cardinal Van Roey, Archbishop of Malines. Two years later he was appointed Bishop of Bruges, and is a member of the Secretariat for Promoting Christian Unity.

At the first session of the Council when the Fathers were discussing the "Sources of Revelation," Bishop De Smedt spoke on behalf of the Secretariat for Promoting Christian Unity and explained the qualities necessary for a true ecumenical dialogue. At the end of his address the Council Fathers broke out in loud and continued applause. Commenting on his talk in *Le Monde*, November 21, 1962, Henry Fesquet said, "This was one of the great moments of the Council." Later in the discussion on "The Church," the talk by Bishop De Smedt proved equally enlightening and provoked widespread favorable comment, both within and without the Council.

In the second session of the Council, Bishop De Smedt's talks on ecumenism and on religious liberty were received with widespread ethusiasm and applause, and our readers will find his treatment of these two topics of profound interest. Thus it is seen that the Bishop of Bruges played an unusually important role in both sessions of the Council. Bishop De Smedt is the author of *Marriage*, which has passed the five hundred thousand mark in sales; *The Great Mystery; Christ in My Quarter; Conjugal Love;* and *The Priesthood of the Faithful*.

TOLERANCE, FREEDOM,
AND ECUMENISM

It is certain that Christ wants unity among Christians. In His Sacerdotal Prayer uttered at the Last Supper, He asked it explicitly of His Father. He did not want it merely for the disciples that were His contemporaries. He wants peace to reign in the minds and hearts of all those who follow Him in every epoch of the history of redemption. He wants it also for our own epoch.

At this very hour the Holy Spirit is awakening a nostalgia among Christians for their lost unity. He is giving the baptized to understand that there is something that is not right in their lives, that their situation has something abnormal about it. Through man's own fault the Word does not exercise the force of persuasion in this world that the fire of the Holy Spirit wants to give it. The hour has come in which humility and repentance are gaining the hearts of Christians. It is the hour of grace. At the Ecumenical Council the Fathers, theologians, laymen, and non-Catholic observers all felt the influence of the salutary uneasiness and anxiety which comes from "the Father of Lights" (James 1:17).

Shouldn't we see in this a first step toward unity? As long as the members of the Catholic Church were content to thank God for possessing the Truth, with hardly a concern that they should possess it in common with their Orthodox and Protestant brothers, they were like the citizens of those flourishing medieval cities who lived happily within their walls, quite unconcerned for the well-being of their country neighbors. At present there is not a Catholic parish that isn't talking about ecumenicism, that isn't praying that the people of God may recover their lost unity. "Where there is a will," runs the saying, "there's a way."

Christian Tolerance

All the press of North America proclaimed as an item of important news the fact that the Ecumenical Council had begun discussion on a schema concerning religious liberty. It would appear that this question preoccupies public opinion there. This news has created a similar stir likewise in Europe, Latin America, Africa, and even in the immense territories of Asia and Oceania. It has been remarked that at the Council itself the Fathers have manifested a particular concern for this problem. The whole world seems to be waiting for the Catholic Church to make a pronouncement on the rights of conscience in the religious domain.

Will this provide a new step toward unity? Without the slightest doubt. Authoritative voices within the World Council of Churches have spoken to the Secretariat for Christian Unity about the need for the Council to confront the question of religious tolerance. They have stressed the fact that the Catholic Church has often been accused of a kind of Machiavellism in this domain. It is said that Catholics make such mention of religious liberty as long as they are a minority within a country, but that they don't speak about this same liberty any longer once they become the majority. On the other hand, in Catholic circles the necessity is seen for a clear and precise declaration in order that the Church may play its full role of pacification in a world that finds itself increasingly divided in ideology. The peaceful coexistence of citizens belonging to different religions, as well as of those who claim no religion at all, is not possible except in a climate where all these different convictions are held in mutual respect.

In what direction does the declaration which is being prepared at the Council point? It is based on a concept of personalism. The Catholic Church has always been concerned with the defense of the dignity of the human person and of his rights. The grandeur of man is that he was created in the image of God. This implies that he was also made to participate in God's liberty. Man is capable of acting freely and he must do it in conformity with the divine law.

But how is man to know what the divine law demands of him? It is here that the personal conscience intervenes. To act according to one's conscience means to want to follow the divine will in so far as this will is known by the effort of a serious act of reflection. Confronted by a decision which will orient his action, one's conscience must answer two questions: what is it that God wants of me, and how am I going to respond to His will?

It is obvious that we are dealing here with an infinitely personal response. In this domain no other person, no human institution, or no established power can take the place of one's conscience. How could they? Can anyone else take my place and say: Here is how the will of God appears to me and how I am going to respond to it freely? It is physically impossible. Besides, it would be a violation of my most sacred rights. It would also be a contradiction of the will of God, which demands that I act as a *free* being.

Let us take a concrete case. After a period of ripe reflection and of assiduous prayer, my conscience tells me that I must serve God in the Catholic Church. I make this decision and I then thank God for having permitted me to respond to the invitation of His grace and to organize my life in consequence of it. All this takes place within the sanctuary of my conscience, in that sacred place where I meet Him Who is my Creator and my Father. Let us suppose that some other human being or institution reproaches me for this decision and sees a reason in it to treat me with contempt.

I have a right to reply: As an upright and honest man, could I have acted otherwise if it was my intimate conviction that God demands this allegiance of me? If I am told that I am mistaken in my interpretation of God's will, I shall reply: Show me that I am mistaken, convince me of my error. As long as I myself don't see the justice of your objections, it is my duty to follow the dictates of my conscience.

In the decree that is being prepared by the Council it is understood that the foregoing argument of conscience holds true equally for the Protestant, Orthodox Christian, and even for the atheist who, in good faith, sincerely follows the judgment of his conscience. Every sincere man who conducts himself in regard to God according to the intimate convictions of his conscience is an honorable man, worthy of respect. Others must act loyally toward him. They may not prevent him from satisfying the demands of his conscience.

Actually, it is rather difficult to prevent someone from having a personal conviction. Outward methods don't take a direct hold on the conscience of another man. But there are methods which, indirectly, may shake one's most intimate convictions. Suppose that I am threatened with imprisonment or death. It may happen also that people try to make me change my mind by enticing promises, or that they subject me to hysterical propaganda in favor of ideas which I do not share, or apply psychological methods of persuasion that affect my personality, as in brainwashing.

All these are examples of what we may call a disloyal proselytism. In this case, it is a matter of methods which aim at trying to make a man say "black" when he himself sees white. The Catholic Church may not allow her members to employ such a method to draw anyone into her ranks. On the other hand, she also declares it inadmissible that any of her own faithful be subject to the same attempts on the part of someone engaged in a propaganda campaign for another conception of life.

The practical application of these principles may, however, lead to complications. This happens when one's personal conscience demands that one manifest one's inward convictions by certain exterior attitudes which are visible to others and which enter therefore into the social scene. Such are all acts of public worship or any preaching of a faith. Thus it often occurs that intimate convictions lead to exterior activities which separate individuals and groups and create a situation of conflict.

It is obvious that all well-educated and right-thinking people will display a reasonable and understanding attitude when presented with these situations. They will make the distinction between that which is essential and that which is of merely secondary importance. They will understand that order and peaceful coexistence would be impossible in any society in which everyone was determined to push his own rights to their extreme limits. A certain *savoir vivre*, an observance of the usages of good society, is required of all. Charity, and respect for the conscience of the other demand that in every society an atmosphere of liberty and of mutual good will prevail.

Liberty is a possession of which any society must be proud, and which it must protect to the greatest possible degree. A civilized nation will consider it a sacred patrimony that witnesses to the high degree of culture attained by its citizens. Certainly there will be cases in which it will be necessary for the public authority to intervene in order to safeguard the religious liberty of its citizens. But in order to prevent any danger of partiality or intolerance in case of conflict, it is best to inscribe in fundamental law the equality of all citizens and religions and their equal right to a reasonable propaganda. Whatever the circumstances, the public authority will prefer to appeal to moderation and tolerance rather than to take coercive measures, and it will limit its interventions to the strict minimum.

The principles enunciated above, we may be sure, will constitute the basis of the declaration on religious liberty which the Eumenical Council is now planning to formulate. If this solemn proclamation of the Assembly helps to create a favorable climate of mutual respect among the whole human family, it is above all the great Christian families which it will lead toward a greater unity, and it is among them especially that it will create a spirit of good will and charity.

The Ecumenical Spirit

It has been said that the Catholic Church displayed a considerable degree of hesitation in the face of the ecumenical movement for a long time, but that since the creation of the Secretariat for Christian Unity, presided over by Cardinal Bea, and particularly since the beginning of the Ecumenical Council, it has assumed more or less the leadership of the movement. For accuracy's sake, it would be well not to exaggerate either of these affirmations. It is certain, however, that since the Council the dialogue between Catholics and other Christians has developed considerably.

What precisely is happening? The ecumenical movement is difficult to define abstractly. This is understandable: it is always difficult to encapsule a living reality in a verbal formula. It is easier to describe its manifestations and its characteristics than to say exactly what it consists of. Ecumenicism is an *élan vital*, a vital force, and a manifestation of the action of the Holy Spirit in the Christian communities. The ecumenical movement is a new encounter of the separated brethren who belong to the same Christian family. God is the Father of this family, Christ is its founder, and the Holy Spirit animates it.

The three Persons of the Holy Trinity can no longer tolerate the present situation. They want Christians to be united, and they want them to be a visible sign and an effective sacrament before the entire world of that unity which should reign in the whole of human society. And what do we see? Where previously prejudice and suspicion prevented any rapprochement between the Catholic Church and the other Christian Churches or communions, today the climate is in the process of changing. This is due principally to the fact that a truly clarifying dialogue is what is being sought now.

In fact, within the ecumenical movement qualified Christians belonging to different confessions are working at the job of getting to know each other better. It isn't simply a matter of good feelings or of prayers for the same intention. The engagement is taking place in the area of conflict itself. Non-Catholics say to Catholics: Here is what we cannot admit in the doctrine and discipline of the Catholic Church. Here, according to our way of seeing things, is where you Catholics are not faithful to the thought and to the will of Christ. Let us add, however, they ask also this preliminary question: Are we correctly informed in this matter? Are things in the Catholic Church *in fact* the way we are accustomed to picture them to ourselves? And, if so, what is the justification of Catholics for this or that position?

In the same manner, Catholics taking part in the ecumenical dialogue are informing themselves precisely concerning the real meaning of the doctrine and discipline of their separated brethren. In the last analysis, it must be said that *every* Christian community must make the effort to understand exactly the real position of every other community. In short, it is a matter above all of mutual clarification. We want to get away from approximations, stereotypes, and confusion. We want a clear and exact inventory.

There is nothing like possessing clear and accurate facts to cure an involved situation. It is on this basis that one can really talk. And what are the results? First of all, to the degree that the dialogue progresses, one begins to discover that the elements of discord are not as fundamental as one has often thought. There are numerous points in common. One begins to discover authentic Christian elements on each side, which one hadn't been paying attention to and which one had simply assumed to have been lost among the others. With the eye of faith, one discovers that Christ is living in the others, that the Holy Spirit is dwelling in their souls, and that finally we all belong to the same large Christian family, whose Father is God.

All this leads to an examination of one's own faith from a new angle. It happens that a particular Christian value is conserved in a more vital manner in a Church other than that to which one belongs. Thanks to this discovery, one begins to understand more exactly or more intensely what one's own Church must do in order to return to its true source or, in other words, to better resemble Christ.

It is easy to understand that this method leads the way inherently to the unity of Christians in the one true Church of Christ. If all the Christian communities become more similar to Christ and more faithful to his doctrine, by this very fact they become more similar to each other. By the same token, prejudices and exaggerations begin to disappear, discord lessens, and different points of view come closer together.

It is then that the fundamental dialogue may be opened. A discussion on the basis of things can be carried on in a serene atmosphere, the interlocutors being animated by a sincere desire to arrive at unity. It is obvious that the realization of this unity is the work of grace. We must wait for the hour chosen by the Lord, while helping to prepare for it by the necessary dispositions. But, humanly speaking, where may we find a better disposition than among brethren, moved by a common nostalgia for unity, who say to each other: Let us gather around the same table and examine objectively the mixture of the truth and alleged error in each of our points of view, while seeking all together to deepen our faith and to approach nearer to our source.

The Catholic Church wants this ecumenical dialogue. There has been presented to the Council a text which sets forth the Catholic principles of the ecumenical movement. The discussion of this matter was long and profound. It showed itself positive and fruitful. To be sure, it was under-lined, as the faith teaches us, that the Catholic Church is the true and unique Church of Christ. It was clearly stated that in order to be faithful to the unity willed by Christ, the unity sought for today must comprise at the same time unity of faith, unity around the sacrifice, and the seven sacraments instituted by Jesus, and unity of direction, the authority for which was conferred by the Master upon the successors of Peter and the other Apostles. The ecumenical dialogue is not fruitful if it is not conducted in clarity and in truth, and thus the Council Fathers have clearly set forth the conditions necessary for the Catholic Church to take part in the ecumenical encounter.

In reality, what is at stake here is a view of the faith and a problem of confidence in the truth. Arrogance and over-confidence in ourselves will not do. We are not without sin in the Catholic Church. Because of our faults, the Church neither displays nor lives that entire sanctity which Christ would like to see in her, and with which the Holy Spirit has endowed her ontologically. The Church is holy because the Holy Spirit renders her so, but she does not live in as sanctified a manner as she should.

On the one hand, the members of the Catholic Church must continue to regret their faults and so purify themselves of them. On the other hand, they must support by their prayers and their penitence those qualified members of the Church who are taking an active part in the ecumenical dialogue. They can and must say to themselves: The more genuine doctrine of Christ is discovered in the different Churches and ecclesiastic communities, the closer we ap-proach to unity. In reality, there is only "one Lord, one faith, one baptism, one God and Father of us all, who is above all and through all and in all" (Eph. 4:5-6).

The Priesthood of the Faithful

In the eyes of many, one of the obstacles to the realization of this unity is what has been called "the hypertrophy of certain organs within the Catholic Church." What is meant here is that the hierarchy would appear to have usurped almost entirely the active role within the Church, to the detriment of the mission of the faithful and in opposition to that priesthood which Scripture attributes to all the baptized.

This observation, which I do not believe to be well founded, will be made less often after the Council. One may await this outcome with confidence, for everything indicates that the Council will make a very clear pronouncement on the faithful and their vocation in the Church. Already the Constitution on the Liturgy speaks of the sacerdotal role of the people of God in these terms:

"Holy Mother Church urgently desires that all the faithful be led towards the full, conscious and active participation in the liturgical celebrations which is required by the nature of the liturgy itself, and which is also, by virtue of their baptism, both the right and the duty of the Christian people, 'a chosen race, a royal priesthood, a holy nation, a purchased people'" (1 Peter 2:9).

But let us go to the root of the matter. Let us look at the source of this doctrine. One finds it set forth in the first letter of Peter, to which the Council text itself makes reference. This letter is the first encyclical addressed by the first Pope to the first Christians. It is, however, an epistle belonging to Holy Scripture, and therefore inspired by the Holy Spirit. This venerable document deserves to be considered the Magna Charta of the priesthood of the faithful.

Before quoting the most important lines of the text, a certain preliminary elucidation must be made. When the Catholic Church speaks of "the faithful," it would be incorrect to think that she designates the laity only by this term, in

opposition to those members who have received the ministerial priesthood, which is conferred by what the Church calls
the Sacrament of Holy Orders. On the contrary, "the faithful" are all the baptized, all those whom the grace of baptism has purified from sin and rendered participants in the
mystery of the death and resurrection of Jesus. Thus, whatever the ministry or *charism* that may be subsequently conferred, all the baptized retain throughout their entire lives
the quality of being among the faithful. They are the people of God by virtue of the fact that they are united to Christ
and participate in His life. But it must be remembered that
Christ is a priest. Therefore all the people of God are priestly
people, and every one of its members is a responsible person
in whom Christ continues His priestly mission.

This is what St. Peter says in the document mentioned
above: "Draw near to him, a living stone, rejected indeed
by men but chosen and honored by God. Be you yourselves
as living stones, built thereon into a spiritual house, a holy
priesthood, to offer spiritual sacrifices acceptable to God
through Jesus Christ." And Peter then continues, as we have
seen: "You, however, are a chosen race, a royal priesthood,
a holy nation, a purchased people; that you may proclaim
the perfections of him who has called you out of darkness
into his marvelous light" (1 Peter 2:4-5,9).

The Ecumenical Council, basing itself on this Scriptural
declaration, as interpreted in the light of the living tradition
of the Church, will proclaim to the Christians of our times
that they must consider themselves consecrated persons,
mysteriously united to Christ, like living stones inserted into
that living temple which is Christ Himself, and members of
a holy priesthood.

What then is the mission of the faithful? It is through them
that Jesus prolongs his priesthood. In them and by them he
wants to offer "spiritual sacrifices agreeable to God." As for
the Father, he regards with complaisance the cult of his people, because in this people He recognizes the love of His

Son, that delegate of the great human family, placed in its bosom in order to praise and glorify its Creator and to offer Him His sacrifice.

But there is more than that. Christ was sent into this world in order to make known His Gospel, the "good news" which must guide a regenerated humanity in its march throughout the whole of its earthly pilgrimage toward the Promised Land of the hereafter. Here again the people of God have a priestly function. They are united to Christ and consecrated to Him in order to be the organs by which He continues to spread His message, in order to "proclaim the great deeds of God."

They must do this as much by the example and the testimony of their life as by efforts to make others understand what the message of the Gospel and an existence guided by its doctrines signify ideally. It is all too easy to establish two watertight compartments in one's life: the *first*, that of a strictly religious life, in which one behaves like a man of faith who follows the doctrine of Jesus and participates in His love for the Father. This religious life is, however, too often separated from a *second* compartment, that of the "practical" life, where the disciple of Christ has likewise the duty to conform his private conduct and his social comportment to the teaching of the Master. No one deserves to be called a member of "the faithful" who is not, in fact, faithful to the light of Christ. Pope Paul VI spoke about this in an allocution delivered in the Vatican Basilica on Friday, January 3, 1964:

"You know that our doctrine recognizes a participation by the laity in the spiritual priesthood of Christ and, in consequence, the capacity or rather, the responsibility of exercising an apostolate. This apostolate, which has been expressed by diverse concepts and forms adapted to the possibilities and character of a specifically lay life, is immersed in temporal realities, and is demanded as the special mission of this present hour. One speaks of a *consecratio mundi* [a consecration of the world] and one attributes to the laity those prerogatives which are particular to the profane and the terrestrial life—a domain in which the diffusion of the light and grace of Christ is rendered possible precisely because the laity may operate *within* this profane world, while the priest, withdrawn as he is from an important part of profane life, is not able usually to excercise an influence on it except indirectly: by his word and his ministry."

Finally, the priesthood of the faithful constitutes a participation in the unifying action of Christ. Sin always provokes a rupture, a breaking apart of things. It is always a division which lies between God and His creatures, but it is also a rupture of one's interior balance and of harmonious relations among men. Christ came in order to restore God's plan, in order to put back into place the debris of the Creation. The plan of God is to "reunite all things in Christ, all that exists in heaven and on earth" (Eph. 1:10) or, more exactly, according to the Greek text: "to replace everything under the same head in Christ."

To participate in the priesthood of Christ means to unite oneself to Christ in that mysterious activity which He wants to conduct in the real world. A member of "the faithful" is a man pledged to action. He is engaged in the service of Christ to the end of realizing that vital current of unification which makes peace reign between men and God, and which leads to that individual and social justice among human beings whose fruit is concord, brotherhood, and charity.

The Catholic Church would like to see this doctrine of the priesthood of the faithful understood and lived by all its members. She wishes the laity to conform their lives to it and the bishops and priests to take it seriously. She asks of the latter to help the laity conduct themselves as adult Christians, conscious of their responsibility at this hour which, it has been justly said, is the hour of the laity in the Church.

Shouldn't we see in this insistence upon the priesthood of the faithful the promise of a better understanding with our

Protestant brothers? The history of the schism in the Western Church reveals that one of the causes of the rupture in unity was a disagreement over the role which the Catholic Church attributed to "the simple faithful." In these last decades the Church's *magisterium* [teaching authority], followed by the theologians, has shown itself very preoccupied with the rehabilitation of the laity in the Catholic Church. In consecrating this tendency, will the Ecumenical Council succeed in eliminating a major cause of disagreement among those who follow Christ?

On the Protestant side, the question will be posed: What becomes then of the powers which the Catholic Church attributes to the Pope and to the bishops? Here we mustn't try to hide the fact that we find ourselves in a domain in which the Catholic and the Protestant vision of things differ profoundly. In general, Protestantism maintains that it is not proved that Jesus intended to perpetuate the mission which He confided to Peter and to the other Apostles. In the eyes of many of our separated brethren, no real power responsible for the organization of worship and the maintenance of the sacred deposit would appear to exist in the Church.

The Catholic Church, on the other hand, considers herself to be continuing the tradition of the first centuries in firmly believing that her divine Founder wanted Peter to be the rock (Mt. 16:18) upon which the Church would repose throughout the whole of her existence, and that the Lord's promise held good for all their successors when he declared to the first Apostles: "I am with you always, even unto the consummation of the world" (Mt. 28:20).

Does this divergence of views have any chance of being smoothed away during the Ecumenical Council? It is a difficult problem. In any case, one may hope that the fraternal contact that the non-Catholic communions will have had with the Catholic hierarchy at the Council will dissipate certain prejudices, and that these communions will see better that having at one's head the sovereign pontiff, a bishop presiding by right over all the local Churches, constitutes an undeniable advantage and a particular grace for the Catholic Church.

Be that as it may, there is a well-founded hope that the presentation of the doctrine on the Church will take into account, in as much as possible, the observations formulated by our non-Catholic brethren. Also, many Fathers of the Council have insisted that the exact meaning of the primacy and of the infallibility of the Pope as well as the nature of the mission of the episcopate in the Church be explained. It has been aptly remarked that when one speaks of the "rights" of the hierarchy, the spirit of the Gospel demands that this triple power reveal also a character of "ministry." It is the "service" of worship, the "service" of teaching, the "service" of direction.

In this perspective, it must be said that if the hierarchy has received a real power from Christ, this power is not an end in itself, but a ministry entirely orientated toward the apostolic activity of the faithful. If the hierarchy has been given charge of the Church's worship and sacraments, it is in order that the faithful may have access to those sources of grace with which Christ endowed His disciples and which enables them to exercise their own priesthood.

In the same fashion, the hierarchy conserves the deposit of the faith and interprets it in the name of the Lord, but this is in order that the priestly people may be and remain faithful witnesses to Christ in the midst of the world. Finally, if the shepherds are charged with the direction of the people of God, it is in order that this people apply themselves effectively to their great mission of introducing a more human and more spiritual orientation into the whole of earthly life, of giving this life a greater conformity with the views of God and with the real good of humanity.

Taking all the foregoing into account, it would appear that the Catholic Church and the other Christian Churches and communities are on the way to unity. Decisive steps have been made in this direction in sessions of the Ecumenical Council. But the pilgrimage of the sovereign pontiff to the Holy Land represents an even greater opening in this direction and the promise of an accelerated rapprochement. At present all Christians must intensify their desire to see unity achieved, and must make their prayer more fervent in order to hasten this accomplishment. One can't do better to depict the atmosphere which must now reign than to cite, in closing, the moving words that His Holiness Paul VI pronounced at Bethlehem, in the grotto of the Nativity:

"The door of the sheepfold is open. The expectation of everyone is loyal and cordial, the desire is strong and patient. The place available is large and commodious. The step to be taken is awaited with all our affection and may be accomplished with honor and in mutual joy. We shall abstain from soliciting any action that is not free and fully convinced— that is to say, moved by the Spirit of the Lord, who will breathe where and when he wills. We shall wait for this most happy hour.

"For the moment we do not ask of our separated brethren more that we propose to ourselves: that the love of Christ and of the Church may inspire every eventual move towards rapprochement and encounter. We shall act in a manner designed to maintain a lively and unaltered desire for understanding and for union; we shall place our confidence in prayer. Even if this prayer is not yet in common, it may at least be simultaneous, and thus mount in a parallel movement from our hearts and from those of separated Christians, so as to meet at the feet of the Most High, the God of Unity."

Qualities for an Ecumenical Statement[1]

All Council Fathers sincerely and positively desire that the tracts treated here should foster unity. The views on a spe-

[1] Statement made by Bishop De Smedt at first session of Vatican Council II, and which was widely acclaimed and exercised a profound and far-reaching influence on the deliberations.

cific tract differ, however, some saying it answers the requirements of ecumenicism, others saying it does not.

The problem is this: What is required in the doctrine and style of a tract in order that it may truly serve to bring about a better dialogue between Catholics and separated Christians?

Here is my answer: All who have the honor of being called Christians have this in common, that they recognize the existence of Jesus Christ. That which has been communicated by the Lord Himself constitutes "the deposit of faith" and we are saved through it. All of us, Catholics and non-Catholics alike, have recourse to this one same source. But when it becomes a question of "how" we come to Jesus Christ then discord begins. We are brothers separated from one another. For very many centuries now we have been cut off from one another.

We know that this discord of ours is contrary to the will of Christ. When will this division of ours ever cease? For many centuries we Catholics have thought it enough to make a clear declaration of our doctrine. Other Christians have had the very same idea. Each side has expressed its doctrine in its own terminology, from its own point of view, but what was said by Catholics was misinterpreted by other Christians and vice versa. By this method of "clearly stating the truth" no progress towards reconciliation has actually been made. On the contrary, prejudices, suspicions, polemical discussions and quarrels on both sides have increased.

In the last ten or twenty years a new method called "ecumenical dialogue" has been introduced. In what does it consist? The characteristic of this method is that it concerns itself not only with truthfulness, but also with the manner in which a doctrine is explained, so that others may understand it correctly. Christians of various denominations help each other arrive at a clearer and more exact understanding of doctrine to which they themselves do not subscribe. Ecumenical dialogue therefore is not a study or tract on bringing about union, it is not a council of reunion, it is not an attempt at conversion. It simply means giving testimony of one's own faith to another in a serene, objective and lucid manner, using the principles of psychology valid in every human dialogue.

It is not an easy thing to draw up a tract in ecumenical style. First of all every trace of indifferentism must be excluded. An ecumenical exposition must faithfully portray the complete and integral Catholic doctrine on a given point. Else how could other Christians come to know from us what Catholicism really teaches if the doctrine that we present is incomplete, distorted or confused? An ecumenical manner of speech is therefore not opposed to an integral presentation of the truth. One who holds this opinion does not understand the true nature of ecumenical dialogue. Such a dialogue is not undertaken so that the two parties may be mutually deceived.

If we wish our doctrine to be understood by separated Christians several conditions must be fulfilled. Here are some of them:

a. We must have a clear idea of the present-day teaching of the Orthodox and Protestant Churches. We must be well acquainted with their faith, their liturgical life and their theology.

b. We need to know the opinions they have of our doctrine, the points they understand and the points they misunderstand.

c. We must know what separated Christians feel is missing or not sufficiently elaborated in Catholic doctrine. (For example, the doctrine on the Word of God, on the priesthood of the faithful, on religious liberty.)

d. We must examine whether our manner of expression contains statements or ways of saying things difficult for separated Christians to understand. I would like to point out that the so-called scholastic manner of speech or the method used in theological schools constitutes a serious difficulty for separated Christians and often gives rise to errors and prejudices. An abstract and purely intellectual manner of speech is not understood by Orientals. On the other hand, a Biblical and patristic manner of speech by itself would avoid and should prevent many difficulties, prejudices and confusion.

e. All forms of sterile polemics should be avoided. Errors should be indicated in a way that is not offensive to the persons who hold them.

Ecumenical dialogue is this new method. The fruit of this method can already be seen in this hall, in the presence of the observers. This is a providential hour, and at the same time a most serious hour, for all those who have followed the lead of Pope John XXIII in prayer and fasting and hope that now, finally, some serious and notable steps will be taken in the direction of fraternal unity among all those for whom Christ our Lord prayed, "May they all be one."

Fred Pierce Corson

Fred Pierce Corson, Methodist Bishop of Philadelphia, has long been active in the ecumenical movement. Born on April 11, 1896, at Millville, New Jersey, he graduated from Dickinson College with Phi Beta Kappa honors and from Drew University, where he was the first recipient of the John Heiston Willey Award for pulpit excellence. After serving as pastor of churches in New York and Connecticut, he organized the Community Church of Jackson Heights in New York City and united twenty-six denominations in its fellowship. Later he served as District Superintendent of the Brooklyn South District of the New York East Conference.

In 1934 he was elected the twentieth president of Dickinson College and continued as president until 1944, when he was elected a Bishop of the Methodist Church. Bishop Corson is a 33rd degree Mason, Grand Chaplain of the Grand Lodge of Pennsylvania, and Past Grand Prelate of the Pennsylvania Commandery of Knights Templar. He has served as President of the Association of Colleges of Pennsylvania and on the University Senate of the Methodist Church, President of the Council of Bishops from 1952–53, and President of the General Board of Education of the Methodist Church from 1948–60.

In August 1961 he was installed as President of the World Methodist Council, and in 1963 received the World Outlook Award as "Methodist of the Year." He was a delegate to the World Council of Churches Assembly in New Delhi and addressed the World Methodist Conference in Freudenstadt, Germany. Bishop Corson has received many honors and awards for his patriotic and religious services and was the official guest of the Republic of China on Taiwan and inspected missions and colleges in eleven countries of Europe and Asia.

A popular preacher to youth, he speaks each year in more than a score of colleges. His interest in good government resulted in his appointment to the Governor's Commission for the Revision of the Constitution for the Commonwealth of Pennsylvania. He is the organizer and head of the Bishop's Crusaders, a youth movement dedicated to Christian service, with more than seventeen thousand members throughout the world.

He is the author of many books, among which are *A Philosophy of Education for the Postwar World, The Minister and Christian Higher Education, The Education We Have and the Education We Need, Free Masonry and the Framing of the Constitution, The Needed Emphasis in Christian Education, Your Church and You,* and *Pattern for Successful Living.* In 1922 he married Frances Blount Beaman and they are the parents of one son. Representing the World Methodist Council, Bishop Corson served as an observer-delegate at both sessions of the Vatican Council, where he secured many insights into the development of the thinking of both the Council members and the observers which are reflected in his article.

UNITY IN OUR TIME

A serious consideration of Roman Catholic-Protestant unity is of recent origin. Less than five years ago it appeared as a purely academic question. Godly men working for the reign of God in the hearts of men and their society said, "Of course it can be. The prayer of Our Blessed Lord that all believers in Him shall be one, will not forever go unfulfilled. But a lot of things must change in Protestant-Roman Catholic relations before it happens."

A divided Protestantism was slowly piecing itself together, but that phase of the ecumenical movement was, in fact, in its infancy. Many of the 175 or more branches of this Protestant communion were actually "separated brethren," not recognizing the validity of each other's ordination, holding exclusively to one particular form and method of baptism, denying one another access to the Lord's Table, not transferring members from one denominational parish to another, unyielding on doctrinal positions and the language of their expression, even divided as to what unity actually meant.

The first real union of major Protestant bodies which brought the three largest groups of Methodists together is only twenty-five years old. Even the term "ecumenical" had not been given its present universal connotation. Protestants and Roman Catholics had not formally exchanged observers at their Church convocations or conducted dialogues before 1958. Church unity, as we now think of it, is in truth a development of the mid-twentieth century, a thousand years removed from the Eastern schism and four hundred years after the Protestant Reformation.

It is in this background that the present status of Christian unity should be judged and evaluated. The amazing thing about it, therefore, is not how much remains to be done or how slow the present proceedings are, but how much closer together the Churches, under these conditions, have moved.

Then on January 25, 1959, Pope John XXIII, of blessed memory, issued the call for the Second Vatican Council, and by doing so fixed another decisive date in human history. Nothing has surprised the sophisticated twentieth century more than what Pope John did. In the first place, little was expected of him except to carry on a kind of "caretaker" ministry in the Vatican. Modern efficiency had decreed that age could no longer be creative. There had, likewise, been no buildup for this unprecedented move in the field of religion. No uncanny commentator had even guessed that it might happen, and consequently the first reaction on the part of the public was that they could not believe their ears.

Church councils were not new. Most of them, however, had been inspired by either fear or despair. They were given over largely to defending the status quo and their effect had been, for the most part, to widen and deepen the gulf which separated Christendom. Pope John's announcement insured the fact that this council would be different; even its name made it different. He called it "The Second Vatican Council" indicating that it would not be an "adjourned session" of the First Vatican Council dealing only with its unfinished business and thus confined to the same areas of action outlined for the First Vatican Council which had been convened almost a hundred years ago.

He directed that its deliberations be centered in two great concerns of the Church, first the purification, reformation, and renewal of the Church itself for which *aggiornamento*, which means updating, became a key word. The second was Christian unity in terms of a new ecumenicity which included all Christians. One evidence of his commitment to this new ecumenicity was his invitation to Christian bodies outside the Roman Catholic Church to send observers to the Council.

The enthusiastic response which the announcement received was beyond all reasonable expectations. Religion became good news. A realistic press seemed to sense that something profoundly significant was happening in the world. All of the reaction, of course, was not on the hopeful and expectant side. Many Protestants at first did not take seriously the invitation to observers. Some even referred to the invitation as window dressing. Many expressed the belief that the Roman Catholic Church would never change. And likewise many Roman Catholics wondered with anxiety where the new Pope was leading the Church.

Several explanations have been offered to account for this remarkable reception. A change in the religious climate of the world is noted. On the one hand there are evidences of greater tolerance among religious people. Pockets of fanaticism still exist, but with nothing like the strength and intensity of the Ku Klux Klan of forty years ago or the political "Know Nothings" of one hundred years ago. The Church, spread around the world, has begun to change its strategy from "competition" to persuasion. The God-desire in every human heart needs the fulfillment Paul gave to the Athenians whom he found seeking a greater but still unrevealed God.

Non-Christian religions also have been experiencing a revival with evangelistic ardor, challenging the presuppositions of Christianity and profiting by the fragmented witness of the Churches. The new wine of a dynamic Christianity could no longer be preserved and contained in old ecclesiastical forms which had changed little in a thousand years. It is true to say that changing religious conditions in the world affected the form which the Second Vatican Council was to take. A static Church became an anachronism in a volatile and changing society.

Others have seen the emerging of the Second Vatican Council as a response to popular demand. It was, they say, brought about by the ground swell of the man on the street and the men in the outposts of the Church who could see no reason, in a world drawing closer together in every other phase of its social existence, why Christianity should remain "off limits" to all except the especially initiated members of a particular religious group. The ordinary man was endorsing the idea of Church unity even though he did not have the faintest conception of what was required to attain it. He, therefore, was ready to respond to a leadership which would forge the way. Great world-changing movements owe much for their opportunity and propulsion to the broad foundations of human concern which support them. And the Church will need to make more of this help in its future efforts.

Still others have said that the Church through the activities of the Second Vatican Council has made virtue out of a necessity. With the secular takeover making rapid progress even in areas where the Christian Church has been dominant for centuries, *aggiornamento* (modernization) and unity became necessities for survival. Certainly from his comments it would appear that Pope John was fully aware of the recession which had come upon Christianity in the phenomenally growing world. It is he who turned the thought of the Church from the outward symbols of its strength to the ominous fact that "the Church has lost the workingman," a statement supported by the statistics on world population which record that while the population of the world has grown 46%+, the Christian population has grown only 5%+.

Roman Catholics have graciously attributed some of the inspiration for the Second Vatican Council to the pioneering work in the field of Christian unity undertaken by the Protestants. Less than twenty years ago the Protestant World Council of Churches was organized but since then, through world convocations and committees working upon every aspect of Church unity, the necessity for Christian unity has been held up before the world as both a divine command and a practical necessity. And the concept of unity, enunciated at the Assembly of the World Council of Churches in

New Delhi as "a unity which enables all Christians to speak and act together as occasion requires in the tasks to which God calls the Church," has been found acceptable in principle and as a starting point for Roman Catholic-Protestant dialogue by prelates and scholars of the Roman Catholic Church.

The only explanation, however, that can account fully for the Second Vatican Council and all that it portends is the simple acknowledgment of Pope John that it is the work of the Holy Spirit. In the fullness of time God sent it forth. Protestants as well as Catholics needed to be reminded, in an age depending on man's ingenuity and his do-it-yourself methods, that God is still at work in the world. The reality of the transcendent power of the Spiritual has been a fading conviction in this age of scientism. The simple acknowledgment of it by Pope John, without an attempt to be rationalistic, has done much to offset the humanistic point of view which, like a jungle growth, has been creeping into the life and work of the Church.

While the Second Vatican Council must deal with procedural and organizational matters, and the world is inclined to measure its achievements by this yardstick, its greatest accomplishment has been a recovery of the experience of God manifested through the Holy Spirit in the affairs of the world. The effects of this acknowledgment upon the cause of Christian unity are many. It is good for the Church to be reminded of her spiritual nature and of her spiritual assets which are withheld from no true follower of Christ. Such a reminder of the Church's spiritual nature is greatly needed in this age of mechanism and organization, and its necessity transcends denominational barriers in its acceptance. The preoccupation of the Church with its internal organization has too long overshadowed its need to heal the broken Body of Christ and to make it whole again through the unity of its members.

The presence of the supernatural, which has been a basic

assumption in the Second Vatican Council from its inception, is providing an effective antidote for the spiritual sophistication which has, as a method and a pose, cast a shadow in both the scholarly and popular mind regarding the Church's supernatural origin, nature, and power. The simplicity and humility evident in the Vatican Council deliberations must not be discounted as signs of intellectual shallowness. They have proven to be the media through which God has so often expressed His Mind and His Power, and their appearance in the leadership of the Council has been to the religious world a breath of spiritually pure air.

A clear indication that Christian unity has been advanced by the Second Vatican Council is the widespread feeling among Protestants and Roman Catholics that God has a hand in it, always, however, taking into account that there are still people in the world who discount anything good by attributing "the power to cast out devils to Beelzebub."

The Second Vatican Council has launched a movement toward Christian unity that nothing can stop. While "a journey of a thousand miles begins with one step," that first step may prove to be the most important. Getting off on the wrong foot has brought disaster to many good causes, espoused by sympathetic and willing workers. The prospects of something tangible coming out of these current conversations on Christian unity is enhanced by the fact that the Council got off to a good start. While some of the procedures could have been improved, none of them turned out to be a blunder. Flexibility was evident in handling emergencies, often averting ruptures which might have occurred within the Roman Catholic Church and between the Roman Catholics and the "separated brethren."

Typical of the effectiveness of these emergency provisions was Pope John's good use of his ultimate authority as Supreme Pontiff when a motion on the report on the nature of revelation failed to secure the two-thirds majority necessary, by only a handful of votes. Had the report rested at that point, old differences could have hardened and new problems between Roman Catholics and Protestants would have formed. But the Pontiff in the interests of final agreement remanded the report to the Committee for further study and added to it a co-chairman so that both points of view under question could have adequate consideration. Had this not been done the Council might have erected another roadblock in the path of unity instead of resolving one.

The timing of the presentation of matters for consideration showed careful planning, with the objective in mind of the clearest understanding and the widest acceptability of the subject dealt with. Naturally, the Protestant world was concerned with many positions taken by the Catholic Church, among them the sincerely motivated Marian Movement, represented by the co-redemptionists. Here exaltation of Christian family life symbolized by the Holy Family was not the issue. Thoughtful Protestants, who saw family life breaking up because the Christian concept was flouted in practice and repudiated in law, welcomed the attention given to the Mother of Jesus. Both Pope John and Pope Paul have taken occasion to recognize the exalted place given by the Church to the Holy Family, and indicated to a world enamored by pagan practices that compromise was not to be the way by which the effort toward unity was to be attempted.

Postponement of an excursion beyond the present position of the Church on this subject meant that many other concerns with which both groups were in position to deal could be settled without the impediment of a new division within Christendom. Often causes come to naught because ultimate questions are taken up before the preliminary questions are disposed of. Protestants have been encouraged in their hopes for Christian unity by the refusal of the Catholic Fathers to be hurried to the discussion of many items in the schemata of the Council until the time has come for the best possible results.

Time, as well as the proper timing, has been another factor

which has aided the prospects of progress toward a genuine Christian unity. The Second Vatican Council has refused to be hurried. The slowness with which it has proceeded has caused questioning and criticism by both Roman Catholics and Protestants. Some of this impatience is prompted by the temper of the age in which we live and the tempo set for quick action and immediate results. Hurry seems to be considered the evidence of accomplishment.

Protestants in their convocations are especially prone to shorten the periods of deliberation and to judge results by the amount rather than the quality of the action taken. To be sure, there was repetition in the speeches made by the Council Fathers in considering specific issues, and some of them shed little or no light to guide the Fathers to right action. But something is to be said for a parliamentary procedure which allows for full and democratic expression in a decision-making body. Moreover, where the application of a decision depends upon a meeting of minds which approach unanimity, as certainly spiritual matters do, it is wise to proceed on the principle of making haste slowly.

The fact that the members of the Second Vatican Council assembled really as strangers indicated that actions must be slowly taken. Most of them had not seen each other before. They came from different cultures and ethnic groups. They had different problems. They needed time for fellowship, for understanding each other, and for exchanging views so that a truly world view of the Church and its concern would provide the proper background for action.

The temptation to debate and not act is likely to grow in bodies where members have the independence and authority in their own areas of responsibility such as bishops do. But at no time has it appeared that both Pope John and Pope Paul were not aware of this and alert to the proper moment when debate should be halted and action begun. Roman Catholics and Protestants have different parliamentary procedures and different philosophical approaches. They too need to be understood and coordinated as both bodies move closer together.

The apparent slowness in the decision-making of the Second Vatican Council has, likewise, aided and prepared the Protestant observers in their understanding and comprehension of all that is involved in the issues under discussion. Hearing the Latin debates and having them translated into English as they were delivered, meeting in weekly sessions with representatives of each of the Commissions for explanation of the schemata under consideration and for the exchange of views, associations with the bishops and cardinals of the Catholic Church who have most freely expressed their personal points of view, have not only acquainted the Protestant world with present-day Catholicism, but has also helped to clarify and identify the challenge which now confronts the Church in all its branches. Protestants, also, feel that these extended periods of debate within the Council have given the Protestant point of view a better chance of being heard and understood by the Roman Catholics and thus enhanced the possibilities that an interpretation of the principles involved in debate will be acceptable to all who seek Christian unity.

Pope John answered the criticism that the Council was not moving more rapidly to decision by recalling the old adage, "He who goes slow, goes safe and goes far." Pope Paul, endorsing Pope John's justification for the apparent slowness of Council action, pointed out that the direction and not the speed of the deliberations was the true measure of the Council's progress. Significantly, Pope Paul in his address to the Protestant observers quoted St. Paul to the effect that he had committed the Council "to press forward."

In matters that have to do with the human spirit, the enactment of law does not always assure the acceptance of the fact. Law is as effective as the sentiment supporting it. So long as separation was the popularly accepted method for preserving truth, even the law and example of Our Blessed Lord made little difference in the relations of Christians.

The tremendous change in sentiment which the Second Vatican Council has fostered in Christian relations and in desire to become more closely identified with each other is an achievement of greatest importance for Christian unity. Without this first, the actions of the Vatican Council for unity would be largely nullified.

Furthermore, the general assumption seems to be that the Second Vatican Council is to be all-embracing and final in the subjects considered and the actions taken. Two facts appear to make such an assumption erroneous. One is the long years of the practice of separation, which have created a multitude of problems which can only be worked through in action as Christians begin to move more closely together. Conduct for the Christian life has been developed for a Christian society which has existed in separate and impregnable compartments. The Churches will have to develop new norms and methods of conduct adapted to the new and hoped-for relation of togetherness. This will need to be done on the diocesan and parish levels, and the principle evolved from the experience must await some later convocation of churchmen to formulate into law.

The other factor is the rapidly changing world situation preventing man from putting his spiritual house in order with a finality which anticipates no necessity for further change. The changeless Gospel must continually seek its relevance in a changing world. "New occasions teach new duties" to the Church as well as the world around the Church, and the understanding and application of the faith once delivered to the saints must therefore be a creative and a dynamic experience. It would be far more realistic to anticipate that these volatile times will require a Vatican Council every decade than that in one or two more sessions the Second Vatican Council can settle the problems of Christian unity for a century.

Let us not forget that the new vocabulary developed by the Second Vatican Council in Roman Catholic-Protestant communication has been a most constructive factor in drawing the Churches closer together and preventing the ruptures which unfortunate language aggravates. Pope John said that it was time "to forget the past centuries when men met to quarrel; let us meet to love one another," and in that way he admonished both groups "to watch their language." He set the example by his own statements. Nothing he said which touched on Catholic-Protestant and non-Catholic relations caused offense or had to be rephrased or explained. His words to the Christian and non-Christian world were like "apples of gold in pictures of silver." He found felicitous ways to substitute new words for old, such as the replacement of "heretic" with "separated brethren."

The old vocabulary which incited hostility was replaced by new words that retained the meaning but eliminated the irritation. Jokingly, a story has gone the rounds that in one of his inner councils a Father referred to those outside the Roman Catholic Church as "lost souls," only to be admonished by the Holy Father, who is reported to have said that if you must characterize this group it will be better to call them "fallen angels." He won the gratitude of the Jews, not by changing the facts of history but by changing the language which referred to these facts.

He treated words as vehicles to be used and not idols to be worshiped, and encouraged changes in terminology in the interests of clarity and understanding. The meaning of "extreme unction," lost to millions living in the twentieth century, has been recaptured by the new wording, "the anointing of the sick." "Infallibility," which in the Protestant mind has certain uncomfortable overtones, might find the way to understanding made easier if it could be thought of as "ultimate authority."

Some doctrines have already been reworded by the use of new language which removes the misconception of old clichés associated with them. Cardinal Bea's statement that, "All those who have been validly baptized in Christ even outside the Roman Catholic Church are organically bound to Christ and His mystical body and belong in a true sense to the Church," will go far to counteract the false impression of intractable finality popularly assumed in the statement of earlier origin that "there is no salvation outside the Church." The Protestant concern for a meeting of minds on the question of religious liberty has taken a hopeful turn through Cardinal Bea's restatement of the fundamental Roman Catholic position that "man's right to choose his religion or no religion is an accepted teaching of the Church" and that "both individuals and society should leave each other free to accept and fulfill his obligations and duties exclusively by the use of his own free will."

The instructions for Roman Catholic-Protestant conversations issued by the Commission on Christian Unity bear out the importance given to a right vocabulary. Catholics were directed to learn what Protestants considered unclear in Catholic teaching, to avoid scholastic terminology not well understood, to choose expressions carefully in regard to their effect on non-Catholics, to avoid useless controversy, and in rejecting errors to do so without wounding sensibilities.

This might well have been a joint statement issued by Roman Catholics and Protestants, since Protestants likewise clearly have a need for such an approach at this critical juncture in Christian relations and would welcome an opportunity to demonstrate such evidence of a working unity.

The dialogues, encouraged by Pope Paul, now taking place in increasing numbers are likewise dominated by a vocabulary which lifts up the highest common factors of belief between the separated church bodies and reflects a new spirit of the reconciliation of differences through tolerance, understanding, acceptance, and change. Our Fathers of a past generation have done Christendom a great service by delineating the differences which characterize its various branches.

Difference is not, however, the contradiction of unity. And the Fathers of the twentieth century have set the Christian family on the road to reunion by a modernized language of description which reveals that some onetime differences can exist without one being dominant, antagonistic, or superior.

Protestants have also been in need of a new vocabulary to describe their position and to conduct their ecumenical conversations. As John Wesley, the Father of the Methodist Church, wrote to a Catholic correspondent in 1749, all of the intransigence and bitterness have not been on the Catholic side. He called, at a time of intense bigotry, prejudice, and persecution among religious groups, for the healing solvent of a language of love and appreciation, a cessation of "endless jangling about opinions," a substitute of words that help rather than hurt each other. He asked for a Roman Catholic-Protestant pact "to speak nothing harsh or unkind of each other, to say all the good we can both of and to each other, to harbor no unkind thought (the mother of words) no unfriendly temper toward each other." Wesley concluded his appeal with words which Pope Paul has indicated by public speech are congenial to him, "Let you and I (regardless of what others may do) press on to the prize of the high calling." The new vocabulary of understanding and reconciliation is a hopeful sign that the moving closer together of Christendom will continue.

The prospects for increasing unity cannot be evaluated apart from the leadership which guides it. Whether or not Christians continue to draw closer together will be determined in the area of human relations. Without a man like Pope John, the new ecumenicity could not have been launched. It required trust and confidence in each other which his approach supplied. Without Pope John's personality and spirit, the favorable conditions under which the Second Vatican Council met would not have been created. Many approached the conduct of the Council "to scoff and remained to pray," in thankfulness for its success. One of the critics spoke for many others when he said, "I forgot my objections when I saw the humility of the Pope." Pope John showed to the world the Church's heart, and he interpreted to his Church the heart of Protestantism. The first sessions of the Second Vatican Council moved within the lengthened shadow of one man.

Without Pope Paul the pilgrimage toward the unity which is in Our Blessed Lord could not have moved forward. For it he continued Pope John's commitment and to it he brought organizing and administrative gifts which such a movement must have to succeed. While Pope John's chief task was atmosphere-creating, Pope Paul's leadership will be needed for decision-making. Charting the course to be followed which, he has said, must be forward, requires a firm hand, a clear head, and indomitable spirit. Pope Paul gives those who have had the privilege of a close-up view the impression that he possesses these qualities in large measure and can be trusted to use them under the guidance of the Holy Spirit.

On the Protestant side, leaders speak with increasing assurance concerning the reality of the new ecumenicity. They are understanding better the Roman Catholic mind and see possibilities of understanding and agreement which is the result of their intellectual and spiritual fraternization. Major unresolved differences are yet to be dealt with. But the assumptions of irreconcilability are not as strong as they appeared to be when the Council was first announced. God, the Unknown Factor, is being given greater significance in finding ways that now appear to be hidden to man.

Certainly, the time has not arrived when all men speak well of the achievements of the Second Vatican Council. Many see no good in it. Others view its prospects with skepticism. Still others find fault with its methods and actions. But few will deny that a new chapter is being written in the history of Christianity and that a new spirit prevails in the attitude of Christian bodies toward each other. Furthermore, there is reason to think that the movement toward unity will continue because there are so many evidences that people, regardless of their denominational affiliation, like it.

The critical period for Christian unity lies ahead. It will come in the area of action-taking after the period of decision-making has laid out the course. Will the organization of church life permit the application of a truly spiritual unity to reach into the personal, intimate daily activities of the 850,000,000 Christians now in the world? This has been a Protestant concern. The question they raise most often is whether or not the fellowship and unity enjoyed on the top levels of the Vatican Council will extend itself to the dioceses and the parishes. Pope Paul has expressed the same concern and voiced the hope that it will.

At this point the clergy and laity must take up the responsibility for the progress of Christian unity. Even where the walls are down, movement back and forth awaits each person's decision to participate or remain aloof. Time and patience will be necessary to become accustomed to these new relationships. Full participation may take generations to be achieved.

Now Roman Catholics and Protestants who are committed to unity are at the beginning. The bridge to span the gulf fixed between these Christian bodies has been projected, and building must start on both sides. If God is the Architect and His followers follow the plans, the construction begun on both sides will meet at some point over the gulf, perhaps much sooner than is now supposed.

Richard Cardinal Cushing

Richard Cardinal Cushing, Archbishop of Boston, was born in South Boston on August 24, 1895, the second oldest of the five children of Patrick and Mary (Dahill) Cushing, emigrants from Ireland. After studying at Boston College he entered St. John's Seminary in Brighton and was ordained in 1921. After a short time in parish work, Father Cushing became Director of the Society for the Propagation of the Faith, spending twenty strenuous years in its service.

On June 29, 1939, he was consecrated as Auxiliary Bishop of Boston, and in 1944 succeeded William Cardinal O'Connell as Archbishop of Boston. Cardinal Cushing is well known for his devotion to the poor, orphans, elderly, and those handicapped physically or mentally. His warmheartedness, kindness, and unfailing generosity have won the hearts of the people of Boston, and Protestant and Jewish organizations as well as Catholic ones have heaped many awards and honors upon him.

On December 18, 1958, he was elevated by Pope John XXIII to the College of Cardinals. Cardinal Cushing has served on various Vatican congregations—e.g., of the Council, of the Propagation of the Faith, and of Seminaries and Universities. In 1958 he organized the Society of St. James the Apostle to supply priests for Latin America, and has allowed many of his young priests to serve in missionary dioceses in the U.S.A. and overseas, with the privilege of returning to the Boston archdiocese in later years if they so desire.

Cardinal Cushing has served on many of the important committees of the National Catholic Welfare Conference and, in general, has played a prominent role in the life of the Catholic Church in the U.S.A. Among the books he has authored are *Meditations for Religious, Gospel Stories for Children,* and *Channels of Grace.* Esteemed and loved by people of all faiths, Cardinal Cushing is one of the outstanding leaders in the ecumenical movement in the United States.

GRASS-ROOTS STEPS TO UNITY

Many are the articles and several the books that have appeared and are appearing on the methods and techniques of "dialogue." These books and articles, however, seem always directed to the professionals: scholars, theologians, clergy and church leaders. But if history and experience have taught us anything about unity and unions among Christians, it should be this: Although unions may be legislated in world ecumenical councils and assemblies, true unity must be born and nurtured in the local parishes and communities. Unity can be lasting only when it is a response to the Spirit moving in the people, breathing in the souls of the laity, present in what is called the grass-roots of the Church.

This fact has prompted me to speak before dozens of Protestant communities and congregations. It has prompted me also to address myself chiefly to the people in my pastoral charge, leaving the theological conversations of the scholars and theologians in the Boston area to men trained for such work, and finally it has prompted me to write the following thoughts and reflections.

This article is not meant to be a detailed guide for dialogue among theologians. It is meant to give some practical counsels for the Christian laymen so that they can create the atmosphere so necessary for the solution of thornier problems pertaining to our separation. This is our work and vocation in our generation: to create an atmosphere, a climate of friendship and brotherhood based upon the teachings and example of Christ our Lord.

The vision of unity is a bright one but it is a distant one. We cannot detect real Christian unity in the foreseeable future; it certainly will not come in our lifetime. But come it must and come it will, for Our Lord has promised it and prayed for it. Our role is to prepare the way, to plant the seed which others will harvest, to prepare the climate for the breath of the Holy Spirit, Who is the principle of unity in Christ's Church.

To this end, then, I suggest that all Christians stress the positive; meet together as brothers; speak with one another in a Christlike manner. In such a dialogue we do not talk to a predetermined end. We converse with one another. To one another, we speak the truth in love. I can think of no better expression of this than one attributed to the late and lamented Father Gustave Weigel, S.J.

"In this matter of ecumenism," he said, "I live from day to day, not worrying about or planning for tomorrow but living with the given and the now. I must practice friendship now without ulterior motive, not only with all men, but especially with the members of the household of faith. There must be talk, much talk and more talk while each side learns how the other understands the Gospel of Christ. We must move into the union of dialogue before we can think seriously about any other kind of union. The Holy Spirit will do the rest."

Stress the Positive

During the Depression years, so the story I heard long ago goes, my predecessor the Archbishop of Boston was visiting a poor parish in the outer and rural region of the archdiocese. The parish had a reputation, or rather a notoriety, for the indifference of the parishioners. Attendance at Mass was very low, church support was woefully small, and parish activities were all but nonexistent. When the aged pastor was asked by his visiting superior how things were faring, he sadly replied, "Badly, very badly, Your Eminence. But then, thank God, the Protestant churches are doing worse."

The humor of this remark does not obscure the uncomfortable grain of truth that it contains. It was not so long ago, in fact, that we Christians looked competitively upon each other's work and progress. We somehow felt that the other's failure meant our success. As if those who lapsed from the Christian faith would surely find their way to *our* Church! The temptation to rejoice (secretly, of course) in the declining membership of "the others" may still be present in some of us. But it reflects a negative and unrealistic and un-Christian attitude. Reversing that old pastor's exclamation, I say, "Thank God, we all are changing."

We recognize that our division and separation are against God's will. We are more painfully aware of our disunity. But we also realize that we share so many things in common, so many truths of Faith, so many traditions, and above all we share the common goal of Christ's calling, calling us to the unity of love in Him with God our Father. Now we Christians are beginning to stress the positive: we are all creatures of our God and Creator, by faith and baptism we are brothers bound by ties much closer than blood, we all share the common task of bringing to the world the kingdom of peace and of justice.

An incident that came to my attention recently might serve to illustrate the positive aspect of the changing attitude that is taking place among us. In a nearby small town the Catholic pastor and the Episcopal rector were very good friends. They met regularly in each other's rectories for dinner, discussed books of each other's favorite authors, and in general enjoyed a fine Christian friendship. The Episcopal church of the town was quite old, badly in need of repair and, since the congregation had increased, it was decided a new church should be built. Naturally, a building fund drive was begun and one of the first to be approached by the rector was his old friend the Catholic pastor.

"I don't know what your Canon Law says about assisting us in building a church, Father, or what your bishop would say about you contributing to the promotion of a Protestant group, but I wanted to give you the opportunity if you wish," said the rector with a twinkle in his eye.

The Catholic pastor thought for a moment, and then suddenly whisked out his checkbook and wrote out a sizable check for the surprised Episcopalian.

"I don't know what the law says about helping build churches," he remarked, "but I am sure that the bishop would approve if I gave you this. Mind you," he grinned, "it's not to help you build the new church; it's more for the necessary expenditures involved in tearing the old one down."

We are all changing, thank God! We are finding ways to be positive, we are tearing down the old walls of division so that a renewed Church may be built up. We are stressing the positive "for the building up of the body of Christ, until we will attain to the oneness of the faith," as the Apostle Paul has told us (Eph. 4:12-13). And for me, in simplest terms, this is the beginning of what is called ecumenism.

This, I hope, will be the pattern of the conversation on every level among fellow Christians. When this is done, then the focus is on Christ and His message and not upon the sad history of separation. Then we shall truly have a manifestation of that love by which Christ promised that all men should know that we are His disciples. We must put aside the rationalization which so easily can come to us to maintain the status quo. We must indeed be unhappy with the status quo of a divided Christianity in whatever fashion it keeps us apart. Even though we cannot expect physical unity among Christians in our generation, we can expect unity of mutual understanding and love; that unity, if you will, mentioned by an apologist of Christianity in its infancy, when he wrote: "Behold how these Christians love one another."

Our task should be to inquire how we can in unfeigned love speak to one another. May I mention one gesture that was tremendously meaningful for me, as I know it was for the widow of our late President. It was a "Resolution of

Gratitude" adopted by the National Council of Churches in Philadelphia in December 1963. It said in part:

"During the recent tragic events we have been profoundly inspired by the power of the Christian faith to cope with the evils and sorrows of this world, as that power has been manifested in the life of Mrs. John Fitzgerald Kennedy. Her dignity and poise under the most shattering circumstances were a demonstration of the grace that enables the Christian not merely to endure but to transform tragic sorrow into triumphant courage. In a day when by the grace of God the various households of faith are being drawn closer together, we have seen clearly in the demeanor of Mrs. Jacqueline Kennedy the majesty and the solace of a Christian commitment. We give thanks to God for this holy witness before the nation and the world."

What could be more eloquent of the way in which "God writes straight with crooked lines" than the way in which men of every faith were brought closer together at the time of the late President's death? And what more touching than the reminder from one household of the Christian faith to another that we share the same fundamental Christian hope?

Meet Together as Brothers

In the past few years some wonderful things have been taking place in the Church. Some wonderful things have been happening in all the Christian churches and communities. The theologians have been describing these by the term "ecumenism," and they speak of the Christian "dialogue" and the "interfaith fellowship" which are growing in our day. Truth to tell, a few years ago I was confused by these terms, and I must admit that even now I am not sure which pronunciation of ecumenism is considered the best.

But to me the important thing is not the jargon but the fact. What is happening is that Christians are talking to each other. This is a great and wonderful thing. We are talking to each other as Christians, as brothers of the same Lord. We are talking with each other as brothers who know that our divisions and isolations and separations are against the will of Our Lord. This fact is giving us a new hope, for it is a sign that the Holy Ghost is moving in our midst, is jolting us out of our smug and self-made ghettoes and pushing us toward the unity which Our Lord wills and for which He prayed on the night before He died.

As a boy, I grew up in South Boston—a neighborhood that was almost 100 per cent Irish—in names, in culture, in loyalty. It was all Catholic. We would never have referred to it as a ghetto and we would have vehemently denied that we had any prejudices. Yet in our homes there were stories and anecdotes aplenty of the persecutions which the English Protestants had carried on against our forebears, and all of us had experienced examples of the discrimination which Yankee Bostonians practiced against the Irish Catholics who were multiplying so rapidly in the land of the Puritans.

I remember more than one black eye received and given in fights with youthful zealots who confused religion and race. We felt quite proud on such occasions that we had defended the faith with our fists and our blood, like the martyrs of old.

As we grew into manhood, the differences still persisted but one didn't show the hostilities in quite so violent a manner. The Boston Irish used the vote and their wits to defeat the Protestants. Political campaigns were not always contests based on political philosophies. Too often there was the subtle influence of differences in faith that aligned us with a candidate. I suppose in a sense this was the inevitable course of events that takes place in an immigrant and pluralistic society like ours.

But as I studied in the seminary and entered the service of God and the Church, I came to recognize that the differences between Catholics and Protestants in America were not so much religious as they were social and cultural. The differences in faith did not divide us so much as the ethnic differences of our parents and grandparents. I discovered that what the ecumenists today call "nontheological factors" were isolating us and setting Catholic against Protestant and Protestant against Catholic more than our creeds or doctrines.

After only a few months as a curate, in which capacity I was not very successful, I was assigned to the office of the Propagation of the Faith in Boston: the society charged with the responsibility of assisting on the local level the missions of the Church. Then it was that I came into contact with people of every social and educational level in the Boston area and elsewhere. Men and women of all faiths soon became warm friends of mine and supporters of the work I was doing to help missionaries to preach the word of Christ and the charitable works of His Church.

When I was called to be Archbishop of Boston, hundreds of Protestants and Jews wished me well. From that day to this, among the most loyal friends behind the program of love of God and neighbor I sponsored were these men and women of good will. The fact that I was a Catholic has not prevented them from helping me to share the burdens we carry in common. Their faith and creed have not restricted me from doing all I could to alleviate the pains of sickness, physical or mental, the indignities of poverty, the problems of the aged, and the other social and moral evils we mortals share in common.

I have realized so often and so well that whenever I showed myself a brother to another human being, there it was that I showed myself as another Christ to another person. Then it was that I received a brother's response; then it was that I saw Christ in my brother. To me, in simplest terms, this is ecumenism. It is brothers meeting and talking with one another and helping each other as Christ wants us to do.

Speak together in a Christlike Manner

The basic attitude of "brother meeting brother" is precisely what good Pope John and his successor Pope Paul have called us to in these recent years. Pope John, as it has been often stated, threw open the windows and doors of the Church so that we could see and be seen by our separated brothers, so that we could meet and be met by them. In receiving and talking with leaders of the major faiths and churches of the world, Pope John in the few short years of his pontificate created such an atmosphere of mutual trust and respect that, thank God, we shall never be the same.

When he insisted that non-Roman Catholics be invited to the Vatican Council, and be allowed to attend all the sessions, he confirmed this brotherly trust. Who can forget the eloquence of the simple words of greeting he preferred to that group of non-Catholic visitors, "I am Joseph your brother."

Pope Paul has not only continued the work of John in the Council, but has given it an emphasis and quality that has made the quest for unity a most important part of the Council's work and hopes. In fact, the address of Pope Paul VI, so movingly delivered at the opening of the Second Session of the present Ecumenical Council, not only reaffirms the unity of Christians to be one of the chief concerns of the Council but also gives what I would call the *practical guides* for our brotherly relations as we seek and pray for unity.

Toward the end of his eloquent speech, which I followed with rapt attention (but which I did not entirely understand until I found a translation) on that morning of September 29 in the great basilica of St. Peter, Pope Paul turned to sixty and more observers who were sitting close to him in special seats and said: "We wish to affirm before the Observers here present some points in our attitude toward reunion with our separated brethren, with a view that they may communicate them to their respective Christian communities. Our manner of speaking is friendly, completely sincere and loyal. We lay no snares; we are not motivated by temporal interests. We owe our Faith, which we believe to be divine, the most candid and firm attachment. But at the same time we are convinced that this does not constitute an obstacle to the desired understanding with our separated brethren, precisely because it is the truth of the Lord and therefore the principle of union and not of distinction or separation. At any rate, we do not wish to make of our Faith an occasion for polemics."

"Our Manner of Speaking Is Friendly, Completely Sincere and Loyal."

This statement is not merely an affirmation of Pope Paul's attitude and approach to men of good will the world over. It is also a practical guide for all of us in the vocation we have today, in what has been called "the ecumenical age."

An incident was reported to me recently which took place in a small New England town. The Protestant community was largely Congregational and would gather each Sunday morning at ten o'clock for their regular service. At about twenty past ten, the formal prayers would be led by the minister, and precisely at that moment the bells of the nearby Catholic church would ring out persistently. The timing of the bells with the beginning of the solemn invocations would occur Sunday after Sunday. The Protestant congregation understandably became more and more irritated and became more and more convinced that the Catholics were purposely trying to annoy them and disrupt their service.

The irritation soon turned to bitter resentment, the resentment to hostility, and what had been a prayer service now was in danger of becoming a hate meditation. At this time it happened that a professor from the Harvard Divinity School was visiting the community and in conversation with the minister and several of the congregation learned of the situation. He was informed by the group that they had had enough and that they had resolved to appeal to the local officials and, if necessary, to the courts to restrain the Catholics from this hostile action. The professor was quite concerned. He had been active in theological dialogue with Catholics and was quite disturbed to see further rifts take place.

"What precisely did the Catholic priest say," he inquired, "when you complained about the bells?"

The minister and the others were stunned by the question.

"Why," replied the minister, "we never mentioned it to him. Naturally not."

"Isn't it just possible," he asked, "that the bells are rung for the ten-thirty Mass each Sunday and that the Catholics have no idea of your worship schedule or that it interferes in any way?"

The Congregationalists did approach the Catholic pastor, somewhat reluctantly, and found that the priest was completely surprised that he had been the cause of hostility among the Protestants of the town. An arrangement satisfactory to all was immediately worked out.

The point illustrated by this true incident is that a lack of friendly relations and of communication was at the root of the misunderstanding. Both groups lacked the concern that friends should have for each other. Both groups had isolated themselves in unfriendly ignorance. Our manner must be friendly. This is the first prerequisite for our relations with each other.

Be Sincere and Candid with Each Other

Another condition which Pope Paul singles out is sincerity. A sincere respect for the conscience and beliefs of our brothers; a frank and honest presentation of our own faith and beliefs. The more I speak with Protestants and Orthodox, the more I see men who are trying hard to be obedient to Our Lord Jesus Christ, trying hard to live their lives according to His Gospel, working and praying for the unity they know He wants His Church to manifest, the more I am humbled by their sincerity and humility.

Many of my priests have mentioned to me that they think that one of the great fruits of the theological conversations they have had with clergy of the Protestant and Orthodox Churches is the practical appreciation of the sincerity of their fellow Christians. One priest confided this conviction to me recently.

"Before I started taking part in these meetings with Protestant ministers," he said, "I am sure that deep down I felt that they must be either fools for not seeing the truth of the Catholic Church or frauds who refused to recognize it. But now I am convinced that these men with whom I talk are being faithful to the Lord as they have received and understood His Gospel. These men speak by the Spirit."

Sincerity too in our presentation of the Catholic faith and doctrines is necessary. I suppose that there is sometimes the temptation for us Catholics, when we talk with other Christians, to gloss over doctrines that we feel might offend them, to convince them that we really have so much in common and that the things which divide us are so trivial. This, of course, would be altogether wrong; it would also be unfair and insincere.

I heard of a situation recently in which a priest was to address a Catholic women's club. The president of the group approached the speaker somewhat nervously and informed him that there were several Protestant women guests present and "would Father be careful not to mention things that might offend the guests?"

"Of course," the priest replied amusedly. "What do you think I should avoid?"

"Well, perhaps it would be best not to refer to the Pope or the Blessed Mother."

When the priest looked a little puzzled, the woman hastened to add, "After all, we should be ecumenical."

Without hesitation, the priest discarded the talk he had planned to give and spoke instead on "some ecumenical problems that divide us." He built his talk around the Catholic regard for the Blessed Virgin and Catholic belief regarding the successor of St. Peter. He felt that this group needed some positive direction in ecumenical sincerity. Suffice it to say that the Protestant women came up to him after the talk and expressed their gratitude for the explanation he had given them about subjects they had never understood before and about which they had been too embarrassed to ask their Catholic friends. Our manner must be completely sincere.

Be Loyal to Truth

Another quality which Pope Paul mentioned in that address of September 29 is loyalty. He said that "we lay no snares" and that "we do not wish to make of our Faith an occasion for polemics." But at the same time he asserted, "We owe our Faith, which we believe to be divine, the most candid and firm attachment."

I feel that it is unnecessary to comment upon this. Uncompromising loyalty to the faith is altogether a prerequisite for our meeting and talking together. Catholic and Protestant theologians alike agree that there can be no true dialogue without loyalty to the truths of one's faith. This loyalty on the one hand does not preclude a frank admission of mistakes many of us and our forebears in the faith may have made. Indeed, it should prompt us to penitence.

Pope Paul VI, speaking in a special meeting he had with the Council observers on October 17, 1963, said: "We have not hesitated . . . to have recourse first of all to Christian forgiveness and mutual forgiveness if possible. Let us all give and seek forgiveness." Then he referred to the beautiful words of Our Lord reported in the Gospel of St. Matthew (Matt. 5:23–24) which counsel us to seek first to be reconciled with our brother before offering gifts at the altar. This is the loyalty of the Church renewing herself in Council.

On the other hand, loyalty requires the firm confidence that the Holy Spirit guides the Church and counsels us to patience. While we welcome a spirit of honest self-criticism, we should not lose sight of the wondrous mystery of the Church. At the Second Session of the Council some of our Catholic journalists did just that. Their reports were colored so often with pessimism that they conveyed a false image of the true picture of the Council.

We too can do this by too much emphasis on past mistakes of either side when we talk together as Christian brothers. As Pope Paul said in the address to the observers: "But it is also best to look not towards the past but to the present and especially to the future. Others can and must pursue the study of history. We prefer now to fix our attention on what *shall* be rather than on what *has* been." Loyalty requires this "look to future." Our manner must be loyal.

Love One Another

These qualities which Pope Paul VI singled out as a guide for Christians talking together as brothers can be summed up in the two words, "Christlike charity." The charity which "is kind, is patient, is not puffed up . . . rejoices with the truth" (1 Cor. 13). This is the charity, the love of Christ Our Lord Who is the Head of His Body, the Church. It is the charity to which we all are called; it is the charity which will unite us in the visible bonds of love in His Church. It is, I know, the charity which prompted Pope Paul VI to go as a penitential pilgrim to the Holy Land in January 1964. It is the charity which he and Patriarch Athenagoras I manifested to each other and the world in their historic meeting.

That meeting of Pope and Patriarch offers us an example and pattern of our meetings—Catholic, Orthodox, and Protestant meeting together. They went out to meet each other and so must we in positive fashion. They met as brothers; so must we meet as brothers. They met in Christlike manner in the presence of Christ; so must we meet. These to me are the first ecumenical steps to be taken on the grass-roots level.

Martin E. Marty

Associate editor of the *Christian Century* and Associate Professor of Church History at the Divinity School, University of Chicago, Martin E. Marty is a prolific writer and a leader in the ecumenical movement in the United States. Born on February 5, 1928, he studied at Concordia Seminary in St. Louis, at the Chicago Lutheran Theological Seminary, and in 1956 took his Ph.D. degree in American religious and intellectual history at the University of Chicago.

He was active as a liturgical artist and served as pastor of Lutheran churches in the Washington, D.C. and Chicago areas. He was the founding pastor of the Church of the Holy Spirit in Elk Grove Village, a Chicago suburb, but resigned his pastorate in 1963 to become an associate professor of Church History. A minister of the Lutheran Church-Missouri synod, he has contributed in the last five years more than three hundred articles to a variety of magazines and has authored and edited numerous books.

In addition to his post as associate editor of the *Christian Century*, Dr. Marty is on the editorial staffs of *The Pulpit* and other journals. He has held a number of theological and historical lectureships and has frequently appeared on radio and television programs. His book, *Second Chance for American Protestants*, stirred widespread interest. In it Dr. Marty argues that the Churches are being "displaced" from their comfortable positions of influence and, in an increasingly religionless world, Christians are becoming once again, in the Biblical phrase, "strangers and exiles."

The traditional beliefs of Protestant Churches have in the past formed the basis in the U.S.A. for a "consensus religion." But this, Dr. Marty contends, has now lost its impact and is like faded wallpaper, visible everywhere but hardly noticed. Change is urgently needed to make the voices of the Churches once more a vital spiritual influence in the life of the nation.

"I tell my congregation," he says, "that their sin is not in being middle class; their sin is not seeing through the limits of their class." Among some of the other books of Dr. Marty are, *A Short History of Christianity*, *The New Shape of American Religion*, *The Infidel:*

Free Thought and American Religion, The Varieties of Unbelief, and *Church Unity and Church Mission.* He is a co-author of *American Catholics: A Protestant-Jewish View.* In 1952 he married Elsa Schumacher. They are the parents of four children and two foster children and the family resides in Riverside, Illinois.

PATTERNS OF PROTESTANT
THOUGHT

Seven years ago, at the time of the last arrangement of my
study library, I had carefully segregated Roman Catholic
books. Today, a Catholic commentary on St. John's Gospel
reposes next to a Protestant one; a Catholic interpretation of
St. Augustine nestles between two non-Catholic interpretations; a Jesuit's book on modern atheism is back to back with
an agnostic's book of self-defense against Jesuits.

What this library arrangement implies is now part of the
public experience of most serious Christian thinkers today. It
is difficult to study the Bible, Church History, or systematic
theology in one branch of the Christian Church without being
mindful of and being informed by the other branches. This
does not mean that some merger between Catholic and Protestant thinkers is in the offing. No capitulations or accommo-
dations are in sight. On almost all the historic points of
difference between communions there still remain great
breaches of understanding. But definitely a new mood, a
common interpretation, and a unified way of "doing things"
in theology are apparent.

These are limited but very important gains. While theology
can be a specialized and technical task, it does, in relating
itself to the concerns of man, involve in the first or last
analysis all people in the Church. What follows is one man's
view of some Protestant concerns which may be important
to Catholics.

The change in relations between Christian thinkers from
coexistence to cooperation has come about, of course, because of the ecumenical movement as well as by the fact that
in the era of modern mass media the same "outside world"
is pushed upon the consciousness of all Christians. This means

that many of the same questions have to be answered afresh by Catholics and Protestants alike, and some of their new answers will fall into the same orbits of overlapping concern and truth.

At first glance, Protestant theology looks plotless to Catholics. Not only are there many denominational brands of thought, but through the middle of each denomination there seems to be a line often marked "liberal-conservative." Further, Protestant theologians are notoriously individualistic. In contrast, Roman Catholics often think of their own theology as more or less homogenized. Because of one final earthly authority, the papacy; because of one official "cast" of theology, Thomism; because of one interconnected hierarchical pattern, it is assumed that Catholic thought is one.

Catholic doctrine may be, but theology is not exactly the same as doctrine. The Catholic layman who could eavesdrop on a meeting of theologians of one Catholic faculty would be shocked (or pleasantly surprised) to hear the variety of viewpoints within the permitted framework. Similarly, he might be somewhat surprised to find that there are certain strands at which he can pull to unify the Protestant picture. Faithful Protestant theologians also want to be obedient to the tradition of the Church and responsive to the Scriptures. Their thought is often disciplined and logical; A+B=C in their world, and the inherited truth of the various branches of the Christian past does dominate their thinking.

In this essay I shall not enter into a discussion about particular points of doctrine. Naturally, a Baptist theologian's view on infant baptism will differ from an Episcopalian's. For our purposes it is more important and more interesting to see how "the whole business" of theology is undertaken, what fundamental grasp of truth characterizes the schools of thought. Immediately we can become lost in labels. They are familiar: "liberal," "modernist," "orthodox," "evangelical," "fundamentalist," and all the same terms repeated with the prefix "neo" in front of each.

Let us picture, instead, a series of strata of thought. These strata explain what is found on the surface. At the base of most Protestant thinking in America is what we can call "evangelicalism." That is a good work for historic main-stream Protestantism. It is centered in the good news of God's activity in Jesus Christ, is warmly conscious of the fellowship of the Church, considers itself to be guided by the Holy Spirit, is judged by the Bible. This evangelicalism toward the end of the nineteenth century tended to form two schools. One, the more liberal, made an easier adjustment to the scientific world view and to critical study of the Bible. The more conservative resisted the scientific order wherever its tenets seemed to clash with the Bible, and totally resisted a critical view of the Scriptures.

In the early twentieth century these emphases hardened into parties. The liberal became "modernist" (a name almost no one likes to have applied to himself today). The modernist was an extremely liberal Christian, often given over to a rather consistent faith in human progress, a hope for God's kingdom in the social betterment of man, and—better than these—a real ethical passion. The well-known Social Gospel of the first two or three decades of the century was largely based in such modernism.

The reactors to what seemed to be a dissolving of Christian truth formed a party called "fundamentalist." Again, this word has fallen into disrepute and not many want to be called by it. The modernist-fundamentalist battle within the denominations was an unlovely one, made famous by the Scopes trial (Darrow vs. Bryan on the issue of evolution) in 1925. Today there are "neo-liberals" chastened by many experiences since World War I, and "neo-evangelicals" who sound much like fundamentalists.

To understand "neo-orthodoxy" as the major event in twentieth-century Protestant thought we must retreat to the nineteenth. Theology in that period came to be "man-centered." The two most influential theologians were Ger-

man. One, an authentic religious genius, was Friedrich
Schleiermacher. We must ruthlessly oversimplify: Think of
him as a romantic. This cultured and immensely learned man
rewrote all Christian doctrines from the manward point of
view. Religion was the *feeling* of absolute dependence. His
counterpart, Albrecht Ritschl, was the historian par excellence and the founder of a school of historians of great
influence. The Ritschlians applied the tools of historical
scholarship to the Bible and Christian doctrine and removed
many supernatural elements (and many "Greek" aspects) and
came up with a portrait of Jesus as the great ethical leader
and teacher.

Dominated by such schools of thought, Christians spent less
time talking about God as the object of faith and more talking about man as the subject. His religious experience became important, and Jesus as example was stressed more than
Jesus the sacrificial Son of God. The Churches tried to ad-
just to the new world views after Darwin and to serve the
world by "Christianizing the social order."

Great Britain and the United States produced slightly less
well-known figures who led schools of thought much like
the two in Germany. These subjective-historical emphases fit
in well with belief in human progress. God's kingdom seemed,
indeed, to be coming into the affairs of men as one after
another of man's concerns became Christianized.

Then came the end of the nineteenth century, and World
War I. Man's most violent war occurred on Christian soil.
Faith in progress was shaken, and the kingdom seemed never
more remote. The theologians tried to listen to the word of
God and relate it to the world of men. A Swiss pastor, Karl
Barth, who survives and remains the "grand old man" of
Protestant theology, responded by writing and publishing a
commentary on Paul's Epistle to the Romans. Later Barth
was to compare his act to a man reaching in the dark in a
tower for something to hold on to; he had grabbed the bell
rope.

Protestant thinkers responded to the tolling of the old theological order and the bringing in of the new. Barth was not alone. He was surrounded by Swiss, German, Scandinavian, and to a slightly lesser degree, British and American thinkers. Soon on the terrain of the "younger Churches" Barthian thought was common. We need not here go into the reasons for the choice of names for the reaction and the new voices: The word "orthodoxy" appeared because Barth and his various colleagues and competitors made a strong appeal to the revelation in the Bible and to the sixteenth-century reformers, especially Martin Luther and John Calvin. Luther had survived the nineteenth century as a romantic hero (Thomas Carlyle contributed to this false portrait). But Calvin's fortunes were low. Suddenly, in the twentieth century, his view of man and man's sin was very much in place.

Barth and his successors reversed the man-centered trend and theology became God-centered. Barth was intoxicated with the idea of God's "otherness" and man's lostness apart from God's action in Christ. It is easy to see why through the years as Barth became more churchly he was more attractive to Catholics than the nineteenth-century options were. He himself regards Catholics to be among the best interpreters of his thought.

Barth's colleague who later argued vehemently with him was Emil Brunner, who also lives in Switzerland. Brunner is anti-institutionalist. That is, he feels that the forms of the Church take captive and distort the experience of the Holy Spirit. Because Brunner was fortunate enough to have good and early translators, he was for a time more read than Barth in America. He has had great impact on American Protestant social thought, preoccupied as he has been with the question of how law and justice relate to love.

We shall have to skip much of interest between the two World Wars and point now to the other peak experience of our century's Protestant thought to date. I refer to a manifesto by the German, Rudolf Bultmann, who lives as a professor emeritus at Marburg. Bultmann had long been known as an expert as Biblical interpretation. But his great blast was obscured from American view for some time because it occurred in a tract, *New Testament and Mythology*, written at the beginning of World War II. Since the war it has become Topic A in Protestant theology.

The Catholic may have more difficulty relating to Bultmann than to Barth. To him Bultmann may seem to be a step away from "orthodoxy" back to man-centered liberalism. Yet Catholic Biblical scholars unanimously must cope with this man and his emphasis and many are greatly informed by him. Why? Because, right or wrong, Bultmann put his finger on a "hot-button" in modern Christianity. In the interest of preaching the Gospel of Jesus Christ he reflected on his problem: Man today not only engages in a different style of living but also a different style of thinking from man of the past, including especially Biblical man.

Biblical people had no difficulty with what he calls a "mythical" world view. (By "myth" Bultmann does not mean a false fable but a necessary way of expressing a reality from outside our experience in terms of our experience.) The Bible pictures a three-story hell-earth-heaven universe, peopled by angels and demons. In the world of electricity and automation, science and technology and explanation, this is meaningless.

Bultmann would—the term is unfortunately negative—"demythologize" the message of the Bible. Now, in a sense, every preacher does this when he speaks contemporary language. But Bultmann goes farther: He comes even to the point of Christ's Resurrection and removes this event as being "mythical." To most Christians this strikes at the heart of the faith. Bultmann does not think of himself as a destroyer. He rebuilds by reference to existentialist philosophy. He has been perhaps overinfluenced by Martin Heidegger, a formidable thinker and—to laymen in philosophy like myself—an

almost incomprehensible one. Bultmann sees the preaching of
Jesus Christ in demythologized form as the way of confronting man in the light of God so that man finds authentic
human existence and faith, which Bultmann considers to be
"openness to the future."

Bultmann has radical disciples who ask: Then why the
Christ-event at all? Isn't he talking about a timeless principle?
Bultmann also has conservative followers who speak much
of a "new quest for the historical Jesus." They have a
developing faith in the reliability of the New Testament portrait which their teacher lacked. We are, no doubt, in a
period of synthesis which will bring modern Protestant
Biblical thought into a somewhat more congenial realm as
far as Catholics are concerned.

Back to America. We have had followers of Barth,
Brunner, and Bultmann. All have been modified and softened
somewhat by the experience of translation. Americans were
a bit less grim, somber, and existential and a bit more
optimistic and liberal. Yet our three best-known theologians
were heavily influenced by the European experience. Two of
the three are brothers: Reinhold Niebuhr of Union Theological Seminary in New York; his late brother, Helmut Richard
of Yale; and Paul Tillich, now of Chicago. These men
dominated and set the terms for American Protestant thought
in recent decades and their influence will no doubt endure
for some time.

Reinhold Niebuhr is best known to the public. Some
political leaders of the New Deal and the succeeding deals
and crusades and frontiers consider him the most profound
political thinker inside or around the Churches in our time.
He shares Barth's view of human pride and is often credited
with reintroducing "original sin" as a respectable category
in common speech.

He was similarly influenced by St. Paul, St. Augustine,
Luther, and especially Calvin. He brought Protestants from
their widespread pacifism to a concern for interpreting power

in human affairs. He has broken completely with Barth on politics. Barth, the most heroic theological opponent to Nazism, has been equivocal in repudiating Communism. Barth thinks (or thought, until a happy first American tour in 1962!) that American capitalism and prosperity can be a greater problem for man's hearing the Gospel than can Communism. Niebuhr's influence began in the early 1930s with publication of *Moral Man and Immoral Society*. Catholic social thought is openly in debt to Niebuhr.

His brother was a quieter, less productive, more analytic thinker; he was less "prophetic" and more reflective. H. Richard Niebuhr kept alive a bit more of the nineteenth-century style of ethics and thought, though his debt to European "neo-orthodoxy" was also apparent.

Third in the triumvirate is Paul Tillich, perhaps the best-known Protestant intellectual of the past two decades in America. Tillich works to "correlate" theology with philosophy and history and art. He is the most live option to Bultmann among many younger thinkers. His thought is not oriented toward history (God revealed in Palestine, in Rome, etc.) so much as toward ontology (God as Being Itself).

Many critics, among them the Catholic Georges Tavard, question whether on the basic issue, the Incarnation, Tillich is actually "Christian." Sometimes the philosophy behind his systematic theology removes him from classic Christian considerations; his widely publicized sermons, however, find him in a role where the decisively Christian stamp is less questioned. He is an amazingly complex thinker who has great influence on Catholic artists, theologians, and philosophers.

Of course, theology is not merely the private experience of great theologians. It will be profitable to leave these giants who make up perhaps the greatest cluster of Protestant theologians since the sixteenth century and draw together some general concerns in which they may have had a smaller part but which equally characterize Protestantism today and which have interest for Catholics.

First among these is a new awareness of the relation between Scripture and tradition. It is often remarked that recent Catholicism is moving toward the Scriptural base and Protestantism toward the traditional; the ecumenical movement occurs at their juncture. Protestantism long used the adjective *sola* before *Scriptura:* Scripture alone was the fountain and source of truth. Like most slogans, this was a half-truth. Luther and Calvin at the head of Protestantism both asserted with Catholics from Cyprian to the present that the Scripture is read *in the Church;* that one cannot have God for Father if he does not have the Church for his mother.

But the Enlightenment and the age of individualism which followed made it seem as if Protestantism was nothing but irresponsible, erratic, isolationistic self-interpretation of Scripture. Historical scholarship, of course, also shows the Church (tradition) to be prior to the New Testament documents. The early Church got along without Scripture *alone*.

Protestantism does not begin, by this, to agree with Catholicism's view of the way tradition is tended. It is extremely careful about what it accepts of "traditions" of men after the Biblical period. But Catholic and Protestant concerns over the place of tradition and Scripture are beginning to converge. The ecumenical movement, with the strong representation of tradition-oriented Eastern Orthodox Christians, is having an effect on Protestant theology, and Catholics, naturally, warm to the growing Church-centeredness of Protestantism.

If the Scriptures represented the formative base of Protestant Christianity, the teaching that man is justified by grace through faith was the first material or substantive point which unified all other Protestant theology. Today this teaching is informed by Catholic thought, just as Catholics are showing a growing congeniality to many of the Reformers' concerns over God's initiative and man's impotence in the acts of grace and mercy in Christ. Meanwhile (the example of uncertain Lutherans at their international meeting at Helsinki last summer is typical), Protestants know that they are not "getting through" to their own membership with this basic teaching and are trying to reforge it. Outlines are unclear at this time, but Catholics should be alerted to watch the discussion.

Second, ecumenical thought about the Church and sacraments has been a major concern of Protestants. I have not stressed that element of evangelical Christianity which should be most familiar to Catholics. Every move at Rome is now watched with respect and hope. For over fifty years Protestants have been drawing nearer each other in their interpretation of the Church. A newer (and older) view of the solidarity of the new humanity in Christ is replacing the old-frontiersy kind of "autonomous individualism," though Protestantism has lost none of its interest in individual freedom in Church or world. Catholics who are interested in non-Roman ecumenical thought will do well to do a bit of research in their libraries on the decades of work in the Faith and Order movement in the World Council of Churches.

Protestant thought is, fourth, strongly oriented toward the ethical. The bomb, racial revolution, and business ethics preoccupy Protestant ethical thought today. There is a constant interest in both individual and personal ethics on the one hand and, even more, on social ethics.

Finally, Protestant theologians are virtually unanimous in their interest in forging a theology for the new kind of secular world around them. Our theological terms were largely "frozen" in the century just before the scientific, industrial, and political revolutions of modern times forced a new vocabulary and style of thinking on people.

One of the inspirations for this new "worldly" theology was Dietrich Bonhoeffer, killed by the Nazis in 1945. (With Barth, Brunner, and Bultmann he makes up the "Four B's" of modern German-Swiss thought.) Bonhoeffer began to sketch a "religionless" Christianity, strongly disciplined by historic faith but free and mobile in a Godless world. In a centripetal or gathering ecumenical era it would be centrifugal, forcing Christians to forego comfort and prerogatives and live the hidden life in the world alongside a suffering and glorying Christ.

A recent book title, *The Secular Meaning of the Gospel*, by Paul van Buren, is typical of this theological concern, and Catholics alert to trends might watch for many more in this family. The controversial, best-selling *Honest to God* by Anglican Bishop John A. T. Robinson was a secondhand popular version of some of these interests. Robinson combined bits of Tillich, Bultmann, and Bonhoeffer to suggest a theology for people in a secular world. His book may not be original, substantial, or adequate, but it does reflect present-day concerns.

I am taken aback to think what I have had to omit out of the amazing variety and richness of a half century's enterprise and trend. New names are beginning to appear: Catholics will recognize names like Robert McAfee Brown and Jaroslav Pelikan. Were it not confusing to introduce a roomful of people and names at a time, we should have said something about the fine tradition of British Biblical scholarship, which has so many American disciples; of natural theology as it is still taught in many American universities and seminaries; of the new interests in the scientific use of language in theology. Perhaps I have whetted some appetites for satisfaction elsewhere. Numbers of Catholic thinkers—Gustave Weigel among them—have written introductions to Protestant theology for Catholics.

My library indicated one man's "do-it-yourself kit" for an ecumenical theology. Others may have more profound ways of suggesting relations between Catholic and Protestant thoughts. Still others may be content with occasional newspaper accounts and passing glances. But all Christians, well aware of the limits of theologians, should partake of some of the sense of adventure that is going into Protestant-Orthodox-Roman attempts to face the enduring truths in a radically changing world.

No corner of the Church can "sit this round out." Those who have been called to love the Lord their God *with all their mind* have not been relieved of their tasks; but once-divided Christians have a growing consciousness of the fact that others outside their communions share the task, and we shall be better off for the sharing.

Karl Rahner

Karl Rahner was born on March 5, 1904, in Freiburg im Breisgau in southern Germany. The son of a professor of Latin, Karl showed early in life his scholarly talents. Joining the Society of Jesus, he studied at universities in Holland, Germany, and Austria and was for a time a student of the famous existentialist Martin Heidegger. He was ordained in 1932. In 1937 he was assigned to teach at the University of Innsbruck, where he remained until his appointment in 1964 to the prestigious chair of dogmatic theology at the University of Munich.

His numerous scholarly articles, lectures, and books have won for him the reputation of being probably the most profound, productive, and exciting theologian of the twentieth century. He is the personal theologian to both Francis Cardinal Koenig of Vienna and Julius Cardinal Doepfner of Munich, and his views on various theological questions discussed at Vatican Council II were eagerly sought by scores of cardinals, bishops, and theologians from Germany, France, Africa, Latin America, and the United States.

Many think that he exerted more real influence on the Council than any other theologian. Pope John XXIII appointed him a member of a select group of *periti*, the official Council theologians. He personally wrote the draft resolution on the relationship of Scripture and tradition that was put before the first session of the Council as an alternative to the one proposed by Cardinal Ottaviani. Using a Socratic method, Rahner keeps relentlessly asking thought-prodding questions, designed to prompt each generation to rethink the problems of theology and restate the answers in contemporary and relevant terms.

Rahner's working day is of staggering diligence and tireless application, extending from 3:30 A.M. until 11 P.M. He was the editor of the *Enchiridion Symbolorum*, the standard compendium of documents expressing the teachings of the Church. At present he is co-editing a massive encyclopedia of theology that is expected to be completed in 1965. Rahner is a profound speculative theologian and writes in an abstract style, and hence it is difficult at times to be sure one has understood his thought.

"When I am an old man and have time," jokes his older brother Hugo (himself a noted Jesuit theologian), "I want to translate Karl's writings—into German."

Dr. Rahner has written hundreds of articles for scholarly theological journals and many books. Among those which have been translated into English are: *Free Speech in the Church, Encounters with Silence, On the Theology of Death, Theological Investigations, Christian Commitments, Happiness Through Prayer,* and *Inspiration in the Bible.*

Dr. Rahner has never written a book summing up his theology, and hence lay people know little or nothing of his theological thinking and views. Hence we regard it as a great achievement that we were able, with the help of Cardinal Koenig of Vienna and Dr. Herbert Vorgrimler of Munich, to secure the interview in which we asked him to express his thought in non-technical language on the ten practical questions we put to him. This is probably the first time that Dr. Rahner has granted an interview of this character, and we are, of course, most thankful to him and all the friends who helped us in securing it.

CLEARING THE WAY
TO CHRISTIAN UNITY

We know, Father Rahner, that practically all of your books are profound abstract studies designed for professional theologians. We wonder, however, if you might not wish to offer a few suggestions that would help Christians in the ordinary walks of life to advance, even in a humble manner, the cause of Christian unity. Do you think that ordinary Christians can help by informing themselves concerning the central issues involved, by cultivating greater friendliness toward Christians of other confessions and especially by praying for Christian unity?

The reunion of separated Christians should be the concern of the simple, ordinary Christian. He should have a special interest where he is actually living with non-Catholic Christians. This ecumenical interest is a duty of love for him and the fulfillment of a responsibility which he has assumed in Baptism and Confirmation. Through these sacraments he has become an apostle, a witness to Christ and His Church. Therefore the Catholic should utilize the media of information on non-Catholic Christians that are offered him in his everyday life by the hierarchy. Where an individual bishop is halfhearted or indifferent to the question of ecumenism, the Catholic with brotherly frankness must ask that this episcopal duty and commission be better fulfilled. Yet the most important thing is prayer, private and common.

Dr. Oscar Cullmann suggests that Protestants and Catholics can foster the ecumenical spirit by having Catholics take up collections in their parishes to help the poor in a neighboring Protestant parish and to have the members of a Protestant parish do the same for the poor of a neighboring Catholic parish. Dr. Cullmann reports that this has already been done

*in a number of communities with good results. Would you
please comment on this proposal?*

Christians should always and everywhere give mutual help
to one another in true fraternal love. A Catholic can help
another Christian in a material way even though this Christian, following the dictates of his conscience, is not a Catholic. The only condition is that such aid does not give the
impression that the assisting Catholic regards the non-Catholic Christian confession on a par with the full Catholic
Christianity.

At present this is not a danger. In practice, a reasonable
and realistic attitude is that in general Catholic and Protestant
parishes should solve their own financial problems. Here and
there, however, concrete help can certainly put into practice
that ecumenical spirit which is the duty of all Christians. This
can happen especially when a sudden need arises in a parish
or when one parish is in a much stronger financial and social
position than another.

*Dr. Robert McAfee Brown thinks that a common acknowl-
edgment of our guilt for the events that separated us in the
past would be a step toward Christian unity. Would you
agree with him?*

Pope Paul VI, in the name of the Catholic Church, has
made an acknowledgment of guilt with regard to the causes
of Christian disunity. I think that the Protestant communities
too are ready for such an acknowledgment even though they
may not yet have made it. However, an individual acknowledgment easily appears as a perfunctory ritual, and so it is
more important for the daily practice of our faith and for the
ecumenical dialogue that we have the continual, vivid conviction that we are *all* guilty. This includes both our Protestant and Catholic forefathers, the laity and the hierarchy—
including the Pope—and ourselves, the Christians of the present who have not given a sufficiently clear witness to
Christianity and who have not offered to the Christians of

different confessions enough of that respect and love which we owe them.

Father Hans Küng has suggested that greater freedom for Catholic theologians and scholars to express their views, provided they are within the general framework of the Catholic faith, and less censorship by ecclesiastical authorities would be helpful for Christian unity. Would you agree with him?

In most cases it is the individual bishops and their delegates who alone exercise ecclesiastical censorship. Thus it is impossible to make a statement which is equally true for every country. One cannot say the ecclesiastical censorship is or is not too strict with Catholic theologians on ecumenical questions. As a whole there exists, especially since the Council, enough freedom for Catholic theologians to express their opinions on these questions. If the bishops are bold and courageous, the theologians in general will have no real difficulties with the Holy Office.

Dr. Douglas Horton thinks that one of the ways of fostering the ecumenical spirit is to pursue jointly some objective in which both are interested and about which both wish to learn more, such as the study of the Bible itself. Instead of confronting one another, they turn to a common objective and this begets a sense of "we-ness" or unity. We would welcome your thought on this observation.

Of course theologians of the various confessions must undertake common studies on the questions of Biblical theology, dogma, the history of civilization, constitutional law, the liturgy, and other problems. Only professional theologians and officials of the Church should undertake such precise, scientific work in general, since discussion on these points will provide little fruit for those not trained in theology. However, theological discussions should not concern only controversial theology.

"Controversial" theology is the term for discussions on those doctrines which divided Christianity at the time of the Reformation. The theological discussions should revolve around the question that is of primary importance to all believing Christians today, namely, how modern men can preach and present authentic Christianity to the non-Christians in their own countries so that it does not appear to them as a spiritual and ceremonial museum piece. This is the urgent task of all confessions. Common effort on this problem will contribute more to Christian unity than a concentration on the old questions of controversial theology.

Theologians must, of course, study the theology of the other Christian confessions in its basis tenets, not in order to refute it but to learn something for their own theology. Such a mutual learning is possible to a much greater extent than most theologians believe. For example, I would say there is no Catholic dogmatic manual which has not taken over many things from present-day Protestant Biblical theology that are valuable for Catholics.

Many Protestant leaders think that a step toward unity would be the declaration by the Vatican Council that all who are baptized in Christ and acknowledge Him as our Lord and Master are actually members of the Mystical Body of Christ and not merely connected in some vague manner with that Body. Would you comment on this?

Presumably Vatican II will declare that all who have received true Christian Baptism belong to the one true Church of Christ in a very real sense. And this, even if non-Catholic Christians do not yet belong to this Church in the Roman Catholic way. There is today, however, much more uniting us with these Christians than dividing us. Baptism, Scripture, grace, and the Holy Spirit are proportionately greater things than the exterior government over which we are divided, even if this Catholic government is an element of his Church willed by Christ. Therefore we can always say to our Protestant brothers that we want to be united with them in the visible unity of the Catholic Church since we know or hope that we are already one in the confession of Jesus Christ our

Lord and Saviour, and in Baptism and the grace of the Holy Spirit.

If we maintain this attitude, we have certainly not achieved unity yet, but we are slowly creating a climate in which an ecumenical dialogue can be carried on more fruitfully. The question of where the true Church of Christ is to be found and what conditions make for full membership in her, remains a dividing controversy among Christians. However, men who are not yet one but wish to be so, will unite more easily, if they recognize in the unity which they already have, the foundation and the obligation for that unity which they do not have.

Canon Bernard Pawley and Frère Max Thurian, along with many other Protestant observers at the Council, think that the affirmation by the Council of the principle of the collegiality of bishops would be a real step toward Christian unity. Would you agree?

Vatican II may declare that all power and teaching authority in the Church in the highest degree rests in the episcopacy with the Pope as its personal head and that the Pope, without prejudice to the position accorded him by Vatican I, is not simply an absolute monarch for whom all other institutions are passive robots. We hope that Protestants and their theologians may also see more clearly that the Catholic Church does have a synodal element which by divine right and the will of Christ belongs to the essence of the Church. Then Protestants will be assured that in the event of their becoming Catholics, they would not absolutely renounce the essential element of brotherhood and synod from their community and belief but would recover it, together with a personal element (the authority of the individual bishops and the Pope), if they bring their own heritage into the unity of the one Church.

Dr. Karl Barth states that to Protestants the most visible demarcation line between the Protestant and Catholic Churches is undoubtedly "the worship of the Virgin." He

CLEARING THE WAY TO CHRISTIAN UNITY

states that Protestants are extremely sensitive about this mat-
ter and have concluded that "the exultation of the Virgin,
that is to say of a person, has been taken much too far by
Rome. We dread the thought that the Catholic Church may
one day elevate to a dogma its conception of Mary as Co-
Redemptress." Would you comment on this?

At the time of the Reformation the doctrine of Mary was
not really a dividing point between Catholics and Protestants.
The old Protestantism also acknowledged and honored the
maternity of the Blessed Virgin even though it believed it
had to combat real or imaginary aberrations in the devotion
to Mary.

With the dogmas of the Immaculate Conception (1854)
and the bodily Assumption of the Blessed Virgin into heaven,
the ecumenical difficulty over the Church's mariological doctrine and practice increased its significance in the ecumenical
dialogue, for practically all Protestants will deny these teachings, at least as binding dogmas of faith. However, we Catholics, in our teaching and practice, must make it very clear
that we consider all our pronouncements on Mary as expressions of the victory of the grace of our one Mediator, Jesus
Christ, and of the perfect redemption which God has
effected for the Church in a visible manner in this person,
Mary.

We Catholics cannot give up the hope that the teaching on
Mary and love for her will one day be common to all, who
acknowledge the true Son of God, His real historical existence, and the abounding victory of His grace. We must
clearly point out that due to Christ and His grace, each member of Christ's Mystical Body is a bearer of salvation to
every other member. Mary's significance for us in the Mystical Body is only that of a bearer of salvation, a role given
her by the grace of Christ.

We ascribe to Mary that position in salvation history which
the Scriptures clearly ascribe to her—a believer and a virgin
who by her free "yes" received the Word of God for us

and who should be praised by all generations. Protestants must understand what Catholic theologians mean when they speak of Mary's mediation and co-redemption. Perhaps we could avoid these words without denying or obscuring the true reality. A Protestant is afraid of these words because for him they imply a denial of that redemption and mediation which is Christ's alone.

Dr. Barth thinks also that there is too much pomp in Catholic worship. "Just imagine St. Paul," he says, "coming back among us and taking part in a pontifical ceremony in St. Peter's. What would he make of it? I myself prefer a simpler and more concentrated form of worship. A Catholic Mass puts me in mind of a play staged in a foreign tongue." Would you comment on this?

The Church's liturgy should be such that the simple Catholic can easily participate in a most personal and real way. If the Catholic liturgy with all its ceremonies can accomplish this purpose (i.e., not a secret cult understandable only to initiated clerics but the worship of God in the Church and especially through the understandable celebration of Christ's Last Supper), then it will not be a hindrance to a future union with Protestants. Vatican II has taken a big step toward this goal.

Hopefully, the bishops and conferences of bishops of the individual countries and continents will make full use of the possibilities for liturgical reform which have been given them in the liturgical directives of the Council. Obviously the vernacular should be used to a great extent in the daily liturgy. This does not exclude the use of a purely Latin liturgy for very festive occasions. If the vernacular is used to the full extent allowed by Church law, it will have a great impact in the pastoral and ecumenical fields.

Most Protestants as well as most Catholics seem to believe that a declaration by the Vatican Council of the right of every human being to worship God in accordance with the dictates of his own informed conscience would be a real step toward Christian unity. Speaking in the name of a number of American bishops at the second session of the Vatican Council, Cardinal Ritter declared "religious liberty to be the basis and the prerequisite for ecumenical contacts with other Christian bodies," and asked for "an unequivocal declaration on religious liberty. . . . Without such a declaration mutual confidence will be impossible and serious dialogue will be precluded." Would you agree?

One can hope that Vatican II will declare that every person has the inviolable right freely to follow his conscience and that neither the state nor society nor the Church may restrict this freedom by physical or moral force. This also holds for the individual conscience which errs unintentionally, provided he does not injure the inviolable rights of another man or of society. True unity among men is not effected by force and power but by personal truth and love. Therefore the striving for a true unity among men presupposes a respect for the religious freedom of individual men. A statement of the Council on religious freedom can only be advantageous to the effort for Christian unity.

Douglas Horton

Douglas Horton, former dean of the Harvard Divinity School, has been identified with the ecumenical movement all his life. Born July 27, 1891, in Brooklyn, New York, he studied at Princeton, Oxford, and Tübingen Universities. He was ordained as a Congregational minister in 1915, and his association with the Congregational Churches doubtless influenced him ecumenically, for these Churches have been leaders in the contemporary effort to reunite Christians.

They were among the communions which formed the Federal Council of the Churches of Christ in America, which grew into the National Council, and they have pushed beyond these cooperative enterprises in conspicuous ways toward organic union. He was the minister of Leyden Church of Brookline, Massachusetts, when the Congregational Churches were arranging the union with the "Christian" Churches, which developed into the denomination known as the Congregational Christian Churches.

Later, as minister of the United Church of Hyde Park in Chicago, he was brought into the front line of local ecumenicity, for this congregation was itself a union of Presbyterian and Congregational groups, and Dr. Horton enjoyed full standing as an ordained minister in both communions. From there, in 1938, he went on to become the chief executive of the Congregational Christian denomination as Minister of the General Council.

As such it fell to him to help engineer the long negotiations, lasting nineteen years, as a result of which the Congregational Christian and the Evangelical and Reformed Churches joined forces in 1957 to become the United Church of Christ. This was a union of unusual significance since it brought together communions which had stemmed largely from two different families of Churches (Reformed or Presbyterian and Congregational) and from two culturally different parts of the world (the Continent and Britain).

At the Harvard Divinity School, where Dr. Horton served as dean from 1955 until his retirement in 1959, there were faculty members and students from many communions. It was while he was dean that the Stillman Chair of Roman Catholic Studies was established there, the first of its kind to be set up in any such institution of Protestant tradition. He was chairman of the American Committee for the World Council of Churches in the years just preceding the creation of the Council in 1948, and in late years has served his term as chairman of the Council's Commission on Faith and Order, retiring in 1963.

He has contributed to many scholarly journals and is the author of *Out into Life; A Legend of the Grail; Taking a City; The Art of Living Today; Congregationalism, A Study in Church Policy; The Basic Formula for Church Union;* and *The Meaning of Worship.* He has been present as a delegate-observer of the International Congregational Council at both the first and second sessions of the Vatican Council, and his attendance as well as his numerous contacts with the Council Fathers enable him to give us an authentic and intimate insight into the deliberations of the Council and to indicate further steps to be taken on the road to Christian unity.

JOURNEY INTO ECUMENICITY

The greatest accomplishment of the Second Vatican Council is something that the Council cannot accomplish itself. The Council can set the sails of the ship, it can head it in the right direction as it makes its course into the future, but unless the crew take their position, stay alert, and do their work, history will say that the Council faltered in carrying out its mighty purpose—and the crew, good reader, is you: it is I. If we fail, the Council will fail.

Take, for instance, the matter of ecumenicity, which includes the whole vast attempt to bring all Christians into unity of heart, mind, and hand, in Christ. The Council has had many other concerns, but none more important than this, and none which has more fully caught and expressed the longings of the broken world of men and nations.

Now suppose the Council should set forth a statement on this subject which would be a magna charta in its field: dreaming in magnificence, conceiving in genius, it might publish the ends and procedures of the ecumenical movement, "the great new fact of this era," with a perfection not before known and not likely soon to be exceeded. But unless priests and ministers at altar and in pulpit and, equally important, Christian men and women in pew and street, at the kneeling bench and in the market, make the Council's thought their own and carry it into effect, the Council itself will be held to have been abortive and disappointing. The Council cannot reach its ecumenical goal without *us*—a truly sobering thought.

With that thought dominant I write these lines, confining myself to the area I have just mentioned—that of ecumenicity.

We cannot do much toward advancing the cause of the Council unless we share the underlying philosophy announced by the Council. This was set forth in the original address by Pope John XXIII in opening the proceedings at the first session. At that time he noted the distinction between the saving truth held by the Church and the mode in which it is expressed to make it understood by others. The former persists from age to age, changeless, but the latter, in order to be fitted into the pattern of thought of any particular age, must be adjusted to that pattern.

It was appropriate, for instance, in the earlier days of the Church after Origen, for thinkers to try to explain the redemption made for us by our Lord as a ransom paid to our enemy, the devil, for this was an explanation helpful to the people used to the customs of the late Roman Empire. But Anselm in the eleventh century with the same truth in mind had to tell a different story: with him the ransom was paid not to the devil but to God Himself, the emphasis being now laid on the moral quality of obedience, which was coming to have a dominant place in the minds of his contemporaries.

Today, however, when ransoms of any sort, paid to people good or bad, are regarded as part of a system from which we are trying to shake ourselves loose, and not as part of normal civilization, these explanations are of little use in trying to help people to understand Christianity. In order to tell the same truth that was told by our spiritual ancestors about Christ's infinite love, we have to use different figures.

This principle, outlined by Pope John, is applicable to contemporary groups as well as to eras. To those who speak only German, I must speak a truth in German, whereas, in order to communicate the selfsame truth to those who speak only French, I must say it in French. Indeed, sociologists tell us that each culture has its own network of presuppositions which constitute a kind of "language" in accordance with which all statements must be made if they are really to be understood.

To tell a boy brought up in a Christian family that God is like a loving father is to communicate a meaning that would be lost on an orphan reared in an asylum such as that in which Oliver Twist had his early years: for Oliver other words for the same truth would have to be discovered. To give the truth such a quality that it can penetrate to the mind of a hearer, it must be fashioned to accord with what the hearer already takes for granted.

This principle of the unchanging truth and the adjustable expression of it avails supremely for the conversations looking toward unity, which the Christian world is now launching.

In the first place, all who participate in this dialogue must apprehend the changeless truth of Christ. Unless they are conscious of possessing this pearl of great price, they have nothing to communicate. And those who have it cannot even dream of compromising it. The words *compromise, concession, adjustment, surrender,* simply do not appear in the lexicon of ecumenicity. Our colloquy is ultimately not about procedures or accidental circumstances: it is about basic conviction, for which men and women have died and will die. Nothing to color or weaken it can be either asked or offered: The inner relationship between the soul and the unalterable truth is fixed and, in ecumenical conversations, inviolate.

As Pope John indicated, however, that relationship is one thing: the relation of soul to soul in communication is another. If a man says, "I not only know the truth but I know also the only true way in which to communicate it," as if he both possessed the truth and, like God, could reveal it, he simply makes ecumenical conversation impossible. The only type of response is either to accept the man's statement or reject it. There is no ground for reasoning together to discover if possible how the truth might be better communicated to meet the hearer's predispositions. If therefore you are a person consciously gifted with omniscience in the imparting of truth, the rest of us can beg you only to disqualify yourself for the ecumenical dialogue: we cannot help you and, to be quite frank, you cannot help us.

If, on the other hand, you are willing to explore your hearer's beliefs so as to speak your own convictions in terms of them, we shall clasp you to our hearts. The groundwork is then laid for honest ecumenical give-and-take, which can refashion disagreements as to definitions into mutual understanding; and this can happen without forcing any person to come over to the position of any other at the deep level of fundamental belief, since the conversation is in the area of mode, not of matter. Any doctrine of verbal inerrancy tends to quash ecumenical debate before it is started, but the repudiation of inerrancy in one's own utterance of the truth, however changeless one may know that truth in itself to be, swings the gate open to a better future. This principle is, in fact, the golden key with which Pope John has already actually opened that gate.

Given the acceptance of this principle by those who wish to make the Council's ecumenical aims prevail, the next step is to apply the principle, that is, to establish ecumenical contact with other Christians not of the same tradition. Only thus can one find out how the expressions of his own faith must possibly be altered to be understood and accepted outside his own communion. In some countries Catholics meet adherents of Orthodoxy or Protestantism every day of their lives, but contact at the new level involves more than random crossing of paths.

The next step is at once extraordinarily simple and excruciatingly difficult. Ecumenical contact: what could be simpler, since it calls only for a little initiative toward friends and acquaintances in other Christian groups: "I am interested in the new ecumenical development: can you let me know more about the life and work of your Church or tell me where I might go to learn more? Are there not some books that I might read, or that we might read together?"

Once the start is made, ideas leading to mutual ecclesiastical acquaintance begin to flow freely. But what could be more difficult than to start? All beginning is difficult, and this is a beginning after over four centuries of studied avoidance of each other in the avenues of religion.

There are two ways of making a beginning, one of them infinitely to be preferred, I think, to the other.

The one way has the apparent advantage of directness, and appears to be scientifically sound. We can conceivably make our first contacts by examining into each other's religious expressions in a head-on sort of way. When anthropologists study a primitive religion, they often divide their research into several parts, examining into cultus, creed, and code of morals, and making as thorough an analysis of each as possible.

I suppose that it is possible for us, in the same analytical way, to study each other's manner of living out the truth in which we believe, putting each other's customs on the laboratory table for purposes of comparison and learning that you worship chiefly in that form, while we do so in this. You say your creed that way, we this way. You stand for this method of birth control, we for this one. For ecumenical purposes, however, the lethal defect in this method is that it is perfectly designed to keep us apart.

I put my eye to my microscope and survey you and your religious habits at the other end of the instrument; and you at your eyepiece do the same with me. Each of us maintains a separately subjective position, holding the other off in a certain objectivity, whereas the whole end of our endeavor should be to see things through each other's eyes, that is, to melt our subjectivities into one, to resolve the I-you polarity into a relationship in which we can begin to say "we." Though we shall eventually want to bring each other's faith and practices into critical focus, this is not usually a fruitful way to inaugurate contact.

The pioneers in the ecumenical field have already built up enough experience to be able to advise us as to a better way of making our contacts initially successful. Instead of entering into conversation *vis-á-vis*, it is best to have some *tertium quid*, some objective in which we are both interested and about which we both want to learn more, or some aim which we both have in common, to which we both turn our attention.

This may be an ethical project, such as the development of world peace. It may be (and this is even more profitable, since it brings us into the properly religious sphere) a study together of the content and historical milieu of some Christian classic, such as *The Imitation of Christ*, or even of one or more of the constitutions and decrees of the Second Vatican Council, such as that on the Sacred Liturgy, already promulgated.

But the best of all materials for study, as has been proved of late years in many countries and by many different types of people, are to be found in the Bible itself. In a group studying the Bible, under a good leader or leaders, the view of the participants is turned away from themselves and toward a *third thing*, which in this case is the very rock from which we all were hewn, the quarry from which we all were dug. What could better give us a sense of "we-ness" than such an examination of our own joint heritage?

The advantages of this type of ecumenical rapprochement were hinted at when, at the second session of the Council, the Pope gave an audience to the observers in his private library. Said Professor Skydsgaard of Denmark, speaking for the observers, "Permit me to point out a matter which seems to me extremely important: I am thinking of the role which may be played by a biblical theology concentrated upon a study of the history of salvation in the Old and New Testaments."

To which the Holy Father replied, "You have opened up . . . a vista which we shall be careful not to neglect. To the idea of developing . . . a theology concrete and historical, centered upon the history of salvation, we most cordially subscribe."

The task of evolving the far-reaching kind of theology these two scholars had in mind is obviously for the theologians, but the point should not be missed that the basis suggested for this dialogue at a high intellectual level is nothing more nor less than the study of the Bible, the story of salvation in the Old and New Testaments. So a standard is set for dialogue at every level—a standard already proved effective beyond expectation.

This way of beginning ecumenical procedure—making a third something (especially the Bible) rather than each other's forms of religious life the object of investigation—accords with the philosophy we have outlined in that it lays no pressure upon fundamental faith, but tends to nurse one's expressions of faith into flexibility.

This procedure also pays dividends psychologically because of its impersonal direction, which frees the persons involved from the embarrassment of having to look at each other eye to eye. But—and this is a further step in the ecumenical process—it also provides positive opportunity for mutual respect to develop between the persons making the study. It holds them together in a collective purpose in such a way as to bring out intriguing sidelights on each.

This may seem a minor matter and really irrelevant, since the Christian Church cannot be built or reunited on the basis of the likings of its members for one another; but I do not think it is. I believe it to be an indispensable introduction to the long course in ecumenicity ahead. Distrust can be dispelled only by acquaintance, and the latter comes as a by-product of common studies. Even where there is no distrust, but only mutual ignorance, there is no stimulus toward better acquaintance comparable to admiration of each other's motives and achievements made evident in a common enterprise. Many men at the Harvard Colloquim of early 1963, for instance—not to mention other similar gatherings of theologians for the exchange of ideas across the Catholic-Protestant line—entered the discussion only as friends of truth, but came out as friends to each other, concerned to know more about each other and each other's positions.

I think I speak for most of the observers at the Vatican Council when I say that I went there with what might charitably be called intellectual belief in ecumenicity, including a lazy hope that God in His infinite providence would some day bring about a reconciliation between Rome and the rest of us. But at Rome I became acquainted with many Council Fathers and *periti*,[1] who also happened to be magnificent human beings. These men were ecumenical catalysts. Thanks to them, we came away with something more than a pious intellectual attitude toward ecumenicity.

We are humanly unhappy to be separated even ecclesiastically from such people as these, whom we enjoy and whose religious insights we respect. It is true that we see no quick and easy way to resolve the differences between us, but our myopia does not affect the vision of Him with Whom all things are possible. These middle walls of partition have been a-building among us in our willfulness and ignorance for centuries: give us now a few centuries to balance the past, and we shall tear the partitions down.

One of the evil effects of the ecclesiastical iron curtain is that the least attractive elements on each side of it—I am speaking of both persons and ideas—seem to make themselves known to the other side by their very extremism, while the best are contained behind their own borders. Conversations between Catholics and non-Catholics, whether upon some Scriptural theme or upon any theme in which both have competence and interest, can go far toward curing this situa-

[1] Expert theologians.

tion. They can give opportunity for the subtle but sure growth of that mutual esteem in Christ which is a first phase of Christian love and the best introduction to ecumenicity. If the relationship developed between Council member and Council observer at St. Peter's can be multiplied all over the world in years to come, ground will be tilled for the growth of good which is today undreamed of.

Once confidence in each other's Christian integrity is firmly established, it becomes as necessary to move into an examination of each other's faith and practice as originally; before that confidence could be taken for granted, it was dangerous to do so. In fact the phrase, "an examination of each other's faith and practice" is ill-chosen. Now there is no thought of either holding off the other and the other's ways as creatures to be dissected like laboratory specimens. A rapprochement has been arrived at which binds the seekers in a common cause, and their work is best described as "an examination by *both*, of the faith and practice of *each*."

The reciprocal relationship in which one plays the object to the other's subject is submerged now in a mutuality in which the two subjects share a double task—the task of knowing all they can about the faith and order, the life and work, of the Churches of both. Note that there is still no question of either's budging a millimeter from his soul's convictions: the research is entirely in the area of expressions, forms, proceedings, methods, but it is paired research, and not opposite-sided. It is, in a word, ecumenical.

This kind of research has already begun in many places and is likely to proliferate in every quarter of the globe. It is a blessed thing which can lead only to blessings. It should take place at every echelon of life in Christendom, and it should be concerned with every aspect of the Church's life. One of the Fathers in St. Peter's hailed the schema on ecumenism as the first grandly pastoral manifesto the Council had put out: "Now we have work to do; now we have direction; now new responsibility has come into the life of every member of the Church!" It is so: new meaning has come into Church membership in every corner of Christianity, and the drive toward unity cannot be accomplished without the concerted striving of all.

Even a brief description of the labors to be performed in making the communions acquainted with each other in the next generations would require a volume in itself. Let me mention here only one feature for study which would seem to me to be the crowning one—the matter of our worship. We must review our theologies in their entire spectra, it is true; we must talk over with each other our ethical ideals, our thoughts about the relations of Church and State, our life together in our cities, towns, and villages.

Let us not forget, however, that the heart and center of the Church lies where, consciously, man meets God or, more accurately, God meets man. Only one thing is needful —to be with Christ. Powers for all the other varied activities of the Church flow from that relationship, and if our ecumenical conversations leave a gap there, they lack their keystone. I hope that these conversations will be oriented from the very outset toward a common understanding of the worship, public and private, of the Roman and non-Roman communions.

a. Here I hope that all Protestants will take advantage of their freedom to attend the worship of non-Protestant Churches. Thanks to Pope John's gracious invitation, reflected and reinforced in Pope Paul, the observers at the Council had the opportunity to be present at Mass every day of the sessions. They came to understand its meaning for the faithful better than if they had read forty books on the subject.

Now and then they had the chance to sit quietly in one of the smaller churches while a friend presided at the altar and went through the now familiar service. It is probable that few of them can accept what seem to be some of the implications of the Mass any better than their fathers did, but they

235

begin to understand what the Mass means to the devoted Catholic, and through him it tends to mean something to them, too. So, and only so, I believe, can the groundwork be laid for the deeper ecumenical dialogue.

b. Catholics as a whole do not today enjoy the parallel freedom of visiting non-Catholic Churches at the time of worship. I am sure that there must be good reasons for this restriction, but I am equally sure that until it is relaxed the generality of Catholics will not understand us at our most important moment. In the meantime I know that special dispensation will be given, permitting specific individuals upon whom peculiar ecumenical charges are reposed, to attend non-Catholic public worship in order not so much to accept as to understand it.

Until a Catholic has waited sympathetically in silence at a Friends' meeting, or watched at a Reformed communion where the bread and wine are the very kind that are used in the homes of the worshipers, symbolizing for them the power of Christ to transfigure common life, or "assisted" (in the French sense) at a non-Roman Mass very like the Roman, to note its correspondences and its differences, he is hardly accoutered for ecumenical discussion of the profounder dimension.

c. One point at which we can come to understand each other is on those ecumenical occasions when we can pray together. At a meeting between American bishops and observers held toward the end of the 1962 session of the Council, after we had asked and answered questions of each other for an hour, one of the bishops said that he was moved to suggest that we say the Lord's Prayer together. That does not seem like an epoch-making event, but I can testify that it felt so.

The momentous element was that in the prayer we suddenly felt a unity we had missed before. The Holy Father similarly led us in the Lord's Prayer at the audience in 1963. It is true that a family that prays together tends to stay together—and if we say our prayers together, we shall surely find there a place where souls can meet. The Council at its 1964 session may give special promotion to this idea: let us pray now that it will.

If the area of worship, though the most important, is only one among many that must be investigated in the course of our ecumenical dialogue, it will be seen that a program is laid out which extends into the future as far as the eye can see. It is simply enormous. It is full of questions, full of difficulties, but people of faith will remember that in Christ no sum of obstacles makes an end unattainable.

It is not only the subject matter of our conversations which is a veritable Behemoth to contemplate: there are the people who must be drawn into the debate. Over nine hundred million of them will need education in the things of the new day, for ecumenicity can mean little *without broad popular support*. All sorts and conditions of men should join in the conversations. The types of encounter are too many and too varied even to be listed here, but if there is one kind more important than any other, it is surely that between the authorized committees or appointees of Rome on the one hand and, on the other, those of the various *denominations*. (And here I confine myself to Western Christians, leaving the matter of Catholic-Orthodox approaches to others more expert in that field.)

Almost nothing has been said about this as yet, undoubtedly because it is so early in the day. But those who are in earnest about the reunion of the Church will soon be asking about denominationally authorized conversations, since these are the only practical channels through which real unity can be achieved. The Protestant observers at the Council have been representatives not of denominations, but of families of denominations, sometimes called confessions or communions.

It would not have been feasible for the Secretariat for Christian Unity to have invited representatives of all the denominations to St. Peter's, because of the simple fact of their numbers: there are in the United States alone, no less, as the saying goes, than 250 sects and insects. Of invited confessional bodies, such as the Lutheran World Federation and the World Alliance of Reformed Churches, there is a more manageable total.

Roman observers have now been present at, and greatly contributed to, such non-Roman gatherings as the Assembly of the World Council of Churches at New Delhi and the allied World Conference on Faith and Order at Montreal. Such contacts are valuable beyond price not only because the eye of the world is on them but because a general look at the *tout ensemble* of non-Roman Christianity is to be had there as at no other spot in the broad ecclesiastical landscape.

Councils and conferences of this sort, however, like their national counterparts, such as the National Council of the Churches of Christ in the United States, are interdenominational, not denominational. As such, though they are well equipped to discuss unity, they have not the authority to negotiate union: that belongs with the denominations.

The same is to be said of the organized world communions represented at St. Peter's: at the present moment in Protestantism and Anglicanism it is not they which are the organs for practical negotiations but rather the denominations which constitute them. The Anglican-Methodist proposal for union in Britain, for instance, though it will doubtless eventually be referred to the world bodies for approval, was worked out not by those bodies but by the denominations chiefly concerned.

With the development of the world organizations, it may be (and many of us hope) that, in the future, organs for negotiating union may be set up at a world level, but that day is not yet. As we begin our conversations, it would seem unfortunate not to draw into them the groups which presently are the only ones equipped to act practically in the field of Church union, and these, in the non-Roman

Western world are, almost without exception, the denominations and the denominations alone.

The dilemma foreseen by the fact that the Roman Church is an international body with its center in Italy, whereas virtually all of the other non-Roman denominations are national groups with centers in many different nations, is now met by the suggestion coming from Cardinal Bea that the Secretariat be authorized to set up sub-secretariats in the various regions of the world. Each denomination would then find in the appropriate sub-secretariat an opposite number with which to enter into discussion.

The importance of such contacts as these can hardly be stressed too much since, in the non-Roman world, many a different system of forms has arisen among the various groups. The Churches of the Anglican persuasion, for instance, have in their own way saved the idea of episcopal succession and built many of their institutions about it. As we look ahead to reunion, it would be uneconomical (to use no stronger adjective) for Rome to deal with all of us non-Romans either on the basis that we all accept the idea of this succession—which we do not—or on the basis that none of us do so—which would be unfair to Anglicanism.

Lutheranism has a distinguished record in maintaining and expanding the theological thought of the spiritual ancestor from whom it takes its name. It would be pure waste for Rome not to treat with Lutheran bodies in terms of that inheritance, or to treat with non-Lutherans as if they too shared the heritage to so full an extent. Something similar could be said of the Reformed family of Churches.

Each one of these and other families of Churches is in turn a congeries of denominations. Each of these denominations, having followed its own line of evolution, needs to be treated according to its own genius, since, as I have said, the denominations as a whole have never relinquished to others —even to the world fellowship to which they hold allegiance —the authority to unite them with other bodies. As soon as the time is ripe—and it is later than many of us may think—all of the major bodies of non-Roman Christians, while keeping in closest touch with the world communions to which they belong, might reasonably initiate conversations with Rome in the capacity of the autonomous denominations which they are, looking not so much to reunion proper as to manufacturing the tools, putting wheels on the vehicles, which may one day bring us to reunion. Such discussions as this cannot be substituted for the innumerable others that must take place in every quarter, but because they would be held by the eventual arbiters of reunion they would give point to all the others.

A final glance into the crystal ball as our conversations get under way. In the course of the debates at St. Peter's many Fathers prophesied that the Church of the future would show diversity in its unity. The non-Latin rites of the Uniate East, which differ from but already have the same standing within the one Church as the Roman rite, were often cited as illustrating the kind of diversity which does not defeat unity, but enriches it. At least one speaker referred to the multiformity of opinion shown in the very hall of the Council, all of it yet being within the reticulation of loyalty to the one Church—and he suggested this as a pattern for a larger tomorrow.

An even more striking example of the kind of differentiation within unification, which permits individual creativity within the limits of orderliness, lies in the existence of the various religious orders. Since many of these came into being, historically, for reasons similar to those which gave rise to the Protestant denominations, we should not fail to examine into their status as a possible design for intrachurch relations involving denominations outside of the Roman Church today. There is no thought that precisely the same pattern could be used. But there is hope that, as a result of asking the same question that was asked when the old orders originally took shape—namely: How can this group maintain a maximum of its own individuality within the context of allegiance to the greater Church?—an answer may be found which would be as consonant to our times as the answer given for the orders was to theirs.

Diversity in unity is indeed our only hope, for each of the non-Roman groups of baptized Christians feels, as does the Church of Rome itself, that the blessing of God is upon it. They all believe themselves to be in touch with the changeless truth, of which we spoke earlier. They will not repudiate their past: they will carry it into the future. They are not going to become Roman, any more than Rome is to become anything but itself. Some way must be found for Rome to remain Rome—Wittenberg, Wittenberg—Canterbury, Canterbury—Geneva, Geneva—but no longer separately. All of them must discover how they can serve their Lord *together* within one holy, catholic, and apostolic Church.

John Cogley

Similar to the ecumenical role played by Father Gustave A. Weigel, S.J., among the Catholic clergy of the U.S.A. is that of John Cogley among the laity. For more than a decade he has been one of the most articulate Catholic laymen in advancing the dialogue with members of other faiths. Born in Chicago on March 16, 1916, he studied at Loyola University in Chicago, where he received the Ph.B. degree. He later studied philosophy and theology at the University of Fribourg in Switzerland.

He is the founding editor of *Today Magazine*, and from 1949 to 1955 was the executive editor of *The Commonweal*. He served for three years with the U. S. Army Air Force, and in 1956 joined the executive staff of The Fund for the Republic, Inc. As staff administrator for the Fund's project on Religion and the Free Society, he played a leading role in organizing a seminar at the World Affairs Center in New York.

Representatives of Protestantism, Catholicism, Judaism, and various shades of non-belief discussed matters of common concern for the free society of America. Out of that seminar emerged a series of scholarly papers published in the book, *Religion in America*, edited by John Cogley. This was one of the first major successful efforts to start a dialogue among top-ranking scholars of all shades of religious faith. The seminar brought together such scholars as Reinhold Niebuhr, John Courtney Murray, Will Herberg, Walter J. Ong, Gustave Weigel, Paul Tillich, and others.

As executive editor of *The Commonweal* for six years, John Cogley carried on the magazine's tradition of expressing concern for every movement that was calculated to promote understanding and good will between the members of the various faiths and races in our pluralistic society. On various occasions when the National Conference of Christians and Jews was unable to secure a priest to participate in an interfaith dialogue, John Cogley was pressed into service. Hence his experience in the broad field of interfaith relations gives him an unusually rich background to make practical suggestions for rendering such dialogues more fruitful.

In his informative article he speaks with the same candor which characterizes his writings and addresses. As a journalist he covered the second session of Vatican Council II and has written a number of informative articles. He is a trustee of the Church Peace Union, in 1960 received the Christian Culture Award, and in recent years has been associated with the Center for the Study of Democratic Institutions at Santa Barbara, California. He is on a leave of absence from that Center to spend a year in Rome, where he is carrying out a writing assignment for the Encyclopædia Britannica.

TEN COMMANDMENTS FOR
THE ECUMENICAL AGE

It has been said that war is too serious a business to be left to the generals. By the same token, Christian unity is too important a goal to be left to the theologians, or at least *only* to the theologians. The theological dialogue, to be sure, is indispensable for understanding between Christians of different persuasions. But only the laity can create the climate of mutual trust and charity necessary for that dialogue to be effective. A theologian approaching another in ecumenical encounter, in a special sense, is representing all the members of his Church.

If the rank-and-file harbor hostility and suspicion toward other Christian bodies, however, the theologian is hopelessly handicapped. He himself may be a model of fair-mindedness and charity, but others, however they may admire him, will be convinced that he is speaking only for himself. He cannot succeed in building unity while the laity of his Church are actually increasing animosity and distrust. *He* may speak with the tongue of angels but if *they* have not charity, his words may strike others as sounding brass and tinkling cymbals.

The masses of laity cannot be expected to be professionally equipped to handle the theological issues that separate believers. However, the cultivation of an ecumenical attitude among them can do wonders. And this attitude is possible to everyone. One need not be an authority on the *filioque* clause or a skilled exegete to share it.

In fact, it might even be said that it is the work of contemporary laymen to undo some of the mischief caused by theologians in the past. For when we ask ourselves how the scandalous division of Christendom came about, the burden of responsibility seems to fall more heavily on clerics and religious professionals than on the ordinary man-in-the-pew. The *odium theologicum* that has poisoned the Christian atmosphere for centuries had its beginnings not at peasants' tables but in the cells of monks, the chanceries of bishops, and the scholarly haunts of divines.

Where bigotry, prejudice, and hostility have been found among the laity, they have been based not so much on theological sophistication as on ignorance. Unfortunately, that ignorance was frequently allowed to go unchallenged by ecclesiastical leaders who knew better; in some cases, they actually cultivated it. Distortions and myths about what other Christians believed were even promulgated from pulpits. The result was that the odium of the theologians, vulgarized, spread to the people, who were allowed to go through life thinking of The Others not as fellow Christians at all but as pseudo-Christians, errant idolators or perverted heretics, and sometimes as the very servants of Antichrist. No charge was so cruel, so outrageous, ill-founded, or absurd, but that somewhere some body of Christians did not hurl it against another.

Appalling Ignorance

Even in the United States, where Protestants and Catholics have lived in civic harmony for generations, the one group's ignorance about the other has been appalling. As a Catholic, I have spent my life denying what some of my Protestant friends thought I had to accept as religious truth in order to stay in the Church. At the same time much of what I grew up thinking about them has turned out to be equally untrue. We found out this much about each other by breaking with convention and actually talking about religion.

At least in the beginning, we were not at ease with such conversation. For discussion of this kind has long been deemed dangerous. In the atmosphere of ecclesiastical cold war that was for so long taken as a fact of life, on both sides, sensibilities were raw and the most innocent remark could set off a bomb. To avoid trouble, then, religious matters were scrupulously avoided in polite company.

Even Brotherhood Week participants went to pains to keep doctrinal questions out of their discussions. Catholics and Protestants meeting at a dinner table or social gathering felt free to discuss every subject under the sun but their common faith in Jesus Christ. The love that should have brought them together was too often a sword of division. In their anxiety for peace and personal friendship, then, they silently agreed to avoid the name of their Lord.

What a ridiculous situation! And yet it was commonplace. Even the partners in mixed marriage frequently agreed to stay off the subject of religion altogether. Maybe because it was felt that clergymen of different Christian faiths would have nothing but religion to talk about, most of them avoided each other's company entirely. Certainly a tactful hostess rarely felt free to invite the local Catholic pastor and the Baptist minister on the same evening. To this day I have friends among the Protestant clergy who have never met a Catholic nun, and friends among the sisters who would not know how to address an Anglican bishop.

In practice, the laity of the two faiths were forced to be more companionable, for there are few places left in the United States where Protestants and Catholics do not play together as children, attend the same schools, work side by side, live as next-door neighbors, serve in the same military outfits, and meet socially. Frequently in fact they are members of the same family. But precisely *as* Protestants and *as* Catholics they often remain strangers. About the things that matter most to both, they have had nothing to say, out of fear of wounding each other's feelings or betraying a disdain for, or ignorance of, each other's faiths. In fact, frequently the more Church-centered the Christian, the less "ecumenical" he was in his daily life. It was the more indifferent and tepid who tended to wander off the reservation.

This is only one aspect of the embarrassing history of Catholic-Protestant relations now hopefully coming to a close. When the final history of Christianity is written in the Book of Life, some chapters outlining this estrangement will certainly be put under the heading of Irony. That friends and neighbors and even relatives should for years and years have carefully skirted any reference to their Christian faith, and have done so precisely in the interests of peace and brotherhood, will seem incredible.

Adjustments Are Needed

It looks now as if such days are behind us—or almost behind us. For there is still a cultural lag. The clergy of all faiths so far have been ahead of their laity in forwarding the ecumenical movement. Events have moved with breathless speed, delighting some but shocking others of the laity.

Take Roman Catholics. The present ecumenical mood of Catholicism is new to them. Many are not yet used to the idea of their cardinals and bishops addressing meetings of the Protestant clergy, of their priests leading joint prayer services, or of their theological experts earnestly exchanging views with Protestant scholars. Some don't know quite what to make of it. It strikes them as a complete reversal of the closed-door, exclusivist notion of Catholicism they grew up with. And to a great extent it is. Remember, only a few years ago it was practically impossible for even the great TV networks to get a priest to sit in on a religious discussion of current issues.[1] Television usually had to settle for a minister, a rabbi, and an uncomfortable Catholic layman. I know, because on more than one occasion I was the layman pulled in at the last minute after all efforts to get a priest failed.

[1] Editor's note. This was not because priests were not willing to do so, but because they could not secure the required clearance from chancery offices.

The Protestant laity, by and large, have also had to make severe adjustments to accept the age of ecumenism. Many of them were brought up with a distaste for anything Romish and a suspicion of the Catholic clergy which was carefully nurtured by the myths allowed to flourish in their communities. Such people were originally doubtful of the good sense, if not the good faith, of those pioneering pastors and theologians who were willing to take a fresh look at Catholicism. They were, it seemed, eternally convinced that nothing good could come out of Rome. As a result, if a clergyman or scholar got a reputation for being "soft on Catholicism," his fate was frequently similar to that of the liberals of the 1950s who were held to be foolishly openminded regarding Communism. The pastor or theologian in question could expect a certain amount of unwelcome fan mail and denunciation as a simpleton or worse in powerful sections of his Church press. Just as the liberal, in defense, finally felt called upon to begin his speeches and writings with a gratuitous affirmation of his patriotism, so many of the early Protestant ecumenists felt it necessary to establish undying loyalty to the principles of the Reform at the opening of every speech.

Ten New Commandments

Even these days may be behind us—or almost behind us. For ecumenism is now "in," and unless something goes terribly wrong—a sudden switch on the part of the Vatican or impossible demands on the part of the Protestant leadership, both of which possibilities seem unlikely—there will be no return to the cold war atmosphere of the past.

A few years ago, Robert McAfee Brown, who has done more than his share to promote better Protestant-Catholic relations in the United States, wrote an article which appeared simultaneously in the *Christian Century* and *The Commonweal*. It was called "Rules for the Dialogue" and it set down a series of *do's* and *don'ts* for those who wanted to partake in serious interfaith conversation. The article, simply worded and superbly timed, had, I believe, more effect on the ecumenical movement in the United States than any half dozen more elaborate works. In trying to figure out what contribution a layman might make to this symposium, my mind turned to Dr. Brown's article. It occurred to me then that I might try to put together a comparable decalogue directed primarily to laymen. In doing so, I hope to pay Dr. Brown the sincerest form of flattery.

Dr. Brown's article was addressed mainly to professional theologians and scholars. What follows is directed to the untutored layman, Protestant and Catholic, who makes no claim to theological expertise but who is eager to participate in the ecumenical experiences of his time. There are millions of such people in both traditions who will not long be content to stand on the sidelines cheering the professional players, but they are still not quite sure what they themselves can do.

They can pray of course, and more and more are doing so, that Christ's will for unity will be fulfilled. But some of the Catholics among them recall the words of St. Ignatius Loyola, the founder of the Jesuits: "Pray as if all depended on God; work as if all depended on you." Protestants can find similar encouragement to match prayerful words with thoughtful deeds, from saintly spokesmen in their own tradition.

Here, then, are my ten "commandments" for the age of ecumenism.

1. *Remember that saints and sinners are to be found in all branches of Christianity.*

In the pre-ecumenical period, what might be called the Age of Polemics, it was customary to play up the saints of one's own tradition and the sinners of other traditions. The villainy of some historic figures was exaggerated and the simon-pure sanctity of others traced uncritically, depending on which side they were found. For example, many Catholics, anxious to belittle Martin Luther, dismissed him simply as a monk who broke his vows in order to marry an ex-nun. The tremendous spirituality of Luther, his anguish of soul, vibrant faith, and awesome love of God were blithely ignored. All that remained of him when these Catholic apologists finished their work was a strong-willed, stubborn, egocentric, sensuous, disobedient cleric who betrayed his priestly vocation and led millions into willful heresy. Protestant simplifiers, on the other hand, portrayed a Brother Martin who was almost a single light shining in the total darkness of monastic corruption and superstition of his time. Neither did justice to the complex man Luther actually was, nor to the tangle of issues that resulted in the Reformation.

The modern layman of whatever faith who wishes to participate in the ecumenical movement has to rid his mind of such stereotypes. The Protestant, for instance, would do well not to be caught exaggerating the number of "bad Popes" and the enormity of their crimes. The Catholic would do well not to be caught denying that any such Popes ever existed or claiming that clerical corruption played only a minor part in creating the scandal of Christian disunity.

Probably both sides would do well not to pontificate on matters of history unless they are quite, quite sure of their facts. For what is important to ecumenism among laymen is not so much the past as the present. The blame for the past is not one-sided, any more than the challenge of the present. As a Catholic, I am of course interested in the past in so far as it helps to explain the present situation, but I do not hold myself responsible for the sins of my forefathers, nor, for that matter, can I take any personal credit for their virtues; by the same token, I have no right to hold my Protestant brethren responsible for the sins of their forefathers. What is clear, in the historic perspective given us, is that in the history of both faiths, God has written straight with crooked lines and brought us both, through no special virtue of our own, to this day when we have a chance to undo some of the hostility of the past and prepare the way for a better future.

But, though a concentration on history may be harmful and distracting, we can both try harder to appreciate the spiritual treasures which Christians of all persuasions have found in their faith. We can also show a more generous appreciation for each other's good works in the present and display more public admiration for each other's saints. One practical way to do this, following the suggestion of Dr. Oscar Cullmann, is to contribute to one another's charities. A collection taken up among Protestants to help, say, the Little Sisters of the Poor, who maintain homes for the aged, would be full of ecumenical significance as well as appreciative of the work the sisters do. Similarly, a collection in Catholic churches to support the efforts of, say, the World Council of Churches international teams working in underdeveloped countries would be a similarly powerful gesture.

The people of one tradition should be better acquainted with the works of charity and prayer carried on by others. Protestant speakers might be asked to address Catholic groups and Catholic speakers to address Protestant groups. They could describe, for example, the work carried on at the Protestant parish in Harlem, the Maryknoll clinics in Korea, the string of colleges established by American Presbyterians in the Middle East or the missions of the Medical Missionary Sisters of Philadelphia, who look after sick and pregnant women in Pakistan.

Protestant libraries might emphasize from time to time the biographies of saintly Catholic heroes and Catholic libraries might do the same for Protestant heroes. Schools, colleges, and the organizations of one faith might honor outstanding work done by persons of the other faith. There is no reason why all Catholic medals, awards, and honorary degrees should go to Catholics or to persons whose religious affiliation is vague (which in the past often seemed to count as a higher recommendation than forthright Protestantism). Nor is there any reason why Protestant honors should not be given to Catholics whose accomplishment, even judged by Protestant standards, deserves recognition.

There are many ways in which we can show that we both take seriously what St. Paul said about the primacy of charity. Unhappily, we are still in disagreement about certain articles of faith and indeed about the nature of faith; we may actually have serious differences about what is to be hoped for, in the life to come; but the greatest of these, charity, can be a point of agreement here and now. There are many different ways of showing that it is. For no Christian community underestimates love of God and of neighbor, and none has a monopoly on it. If that were not true, the ecumenical movement would be doomed from the start.

2. *Do not look to conversion as the proper result of ecumenism.*

I heard a conversation in Rome during the second session of the Ecumenical Council between a priest and a layman, both converts to the Catholic Church. The priest was converted from Judaism and is today an outstanding ecumenist; the layman, formerly a Protestant clergyman, is now a well-known Catholic journalist. He, like some other converts I know, was not overly enthusiastic about the ecumenical movement. It disturbed him that the Catholic Church, which he reached at the cost of great personal sacrifice, seemed to be drifting into a kind of indifferentism. He became a Catholic, the journalist said, because he was convinced that the Church of Rome was right in its claim to be continuous with the Church founded by Christ.

It was certainly not because he found Catholics more attractive than his former Protestant parishioners or because he was dissatisfied with the work of a Protestant parish that he made such a costly change, but simply because after prayerful consideration he followed the guidance of conscience. All his life since, he has dedicated himself to persuading others to do likewise, to preaching the Gospel as he now understands the Gospel's demands. It is the Church's obligation, he said, to "teach all nations" the full Christian truth, including the whole Catholic doctrine. But the present ecumenical emphasis seemed to be belittling the work of the convert-maker and suggesting to the potential convert that he would do quite as well to stay where he is and work for ecumenicity.

The priest was sympathetic. His own conversion, he said, was also paid for by the loss of friendship, affection, and misunderstanding from people who were dear to him. His motives were misjudged; he was both denounced and pitied by some whose opinion he valued highly. But, in conscience, neither did he have any other choice but to do what he did, once he became convinced that the Catholic claims were true.

"You and I solved *our* problems," the priest said. "But we did not solve the problem of Christian unity. At the same time you were becoming a Catholic, some cradle-Catholic was becoming a Protestant. Conversion is a busy, two-way street."

That does not mean, the priest said, that the journalist should have stayed where he was. A half-hearted, unconvinced Protestant parson who feels that he belongs in the papal fold serves neither Church well, nor is he being true to his conscience. But individual conversion is always highly personal and mysterious. It has to be sharply distinguished from ecumenism.

The ecumenist who tries to exploit the desire for Christian unity to make converts to his own faith is doomed to failure, on both counts. For he is not forthright about either of his two purposes. The convert-maker has one end in view, the winning of hearts and minds to his idea of what is true—a perfectly laudable, apostolic motive. The ecumenist has another aim: the creation of bonds of charity between different Christian communities and the healing of Christian schism in accordance with the will of God. Any "fifth-column" proselyting activity on the part of the ecumenist, Catholic or Protestant, will quickly undo what he set out to accomplish.

His proper role in relation to other Christian communities engaged in the common pursuit of unity is then not so much to preach the Gospel as to live it.

Of course it is always possible that as a result of ecumenical activity some conversions may follow, from Protestantism to Catholicism or from Catholicism to Protestantism. This is one of the risks involved in the movement. But such an effect is accidental and unsought, so to speak, and based on a purely personal decision, which must be respected. It can never be counted on.

Convert-making involves a persuader and the one persuaded in a teacher-student relationship. Ecumenicity, on the other hand, involves a confrontation of persons who regard each other as equals. Neither sets out to "work on" the other. The purpose of ecumenism is not to persuade but to understand a position other than one's own, to build bridges across chasms of historic hostility, and to seek out what is held in common rather than to sharpen differences.

From the beginning the ecumenical movement has been inextricably tied in with the idea of dialogue. Dialogue should not be confused with debate or argument or dialectic. As Martin Buber, the great Jewish thinker, explains it, it does not involve the conflict of ideas so much as the confrontation of persons, each taking the other as he is. No one comes out of a dialogue a winner or a loser but simply as a fuller person enriched with a deeper understanding of how another person thinks, why he thinks as he does, and what at the innermost core of his being are his convictions.

Charity is built on such knowledge. And it is the belief of ecumenists, whatever their faith, that if, in the providence of God, the unity of truth is one day to be realized among Christians, it must first be preceded by the unity of charity. Achieving that unity—the oneness of love—is the special task of our generation. It is sought in the belief that if it is found the rest will one day be added unto us, in a manner and according to means which God has not yet revealed.

3. *Do not attempt to achieve charity at the expense of truth.*

During all the years since the Reformation, especially since the Council of Trent, the Catholic Church has laid down very strict rules regarding the participation of Catholics in non-Catholic worship, the acceptance of non-Catholic sacraments, etc. In some places at certain times, these regulations may have been too rigidly enforced, as they still seem to be in a few dioceses where Catholics are forbidden to pray together with their Protestant brethren, sing mutually accepted hymns together, or listen to a reading from the Scriptures. Since the Ecumenical Council began, though, there is a general loosening up and the joint prayer meeting or Bible service is fairly commonplace.

Still, the Catholic Church has not completely backed away from its former position, nor is it likely to. The reason is that the Church does not believe that charity can be bought at the expense of truth, for God is the Author of both. Catholics are forbidden, by their active participation in Protestant services, to seem to be endorsing Protestant theological teachings and the principles of the Reformation. In accordance with the same reasoning, Protestants by and large would not think of participating in the Mass to the extent of receiving Holy Communion, presenting themselves for Confirmation to a Catholic bishop, or telling their sins in a confessional in order to receive a priest's absolution.

No intelligent Catholic would expect them to do so. Nor would any Catholic with a brain cell working expect his Protestant neighbors, in the interests of ecumenism, to abstain from meat on Friday, attend Mass on the Holy Days of Obligation, or submit themselves to the Catholic Canon Law regarding marriage. Ecumenicity makes no such foolish demands.

Most people became Catholics or Protestants because they were born into one or the other faith; they had no choice in the matter. Hence conversion is always a possibility. But the mature Christian stays with his faith because he is convinced that it provides the means of salvation in accordance with the will of the Lord. Because Martin Luther no longer believed that of the Catholic Church he was born into, he bolted it. His famous "Hereon I stand . . ." is a magnificent statement of the claim the truth and personal conscience should have on the Christian. In its way, it is the basis of all Protestant thought, as the ancient Catholic proposition *extra ecclesiam nulla salus*—understood as meaning that Christ and His Church are one—is the basis of the Catholic claim.

There is no reason, then, why either Protestant or Catholic should feel that the ecumenical spirit requires them to slight particular doctrines, state other than true beliefs, act as if one belongs to a community of prayer based on theological positions one does not truly accept, or settle for a vague indifferentism which holds it really doesn't matter what one believes as long as one's intentions are good. That attitude used to be described by conservative Catholic theologians as a "false irenicism." Many of them feared that the laity, being unschooled in theology, would quickly fall into it if they were encouraged to participate in the ecumenical movement.

I believe that these theologians underestimated the intelligence of the laity and the layman's grasp of the theological essentials. But, in recognition of the danger so assiduously pointed out by them, and so as not to raise any false hopes among a certain kind of Protestant who sometimes seemed to feel that Catholic "exclusiveness" was based more on fear of exposure to Protestant worship than on devotion to Catholic truth, it is included in this list of "commandments."

4. *Do not attempt to serve truth at the expense of charity*. If the foregoing "commandment" is one more likely to be broken by Protestants, the fourth is particularly directed to Catholics.

Not long ago, a reader asked Monsignor Conway, who conducts a question-and-answer column in a number of diocesan papers, whether a Catholic who is innocently served meat on Friday by a non-Catholic hostess must turn it down. The good monsignor said that he saw no reason why the guest should not eat the meat without comment, in order to avoid embarrassing the hostess. After all, the law of charity comes before even ecclesiastical laws, as our Lord Himself indicated when he had no hesitations about performing cures on the Jewish Sabbath. It was not, Monsignor Conway pointed out, a matter of choosing between the service of God and the service of man, for charity toward one's fellows is a kind of service to God.

This, of course, is a small issue, but the question was significant. The lady who sent it in to Monsignor Conway said that she had been told by other priests that she would be obliged, under such circumstances, to abide by the letter of the law. Monsignor Conway did not attribute his own opinion, which was not the traditional one, he admitted, to any spirit of laxness invading the Church but to the new ecumenical spirit in Catholicism. In the Age of Polemics, the confused guest might have been encouraged to pass up the meal, if only to "make a point" by stressing her loyalty to the Church and acceptance of its authority, he acknowledged.

But the primary emphasis of ecumenism is on charity. This means that, while one never denies his faith or says it is other than it is, one does not at the same time deliberately wave red flags which might needlessly arouse the anger and annoyance of others or bring the personal encounter to a bad end. For instance, the Catholic does not flaunt his belief in the prerogatives of the Blessed Virgin Mary before he has established his belief in the uniqueness of Jesus Christ Who alone gained eternal salvation for mankind. An ecumenical-minded Anglican does not immediately proclaim his disbelief in the authority of the Pope before he establishes his belief in the authority of the Apostles. Catholics do not launch into a discussion of the miracles of Lourdes or Fatima, to get an ecumenical discussion off the ground, any more than Presbyterians demand to know immediately why Catholics put so little stress on the Bible in their worship.

In time, even issues as touchy as these can be discussed, and should be. But in ecumenism as in everything else, a sense of timing is all-important. There is a time to speak and a time to remain silent. Not every misunderstanding has to be corrected immediately nor does every thoughtless or tactless statement have to be challenged on the spot. This requires, of course, a certain comprehension of another's feelings and at least some understanding of another's mind-set—and such insight does not come easily to some people. Perhaps the best thing for them to do then is to avoid ecumenical conversations and let others carry that ball, while they confine themselves to the sidelines.

I recall some years ago talking at a religious conference conducted on the campus of an Ivy League university. I was there as a Catholic. After the meeting the Catholic chaplain sent word to me that I had been too timid and should have been infinitely more vigorous in the defense of the faith on the platform. The reproof shook me at the time, but I have since become convinced that in letting certain things pass in the interests of establishing a meeting of minds with others on the program, I really acted properly.

The same chaplain, I learned later, had never been able to "get through" to non-Catholic students, despite all the good will in the world, but, rather, fulfilled all their stereotype notions of the proselytizing Catholic priest. He insisted at all times on playing the *Defensor Fidei*. As a result the students found his defenses unconvincing and his attitude forbidding. Some who were interested in Catholicism avoided approaching him because they were afraid he would bite their heads off if they so much as stated an honest doubt. That chaplain, unless he has changed, should not be engaged in ecumenical work.

A small but significant application of the fourth "commandment" has to do with terminology and titles. It is true that it is the common view of the Catholic Church, for instance, that Anglican clergymen have not received validly the Sacrament of Holy Orders. Some Catholics, to point up this position, refuse to call any Anglican clergyman a priest or to address him as "Father" even when he introduces himself that way. "I am Father Snowden, the priest in charge of All Saints." "Mary, I'd like you to meet Dr. Snowden, the minister in charge of All Saints." These few words are enough to nip any ecumenical encounter in the bud. Interestingly enough, though, Catholics who indulge in this kind of point-making almost invariably speak without hesitation of *Bishop* Pike of California or the late *Bishop* Oxnam of the Methodist Church.

There are point-makers among Protestants, too. An excessive, persistent emphasis on *Roman* Catholicism, despite the common usage among Catholics, can be jarring. Of course other communions claim to be part of the Catholic Church founded by Christ, and that is the point being made by such insistence on the *Roman* qualifier. But Catholics might also insist that they too are members of an Episcopal Church, a United Church of Christ, a Baptist Church, an Orthodox Church, etc. I recall hearing a friend say that he felt it perpetually necessary to make a point of the Romanism of the Catholic Church in order not to mislead anyone about how he felt about papalism—but it turned out that he belonged to the Christian Church. It never dawned on him that here was another large titular claim.

The only polite thing to do is to use the titles commonly accepted by the Church involved and let the "points" be made some other way. Let "Fathers" be Fathers, "Sisters" be Sisters, "Brothers" be Brothers, whether the people in question be Jesuits or followers of the Reverend Dr. Divine, Dominican nuns or Salvation Army lasses, Brothers of the Christian Schools or Baptist preachers. If the Pope is called His Holiness, so be it. If the Archbishop of Canterbury is His Grace, so be it. If an Orthodox Patriarch is His Beatitude, so be it. The important thing is that all call on the same Father Which/Who art in heaven.

5. *Do not question another's sincerity or lightly impute superstition, ignorance, or fear in order to explain why they believe as they do.*

Father John Courtney Murray, the eminent Jesuit theologian, once pointed out that as our various religious traditions have developed, even in the Christian West, they have produced not only strikingly different ideas and concepts but even different modes of thought. The modern Catholic, for example, tends to be "rational" and studiously "logical" even when he is thinking theologically. The Orthodox characteristically put more emphasis on the mystical. It is hard to generalize about Protestantism, but it might be said that Protestant thought is more Hebraic and "Scriptural" and less Hellenic and conceptual than either the Catholic or Orthodox. The result of such diversity is that even scholars of the different traditions have a difficult time understanding each other. Protestants are frequently appalled by the "logical" treatment of the Christian mysteries they find in Catholicism; Catholics in turn are upset by the "looseness" of much Protestant thought and the tentativeness they find in its doctrinal pronouncements. Unfortunately, the result has been that one group sometimes actually suspects the sincerity of the other's commitment to Christianity.

I have known Protestants who felt that the Catholic Church was little more than a cultural relic, a vast sociopolitical phenomenon that had almost lost touch with the life of faith. Its customs, traditions, liturgy, and the mental processes of its members seemed so alien to them that they found difficulty in even connecting Catholicism with Christianity. I have likewise known Catholics who felt the same way about Protestantism. They felt that the average Protestant's attitude toward doctrine was so cavalier as to cut the Churches of the Reform from the living Christian tradition.

Though Protestants, by and large, find satisfactory Biblical justification for their position on such matters as birth control and divorce, these Catholics took it that only capitulation to the world or compromise with basic Christian teaching could explain it.

There are Protestants who regard the Mass, the central act of Catholic worship, as a meaningless mumbo-jumbo of superstition, and Catholics who look on the Protestant emphasis on private interpretation of the Scriptures as a kind of moral and theological anarchy. Of course each is judging the other by different standards from those arising out of the total thought-system of the two traditions. Each, consequently, is unjust to the other, as a deeper understanding of the unknown system would reveal. The Catholic, for example, may look amiss at the Protestant's neglect of the Mother of Christ, asking how one can honor the Son by giving so little attention to the Mother; but the Protestant in turn may be equally put off by the Marian emphasis he finds in Catholic life, asking if the Son has not been deprived of his due rights by the glorification of the Mother. Each as a result may be tempted to make cruel and uncalled-for charges against the other. But to do so, each has to speak out of an ignorance of the other's total theological orientation.

To avoid misunderstandings of this kind, then, one should be very, very slow indeed to make charges. Protestants, for instance, might do well to realize that Catholics in obeying their Popes, bishops, and even parish priests, do so because they believe that Jesus Christ established a hierarchical Church and that in obeying the men set over them they are obeying the Lord Himself. It is not because they fear men but because they love God that they obey. Catholics, for their part, might do well to understand that in rejecting any final ecclesiastical authority and relying on the Scriptures alone, the Protestant is also obeying the Lord, according to his best lights.

Imputation of unworthy motives can be death to the ecumenical spirit. Charges, made out of ignorance of a tradition other than one's own, can not only be unjust but cut off any possibility of future understanding.

6. *Respect what others deem holy.*

A Protestant who believes the doctrine of the Real Presence is a total misunderstanding of the Lord's Last Supper cannot reasonably be expected to genuflect before the altar in a Catholic church. He can, however, be expected, and properly so, to behave decorously and with a reverential attitude in the place his Catholic brother holds sacred. A Catholic who finds himself in a bare Protestant church where the center is the pulpit rather than the altar may find the setting strange. But he would be a boor to show that he looks upon it as nothing more than an auditorium. It is a dedicated place of prayer and he should acknowledge that fact by his deportment. Such behavior can be taken for granted in a civilized society. It is only in most unusual cases that this "commandment" is broken.

But ecumenism would seem to require that the attitude of reverence be carried further. For instance, one would hope that the new spirit would mean the end of the tasteless "theological" joke. An after-dinner story involving the confessional, for instance, may seem perfectly harmless to one who does not believe in the sacredness of the confessional, but it can wound and embarrass those who do. A raucous rendition of a Gospel hymn may be a source of delight to those who are not used to such music in their worship, but it may easily shock the sensibilities of those who are. Funny stories involving the flippant use of the name of Mary, like some I have heard, can be a source of great annoyance to Catholics. Tasteless stories involving priests, ministers, nuns, and other consecrated persons certainly don't promote better feelings between religious groups. If through the ecumenical spirit they disappear completely, the benefits to religious brotherhood will only be exceeded by the contribution made to lessening of the total amount of boorishness in the world.

Religious communities don't think of their tradition in abstract, conceptual terms. The tradition, rather, is incarnated in certain rites, ceremonies, customs, music, buildings, monuments, shrines, and even persons. The ecumenical spirit requires that all these be treated as holy because they are invested with a symbolic as well as a real meaning by those who identify with what they stand for.

7. *Don't defend the indefensible.*

Religious history, involving as it does sinful man, has many dark chapters. Intolerance, persecution, ignorance, and social reaction have all played a part. Protestants have persecuted Catholics, and Catholics have persecuted Protestants. Both groups have in their collective past examples of cruelty and barbarism, carried out in the name of religion, which are a shame to Christianity. Both can claim martyrs who bore witness to one or the other faith with great courage and integrity. In the Age of Polemics, out of a mistaken sense of loyalty, it was commonplace to hear even gentle, saintly religious folk justifying and explaining away the most monstrous deeds committed by their spiritual ancestors and finding excuses for the most outrageous intolerance.

If there is, for example, a "black legend" history of Catholic Spain, so is there a whitewashed history of Spain such as was thought suitable for Catholics. If there is a "Bloody Mary," villainess of Protestant tradition, so is there a Jesuit-killing Elizabeth I to match her in Catholic tradition. Frequently, the trouble in the past was that Catholics were unwilling to acknowledge Mary's intolerance and Protestants brushed off Elizabeth's. It is characteristic of the ecumenical spirit that French Catholics are now making penitential pilgrimages to the shrine of the Huguenots killed in the St. Bartholomew's Day slaughter. This gesture has gone a long way toward improving Protestant-Catholic relations in France.

But perhaps, in this regard, the contemporary is even more important than the historic. Intolerance, persecution, and ignorance have not disappeared from the world. When they appear, victimizing either Catholics or Protestants, it would be reassuring to see members of one group come to the defense of the persecuted in the other. For example, American Catholics stanchly and unmistakably using their influence to protest against unfair, intolerant treatment of Protestants in certain European and Latin American countries would point up the fact that there are Catholics who are genuinely interested in religious liberty. A more vigorous defense of persecuted Catholics in Communist countries on the part of Protestants would certainly promote interfaith amity.

A mistaken, sectarian sense of loyalty on either side which feels it necessary to defend the indefensible can be most harmful to the ecumenical spirit. In the first place, it gives the impression that the intolerant, the dishonest, the cruel, or the doubledealing, when all is said and done, are really representative of the faith. Secondly, it gives the impression that loyalty to the group outweighs loyalty to the standards verbally upheld by the group. Thirdly, it gives the impression that Catholics feel that any Catholic is better than any Protestant, or that Protestants feel that any Protestant is better than any Catholic, and hence more worthy of defense and support. A man who gets that impression really has no reason to look forward to Christian unity, since he comes away with the idea that what is being offered is a kind of second-class citizenship.

8. *Work together for the common good, as citizens equal before the law.*

One of the better developments of modern times, without which ecumenism might have been totally out of the question, is the constitutional establishment of religious liberty, or the civic equality of all persons whatever their faith. This means that Protestant and Catholic (and Jew and unbeliever as well) share a common obligation to promote the public welfare. It also means that cooperation between members of different faiths is a necessity as well as an opportunity.

It is foreign to the ecumenical spirit for such work to be

conducted in the spirit of warfare as between competing religious blocs or pressure groups. Any suggestion that Catholics are ganging up on their Protestant fellow citizens to get more than their share, for example, can hurt the ecumenical movement. Likewise, any hint that religious prejudice is keeping one or the other group from getting a full share is harmful. Preferential treatment of whatever kind—and the "preferred" can change from place to place—is sure to be resented.

In this area of life, the political order, arise many touchy issues that can be the source of tensions between different religious bodies. In the first place, depending on the interests involved, the groups see things differently. Currently in the United States, the school question is a prime example. Deeply held doctrines have also led to controversies—over birth control, for example, or divorce laws, Prohibition, and gambling. All the good will in the world, plus great measures of patience, intelligence, and political prudence, are necessary to resolve such issues. Ecumenism provides no magical formula by which they can be resolved.

But the ecumenical spirit does add a new ingredient. The ecumenical spirit means that one side will go to great pains to understand the position of the other; that both sides are as interested in protecting the rights and needs of the others as of their own; that neither side is imperialistic in its demands or dedicated to translating its particular beliefs into the law that is binding on all. Such issues are too complex, manifold, and far-reaching to be fully discussed here. It is enough to say that the ecumenical spirit can be an important contribution to their ultimate solution.

It is important to note, too, that Protestant-Catholic collaboration in the civic area is not all controversy-laden. There are goals for our society—peace, civil rights, public education, and abolition of poverty come to mind—which members of both groups share. Here the possibilities for united Christian action are unlimited, especially as between laymen and indeed entire parishes. We shall be sure that the ecumenical spirit has taken hold when it becomes commonplace for the members of Blessed Sacrament parish and the congregation of the Elm Street Methodist Church to hold meetings with a view to, say, desegregating the north end of town, providing employment for the drop-out teenagers in town, or improving the standards of science teaching at the local high school. "By their fruits you shall know them." By the work they accomplish together, Protestants and Catholics may yet come to recognize each other as true Christians.

9. *Pray together.*

Here of course there are certain limitations. Until the great day when full unity has come, Protestants and Catholics cannot share the Sacrament of Unity. But there are many opportunities for joint public prayer—common public displays of faith, the celebration of feasts held in common—and, if a common Bible is approved, reading of the Scriptures together.

There are also opportunities galore, so far generally unused, for study clubs to bring together Christians of both faiths to investigate the conditions of our society, judge what is needed to Christianize it, and make plans to act as a "leaven in the loaf." There is no special reason why the two laities should confine their joint activities to insipid church bazaars or bake sales.

The important thing is that there be more contact *as Christians*, more public acknowledgment that both groups worship the same Lord, acknowledge the same Scriptures, and yearn for ultimate unity. This yearning cannot be left forever an abstract commitment but must be expressed visibly, humbly, and penitentially. Only then will it become meaningful to the millions whose imaginations have not yet been aroused by the ecumenical movement and who take the present scandalous division of Christendom as inescapable.

10. *Leave theology to the theologians.*

At one level of the ecumenical encounter the laity will,

by and large, be out of place, because they do not have the knowledge or training for it. This, of course, is the meeting of theologians who are dedicated to straightening out the doctrinal issues that must be settled before unity can, at the official level, move forward. This is an important aspect of the movement but, to my mind, far from the most important. Because it is so specialized and has involved such articulate, thoughtful people, I believe its importance has been exaggerated. What the parish minister and the local priest do and the attitudes prevailing among their parishioners strike me as much more significant in the long run.

Nevertheless, the theological dialogue is essential—and it can only be carried out by theologians ready for it. An untrained layman sounding forth on issues he really knows little about is an absurd figure. The theological dialogue requires subtlety of thought, the study of history, a grasp of two theological traditions, and a sharp awareness of where doors may be opening or of where lines must be drawn. Even a thorough knowledge of the catechism or a teaching certificate from the Sunday school association is not enough to meet that challenge.

There may be a few laymen better equipped than most clerics to meet it. It is only realistic, however, to accept the notion that most laymen are not ready for it, nor can they be expected to be. The layman, unprepared for it, might do more harm than good by trying to engage in theological dialogue. He may well mislead the other participants, closing doors that should be left open and drawing lines that should be left undrawn.

Gregory Baum

A leader in the ecumenical movement in Canada and the United States, Gregory Baum was born June 20, 1923, in Berlin, Germany, of non-practicing Jewish parents. He was brought up without any religion, save the Protestant instruction at the German state school. In 1939 he was able to immigrate to England, thus escaping the fate that befell so many German Jews.

A year later, after the outbreak of World War II, he was interned in England as a German national and brought to an internment camp in Canada. Together with a large number of refugees from Germany, he spent about two years in the internment camp, until his release in the spring of 1942. Fortunately he was able to study mathematics and physics at McMaster University, Hamilton, Ontario, where he received his B.A. in 1946. He then went to Ohio State University, where he secured an M.A. in mathematics a little over a year later.

After the profound experience of reading St. Augustine's *Confessions* and a period of six months' intensive study, he became a Christian and a Catholic in 1946. His immediate desire was the religious life, and in 1947 he joined the Augustinian Order. He spent two years in the U.S.A. studying Greek, Latin, and philosophy, then had his novitiate year in Canada, and in 1950 was sent to the University of Fribourg, in Switzerland, where he studied theology, receiving the licentiate in 1954 and the doctorate in 1956.

Father Baum spent three more years in Switzerland, teaching philosophy at Georgetown-at-Fribourg, working at a parish in Neuchatel, and continuing his studies and writings. In 1959 he returned to Canada, where he was invited to teach at St. Basil's Seminary, Toronto, and a little later, at St. Michael's College, University of Toronto. Since then the college has opened a Centre of Ecumenical Studies, of which he is the director, and a Graduate School of Theology, of which he is now a faculty member. In 1960 he was appointed consultant to the Secretariat for Promoting Christian Unity, Rome, which involved him in the preparatory work for the

Vatican Council and the attendance at the sessions as a *peritus* or theological expert.

He is the author of *That They May Be One*, *The Jews and the Gospel*, *Progress and Perspective*, and is the editor of *The Ecumenist*, a journal for promoting Christian unity, published by the Paulist Press of New York, which is doing so much to promote the ecumenical movement in the U.S.A. and Canada. Father Baum's articles are featured frequently in this journal, and he is playing a vital role in stimulating interest in the ecumenical movement in North America.

DRAWING CLOSER TOGETHER

All Christians acknowledge that the multiplicity of Churches is an evil, the fruit of sin, and a state of disobedience to Christ. From the Scriptures we realize that Jesus wants His followers to be one. The New Testament teaches us that the followers of Jesus have been constituted a new people, the people of God.

In the past we often regarded our divisions as the result of the sins of others, and if there was anything sinful in the present situation we thought that it was really the unwillingness of these others to think and act as we do. For the sake of Christian unity, Catholics were trying to make Catholics out of Protestants, and Protestants were trying to convert Catholics to their Churches.

The ecumenical movement has taught us, through dialogue, friendship, and a deeper understanding of history, that our divisions are not only due to sins of the past, sins in which the whole Christian people were involved, but that these divisions are also an evil in the present, an evil confirmed by our selfish actions, an evil preventing the spread of the kingdom among men today. It has become honorable for Christian Churches to acknowledge their own involvement in the sin of our divisions; and even if the Catholic Church has been slow in acknowledging her own share in the responsibility for the divided state of Christianity, since the Vatican Council Catholic voices have not been lacking which have acknowledged, in all humility, our own involvement in the common guilt. In his opening speech at the second session of the Vatican Council, Pope Paul himself asked pardon of God and men for the harm done by the Catholic Church in the history of our divisions, and he expressed his sincere desire to forgive also the harm done by Christian brethren to the Catholic Church.

The Catholic Church regards itself as the true Church of the Lord of the world and, trusting in the promises of Christ, we believe that the gates of hell shall never prevail against her. Basically, therefore, the Church always remains holy. Christ always remains present in her, transforming our hearts, leading them away from self-seeking to the love of God. It is precisely for the sake of the Church's holiness that the acknowledgment of our sin, such as was made by Pope Paul, is so important. The grace of the Lord, which forgives, heals, and builds up what we have pulled down, will not be operative in us unless we repent. This attitude of humility is, therefore, the first of a series of divine gifts leading to the final gift which is a perfect unity.

At the Vatican Council many bishops from various parts of the world acknowledged the involvement of the Catholic Church in the guilt of Christian disunity. One day a certain bishop had enough of this. He said that he was tired of listening to these public acknowledgments of sin: if these bishops, he said, felt so guilty, they should find for themselves a good confessor and leave the Council Fathers in peace. Fortunately, the bishop did not have to wait long for an answer. Another Council Father bluntly suggested that it would not do to be penitent in the confessional if one wishes to be a pharisee outside of it.

It is generally admitted that the acknowledgment of one's weakness is a sign, not of weakness, but of strength. It is precisely because we believe in the divine mission of the Church to unite all men and express the gift of charity in the unity of her members that we feel the weight of our failure and realize that all Christians, including ourselves, are responsible for the dispersion.

God continues to speak to his Church through the events of her history. He speaks to us even through our divisions. Our schisms remind us of our past infidelities and of the present unwillingness to obey the Lord in all things. As the chastisement of the people of Israel and especially the division and dispersion of the twelve tribes were part of God's plan to teach his people their involvement in infidelity and to lead them to greater faithfulness to the divine call they had received, so are also the schisms in the Church signs of God to which we must listen, signs reminding us that we have sinned and signs initiating the divine remedy for our failures.

This last point is important. We believe that God permits evil in the midst of his people only for the sake of showing greater mercy. We believe that God, Who is the Master of history, will always draw good out of the evil men have produced. Since the history of salvation which began in Israel and came to a climax in Jesus did not cease with the Lord's exaltation but in a real sense continues in the Church, we have every confidence that the events of the Church's life, despite the human involvement in it, are guided and directed by the Lord.

Just as, according to the teaching of St. Paul, God permitted the unbelief of a large section of the Jewish people for the sake of extending salvation to the Gentiles, so he has permitted the schisms and divisions in his Christian people for the sake of the ultimate reconciliation of all men. Schisms are not solely signs of sin, they are at the same time signs of God's mercy, for no chastisement will come upon the people of God unless it is destined to renew them and reconcile them more profoundly with their Lord.

This may appear as a new idea, and some readers may find it a little daring. After all, the evil of our separation is so obvious. The missionary impulse of the Church is greatly hindered by our schisms. Men in our countries and, more especially, men in missionary territories often do not believe the message of Christ because the witness to the deeds of the Lord is divided. The Churches seem to have struggled against one another, and in distant countries missionaries seem to have spent their time stealing parishioners from one another.

Our divisions, moreover, place us in a position where we are constantly tempted to fail against charity. Because Christians of other Churches belong to what may sometimes seem to us as competing organizations, it is difficult to love them. Our divisions, moreover, give us a sense of insecurity and put an obligation on us to be on the defensive. Not only our writing of history and our reporting on present developments in the Church become influenced by this apologetical tendency, but even our theological reflection on God's Word has often been elaborated with an eye to proving our position against the attacks of others. Thanks to the progress of the ecumenical movement, it is today a common realization that the conflict between Catholics and Protestants has impoverished the religious heritage of both sides and that it is only in our age that the Churches with a renewed sense of security are able to regain some of the balance and fullness which should be theirs.

If this is the state of affairs, how can we then talk about the good which will come from our divisions? The reply here is by no means obvious. The answer must, first of all, be given by faith. The man of faith acknowledges that God is the master of history. Therefore he believes, even if the evidence is not available, that God permits the schisms in His people ultimately for the sake of showing them greater mercy and healing the very ills that have caused the schisms.

This is our faith. It is supported by the story of salvation told in the Scriptures. Whether the ills that befall the Christian people are shadows of the cross of Jesus—from which the Church never wants to withdraw—or whether these ills are the fruit of our infidelities, God, the Lord of the Church, has ordained the history of his people in such a way that good will come out of evil, holiness out of suffering, firmness of faith out of controversy, and steadfastness of hope out of situations which look, humanly speaking, hopeless.

This is our faith. But is there anything in our experience which confirms this divine activity in our divided Christianity? Is there a way of looking at our division which reveals to us its positive side? We must study our schisms and the movement to overcome them in order to discover the good gifts which the Lord wishes to bestow upon His people.

Is not the ecumenical movement itself, inspired by the Holy Ghost, a divine action to derive good from our divisions? We have discovered, first of all, new ways of charity. We have learned anew what it means to follow the Lord and to love all men. We have become aware of certain tendencies in our hearts which we used to attribute to passion for truth or the love of the true Church but which we now know to be expressions of group egotism from which no Church is free.

The love of the Church, properly understood, will produce love of other men. If it produces resentment, prejudices, unwillingness to listen to others, self-righteousness, phariseeism, and the postures of superiority, then it cannot be the love of the Church, which Jesus gives those who seek Him. The ecumenical movement has purified our charity. We have learned how to speak about others with respect and appreciation, even when we differ.

The ecumenical movement has taught Christians of various Churches new ways of collaborating. While we have always known that we must collaborate whenever possible, without compromising our principles, to improve the conditions of life in society and assert as far as possible the laws of justice among men, we often hesitated to stretch out our hand to our fellow man, especially when he was a Protestant. We did not seek his help or offer our own. We have discovered in the ecumenical movement that we can collaborate, not only on purely temporal issues, but even in certain areas which are properly religious and supernatural.

In many situations in mission territories and in our own countries we should try to give a common witness to Jesus Christ before a world which does not believe. Whether we think of our village, our city, our university, our factory, or our company, we can easily imagine situations where a common Christian witness given by Catholics and Protestants will increase the credibility of the Christian message and the sanctifying influence of the word of God.

On many university campuses there are small student groups of various Christian denominations, the Newman Center for Catholics, the Canterbury Club for Anglicans, and so on. In their dispersion hardly any effective Christian witness is given before the student body as a whole. But as soon as the ecumenical movement is introduced to these student groups they will come together, on certain occasions, to give testimony, not to perfect unity—for this does not exist among them—but to a common search for unity in the same Lord into Whom all are baptized. Through this common action the voice of the Gospel is heard with more power at the university.

The ecumenical dialogue among theologians has been of unexpected fruitfulness. Not only do we take the criticisms of others seriously and hence are willing to re-examine more carefully, in the light of Scripture and Tradition, many of our positions and practices, but we also learn to enter more deeply into the meaning of the Gospel. It may sound strange that after almost two thousand years of Christianity we should still be penetrating more deeply into the meaning of God's word, but so inexhaustibly rich is God's self-revelation that we will always grow in the understanding of it.

Why is it that we discover certain aspects of God's word today which were hidden even to the great theologians of the past? The reason is that God Himself, through the historical situation in which we find ourselves, makes us more sensitive in certain areas and we suddenly understand an implication of the gospel message which had escaped us before. The ecumenical movement, therefore, has been a source of renewal in all the Churches.

To give an example of this doctrinal renewal—an example drawn from the life of the Catholic Church—I refer to the very meaning of the gospel, or the good news. For many centuries we have tended to regard the good news of salvation as a doctrine or a set of doctrines revealed by God to the Church, which we must faithfully accept and preserve. In our own day, however, thanks to the ecumenical dialogue with Protestants and the biblical movement, we have become more conscious that the gospel is, first of all, the good news, liberating us for a new life.

We are told by Jesus that God is good, that He loves us, and that He has prepared a universal redemption for mankind. We are assured that we have received the forgiveness of sins and have been established in the friendship of God. We belong to Him now, we have been written into the palm of His hand. Whatever the Church teaches is part of this good news. She announces the wonderful things God has done for us, and even the exhortation to holiness which has gone out to us is the magnificent possibility to respond to the call God has extended to us. The Christian life is, first of all, what God does to us in His Son Jesus Christ.

That this understanding of what the gospel is has a profound influence on our preaching, on the teaching of religion and the language in which we speak about the things of God, is not surprising. This emphasis on God's doing, I may add, does not encourage passivity on the part of Christians, nor create the impression that we do not have to do anything. On the contrary, believing firmly that God is our Saviour, we trust that He will make us free and active and invite us to collaborate in the transformation which He works in us.

We shall act and do in the Christian life, not because we fear that otherwise we shall go to hell, but because God really works in us, touches our hearts in order to produce a new freedom there, and inspires us to give what we have into the maturing process of becoming holy. This deeper understanding of the meaning of what God has done for us is, at least in part, due to the ecumenical movement. Many other examples of doctrinal renewal could be given. It is not unrealistic to praise the movement for Christian unity as a divine action in the Churches.

One of the great dangers to the Christian faith is indifferentism, not atheism nor a philosophical materialism, but the belief that all religions are equally good and useful and that the distinction between true and false has no application in religion. This, in our country, is the real enemy of Christian faith. If religion is not based on truth, but on feeling, it cannot last long; and we find that in some countries this movement of indifferentism has progressed so far that churches have become empty and the people are Christian in name only. We notice that this is true particularly in countries of one religious confession, such as Sweden or Italy, where Christians are not obliged to contrast their teaching and their positions with those of others. There is a great deal of evidence for the opinion that confrontation with others is a necessary requirement for the vital Christian faith of a people.

The divisions of Christians and, more especially, the ecumenical movement seeking to overcome these rifts, are often a source of greater fervor among Christians. Sometimes the fear is expressed that the movement for unity will lessen the attachment of Christians to their Church and make them regard all truth as relative or optional; but it seems to me that the opposite is true. The ecumenical encounter and the greater awareness of similarities and differences among Christians create a greater attachment to doctrine and their meaning. What changes is our approach to doctrines. Our main effort is no longer how to "prove" doctrines from the Scriptures and the Church's tradition, but rather how to discover their real meaning for the Christian life.

Indifferentism is a terrible thing; but there is a contrary disposition which is equally bad, namely an exaggerated attachment to doctrinal truth. It is possible to be so attached to doctrinal propositions taught by the Church that they become an end in themselves and we forget that doctrines are precious only because they communicate new life to us. Doctrines are for us a way in which divine truth, which is God Himself, comes to us, and if doctrines do not become sources of life for us then they are unable to save and sanctify us and hence are useless. It is possible to imagine a very orthodox person who knows by heart the whole doctrinal tradition of the Church and yet be little embued with Christian wisdom. Correctness of faith cannot be equated with vitality of faith, and the correctness of doctrine does not yet mean that one has assimilated Christian doctrine as a principle of life.

The ecumenical movement teaches us the sound and holy middle position between the two extremes: indifferentism on the one hand, and an exaggerated dogmatism on the other. It teaches us to make doctrine a *listening* to God. As we reflect on the gifts God bestows upon the Church through the movement for Christian unity, we begin to understand that no one should call the ecumenical movement a failure just because Christian unity has not yet been achieved or will not be achieved in the near future. Even as we strive for unity, we are blessed by God. We must, moreover, admit that the visible unity in a single Church is not a happy thing unless it be a unity in holiness. Visible unity of Christians is not an end unless it includes unity with the Lord Jesus. One could easily imagine Christians of a certain country all belonging to a single Church and yet being without much faith, lacking in hope, and not deeply moved by divine charity. In such a situation, the division of Christians, if understood as a sign of God and a source of renewal, could even be a blessing.

We have traveled a good distance in our reflection on the positive role of schisms in the Christian people. We know that God, who has permitted divisions because of our sins, will draw good from these schisms to heal our infidelities, and we have seen what this could mean in a practical way. Without, in any way, restricting the article of faith that the Catholic Church is the one true Church of the Lord, we are able to see that in the divine economy of grace, the divisions and the movement for unity may have a redemptive role in God's universal plan.

Should we not go a little further? Should we not admit that ever since the Church came into existence Christian groups have lived outside of it? Every century has known its schisms. Even while we strive for unity, we should recognize that in the present age, determined as it is by the freedom of fallen man, the unity of the Church will always be threatened. Even if the ecumenical movement should succeed in bringing about the unity which is Christ's will for His people, what guarantee do we have that this unity will continue for long? In the light of the Church's history it is not unreasonable to expect that there will always be Christian divisions.

If schisms are a sign of God's recalling to the people that they are sinners and are a source of fervor, purification, and renewal among them, we are justified in saying that in every age the Christian people are in need of this message. The Church must always strive for unity, but she must do so with patience and trusting in God's time, realizing that the gifts of God are with us in the very striving for unity.

These considerations show quite clearly that the ecumenical movement is not concerned with bringing individual Christians separated from the Church into communion with us. It is true that we believe that the Catholic Church is the authentic Church of the Apostles and we affirm that if a Protestant recognizes this claim of ours, he is in conscience bound to join us, whatever the sacrifice this may entail for him. But the destiny appointed by God for certain individuals has nothing to do with the ecumenical movement. This movement tries to reach all Christians, tries to deal with all Christian Churches, tries to find greater areas of collaboration, tries to enable Christians to give a common witness in the modern world, tries to expand the common ground among the Churches, tries to make all Christians more Christian. And if we do become more Christian then we are on the certain road to unity.

The ecumenical movement has begun between the Catholic Church and the Christian Churches belonging to the World Council of Churches. Dialogue exists, though not yet on the official level. We have begun to discuss matters of theology, but we have not yet attacked the great practical problems, such as the notion of Christian marriage, the problem of mixed marriages, and the meaning of Christian education. For some of these difficult problems solutions or agreements may be found, for others they will be impossible. But what we must hope is that the near future will introduce dialogue on these questions on the official level.

What do I mean by this official level? Let us consider, for instance, the problem of mixed marriages. From one point of view, a mixed marriage is a contradiction in terms since the unity between husband and wife which excludes the unity at the table of the Lord is not complete. And yet mixed marriages occur frequently and, because of the pluralistic society in which we live and the unpredictable way men fall in love, mixed marriages will increase. At present the legislation of the Catholic Church is quite severe. The marriage must be performed before a Catholic priest, and yet the ceremonies are quite restricted; the partners must sign promises that the children be brought up Catholics; and if a marriage is performed without the consent of the Catholic authorities it is not only regarded as illicit but even as null and void. This legislation hurts Protestant Christians. Is there a way of changing it? If we respect the Christian faith of Protestants and acknowledge that they are brothers, even if separated, is there no way of legislating so that their consciences would be more respected?

It is to be hoped that the Catholic authorities responsible for the legislation of the Church will enter into dialogue about these matters with the leaders of the other Christian

Churches. This is dialogue on the official level. Not that thereby all the difficulties can be solved, but at least we must examine, by listening to all parties, whether we cannot do more justice to the Christian conscience of others.

In the matter of mixed marriages all hardships cannot be removed. Since a mixed marriage is, in some real sense, a theological contradiction, there can be no legislation for it which will not introduce some elements of injustice. It seems to me that the Catholic Church could easily introduce a full liturgical celebration for mixed marriages performed before her priests, and she could recognize as valid, even though illicit, the marriages of Catholics and Protestants performed without the consent of the Catholic authorities.

Greater difficulties occur in the area of the education of children. It seems to me that, according to Catholic doctrine, the children of Catholics should be Catholics, and, even if we need not burden the Protestant party with the signing of promises before the priest, the obligation rests on the Catholic party who will see to it that the children receive a Catholic education.

But official dialogue on the highest level is of greatest importance here as it is on other practical questions. Church leaders must really understand the problems as they appear to those outside their own Church, and this can be done only through dialogue. Even though the Catholic theological ideal demands that the children of Catholics be Catholics, the Church has been content with less in certain countries in the past—for important reasons such as political peace, or freedom of exercise for the Catholic faith. Though I do not regard it likely at the moment, it is not inconceivable that the Church, for grave reasons, would permit mixed marriages even if no promises for the Catholic education of children are made. One could imagine that, in certain countries where the Catholic Church is faced by a single non-Catholic Church of equal size, fraternal peace between the Churches and the consequent greater Christian impact on the whole people could be regarded as so important that the Catholic Church would legislate, not according to its theological ideal, but to a lesser standard. Or, in other cases, where a Catholic who is not practicing his religion marries an ardent Protestant, the only assurance of a Christian upbringing might be the permission to have the children brought up in the faith of the actively Christian partner. Since there are, then, conceivable exceptions to the present legislation, it is to be hoped that official dialogue will take place on this issue.

In order to hasten the day when we can fruitfully dialogue on mixed marriages, we hope that Protestant theologians and churchmen will reflect more deeply on the scriptural doctrine of marriage and the meaning of married life according to the word of God. This would reassure Catholics that the Protestant Christian also seeks obedience to God's self-revelation in Christ when he explains what marriage means to him.

Dialogue with the large Churches which are part of the World Council of Churches is easy, and a rewarding experience. More difficult, if not at first impossible, will be dialogue with the so-called sects, the evangelical movements in their various forms. There we often find great hostility to the Catholic Church and to the ecumenical movement in other Christian Churches. There we often find an unwillingness to engage in dialogue, in reasoning, in careful examinations.

On the other hand, the fruits of charity, patience, sacrifice, dedications, and joy are often so great in these evangelical sects that one cannot seriously doubt that the Holy Spirit is at work among these Christians. Perhaps the established Churches have been too cold, have compromised too quickly with the spirit of the age, are lacking in family spirit, in mutual service, and in liturgies in which freedom is granted to the promptings of the Spirit . . . and so a reaction has been permitted by God in the form of sectarian movements.

It is surely the task of ecumenism to approach these groups

in ways that must still be found so that we do not deepen the gap that separates ecumenically minded Christians from the sectarian movements but manifests to them and to the world that we will never be content with a Christianity which excludes these millions of evangelical Christians of good will, who are often our opponents and sometimes even regard themselves as our enemies. When Jesus prayed that all may be one, He thought of all His followers without exception; and since the Christian lives by hope, he will confidently try to apply the principles of ecumenism to the independent evangelical communities.

Augustin Cardinal Bea

Augustin Bea was born on May 28, 1881, in the German village of Riedbohringen on the fringe of the Black Forest. He entered the Society of Jesus and studied at Innsbruck, Valkenburg, and Berlin. He was ordained in 1912 and was later appointed Jesuit Provincial of Upper Germany, and in 1930 was made rector of the famous Pontifical Biblical Institute in Rome. A specialist in Scripture, he sought to harmonize the exegesis of Holy Scripture with the latest findings of modern research in history, archaeology, philosophy, philology, and theology.

He edited two reviews, *Biblica* and *Orientalia*, and in addition to his two monumental works, *De Pentateucho* and *De Inspiratione Sacrae Scripturae questiones historicae et dogmaticae*, he wrote more than 150 scholarly articles in German, Latin, and Italian. He was closely associated with Pius XII and was appointed a cardinal by John XXIII in 1959 and, the following year, was named the president of the newly created Secretariat for Promoting Christian Unity.

Ideally equipped by nature and training for that important post, Cardinal Bea has won the esteem and admiration of all Christians and probably exercised an influence at both sessions of Vatican Council II second only to that of the Supreme Pontiff. He sums up the great task facing all Christians in the following words: "Let us leave the judgment of the past to the historians insofar as they have the sources and the means of making such judgment. Let us leave it even more to the judgment of God, and let us try to regain today what was lost centuries ago: the unity of all baptized in Christ!"

LIBERTY OF CONSCIENCE

Taking his cue from the well-known saying of the ancient Latin poet, *"Trahit sua quemque voluptas"* (Pleasure attracts each one), St. Augustine said, with his usual sense of reality and depth, "If the senses have their joys, will not the spirit have its own?" And he exclaimed, "What more does the human spirit want than truth?" And he who had sought it among all the currents of ideas and along all the roads in Africa and in Italy, knew a lot about this desire! But through how many paths and detours does this magnificent and most profound tendency of man pass when it painstakingly seeks truth!

It is, then, not surprising that precisely the love of truth and the search for truth have been more than once in history, and are still, always, every day, the cause of disputes, of conflicts, of clashes, and sometimes even of the most painful and implacable strife of one man against another.

There are, for example, people who identify truth with their own thought or with those who think as they do, precisely when their thought is in conflict with that of others. What we should learn, however, is how to put ourselves "in the place of others," that is to say, how to understand the other's point of view, which is like placing ourselves in another's place and seeing things as he sees them.

One should also remember that reality has a thousand different aspects, a thousand different facets, while the mind of the individual man, even though he may be most gifted and intelligent, notices barely a few.

Obviously, it is here not a question of making truth a relative and undetermined thing. It is, rather, a question of a real and binding love of truth, and it is precisely this love which admonishes us to bear in mind the limitations of our knowledge and recognize also that side of truth which others see, without denying, however, that which we ourselves really know about truth. Neither is it a question of leveling out everything, the true and the false, in the name of respect for another man's point of view, holding that all assertions—as is sometimes stated bluntly—are equally true and equally false.

This is a most important point in this modern world, where we are surrounded by a real chaos of ideas, and where sound firmness in affirming truth, both in respect of purely human knowledge and of religious faith, is easily taxed as being transigent fanaticism and, therefore, abhorrent.

Yet, modern man really thirsts for certainty, for sure and definitive knowledge. But on the other hand, the real love of truth requires us to recognize it wherever we come across it, wherever it may come from, and therefore also requires a readiness and effort to hear the voice of truth wherever it makes itself heard.

Divisions and disputes also arise from the difficulty in explaining the truth in human language. Language is, without doubt, a magnificent gift of the Creator, enabling us to open our minds for others and to communicate from one to another among ourselves the treasures of the spirit, knowledge, and mutual love. At the same time, how imperfect, how changeable, and how limited is often our knowledge of this communication. It engenders a thousand misunderstandings, even in the sacred area of religious faith.

It is well-known that the Catholic Church is rather conservative when it comes to the formulations in which her doctrinal heritage have been expressed. Yet the Holy Father himself declared, at a solemn moment—his opening address at the Council—that the truth of which the Church is the custodian must be explained to the modern world in a new language, that is, in the language of the men of today, the only one they understand. And the Holy Father gave this reason for it: an idea is one thing and another is its concrete expression in words. Therefore, while faithfully preserving the pure doctrine, one may well express it in other concepts, according to the mentality and language of men.

Another error of misunderstood love of truth were the painful wars of religion, when attempts were made in the name of truth to impose with force certain convictions on other men, while overlooking a no less fundamental point of the love of truth, namely, the freedom of man.

This freedom means the right of man to decide freely and according to his own conscience regarding his own destiny. From this freedom is born the right and duty of man to follow his own conscience, and it is the duty of the individual and of society to respect this freedom and this autonomy. You are aware that the Secretariat for Promoting Christian Unity has prepared a project on this theme for examination by the Council.

To those who might wish to object to this that error has no right to exist, we propose to answer that error is something abstract and hence not a subject in which rights may exist. It is man, even when he errs invincibly, i.e., without being able to correct himself, who is the subject of rights. He has the right and duty to follow his conscience, and the right that this independence be respected by all.

Having considered a few forms which aberrations in the love of truth may take, let us ask what is the best way of avoiding these pitfalls and many others which threaten charity and the quest for truth? The best way is without doubt authentic love of one's neighbor.

When we consider, for example, maternal love or the love of a real friend, we observe how this love teaches us to place ourselves effectively in the place of another, to consider his point of view, to endeavor to understand what he thinks, what there is of truth in what he thinks, to strive to understand his thoughts or to make ourselves understood, always using new terms, new comparisons, and new ideas. Here love is able to respect with sympathy the loved one and hence also his opinions.

And why is this so? Because there is love; because, as St. Paul said, "Charity is patient, is kind . . . it rejoices with the truth; bears all things, believes all things, hopes all things, endures all things" (1 Cor. 13:4–7). These words of St. Paul express the experience of every authentic love.

But here we must unfortunately add a warning: we must beware of pitfalls and aberrations. The very examples we have just mentioned suggest this warning, for it is easy for maternal love to become unintelligent and soft, to transform itself into a harmful weakness, incapable of refusing anything, thus ruining the beloved child. Why does this happen? Because, among other reasons, one does not take into account the truth of certain principles of reason, of common sense, of other factors. In this case, charity is not combined with an effective love of truth.

Both are therefore necessary: the love of truth and the love of the person, that is, charity toward one's neighbor. Both united harmoniously, each in its own place and according to its importance. United in this way, they are able to unite men and create harmony in a most efficacious manner.

We actually deal here with a union of men according to their most profound tendencies: the love of and the quest for truth, and the real love of friendship. What greater union can one imagine than that in which one spirit kindles another and one is lighted by the flame of another, where one heart warms another and is warmed by the spirit of his neighbor, by his love?

The whole difficulty depends on knowing how to combine both tendencies harmoniously, on giving to each its own place, its own importance, without harming one to the benefit of the other. For we know that the love of truth without charity becomes intolerant and is repulsive, and charity without truth is blind and cannot endure. We must, therefore, constantly react against any inclination in us to separate love from truth.

It is only by resorting to God in prayer that we will find the harmony, so hard to achieve, between the love of truth and the love of neighbor.

AN EXCHANGE BETWEEN POPE PAUL VI
AND THE OBSERVER-DELEGATES
AT VATICAN COUNCIL II

K. E. Skydsgaard

An Address on Behalf of the Observer-Delegates and
Guests at the Audience with Pope Paul VI, October
17, 1963

WE HAVE MADE SOME PROGRESS

In receiving us here, Your Holiness will certainly understand that we who are guests and observers at this Council
would like, above all, to recall with affection and respect the
memory of your predecessor, Pope John XXIII, who greeted
us in this very place last year.

The news of the death of this great pope filled us with
sadness. We shall never be able to forget him, so full was
he of spontaneity and of love, of wisdom and of courage.
It is my privilege today to express to Your Holiness, in the
name of the guests and observer-delegates, our deep gratitude
for the renewal of the invitation to this second session of
the Council, and for the friendliness with which we have
been received both at the opening ceremony in St. Peter's
and also now in this audience.

We are aware that we are witnesses of an event which is
so decisively significant for the Roman Catholic Church of
our day, and we would like to tell you with what interest

and attention we follow the deliberations of the Council where diverse opinions are sometimes expressed by the Council Fathers, but always in an atmosphere of objectivity and loyalty. Each day we experience the good will of the Council Fathers towards us, and the unfailing readiness of the Secretariat for the Promotion of Christian Unity to help us. The cordiality and frankness which surrounds us makes it easier for us to fulfill sincerely and in good faith our tasks as observers. We are especially grateful to His Eminence, Cardinal Bea, who has generously invited us to express both our positive and negative reactions to the work of the Council.

The schema *De Ecclesia*, which is at present under consideration, is certainly—today as in the past—one of the most difficult and debated of subjects. One could say, in fact, that the doctrine of the Church is the point at which all our divisions culminate so that it is precisely here that they seem insurmountable, despite our sincere efforts to understand each other. Yet in this sad and discouraging situation, we have made some progress simply by reason of the fact that we jointly experience this difficulty and together bear its burden.

In these times, one sometimes meets a naïvely optimistic or superficial ecumenism which appears to think that the visible union of Christians can be quickly achieved. This is certainly not our view, and it is for us a real relief to know that Your Holiness does not share this opinion. Your sober and realistic words on Sunday, September 29, clearly testify to this. As Your Holiness said, there are grave and complicated problems to be studied and resolved, and their solution presupposes conditions which at present do not yet exist.

Permit me in this connection to refer to a development which seems to me extremely important. I am thinking of the role of a Biblical theology which concentrates on the study of the history of salvation in the Old as well as in the New Testament. The more we progress in understanding the hidden and paradoxical history of the people of God, the more we shall begin truly to understand the Church of Jesus Christ in its mystery, in its historical existence and in its unity.

Once again allow me, Your Holiness, to express our living hope that the light of such a concrete and historical theology, that is, a theology nourished by the Bible and the teaching of the Fathers, will shine more and more in the work of this Council.

We also rejoice wholeheartedly at the new ecumenical spirit which is becoming manifest in this Council. We find ourselves meeting together at the beginning of a road whose end God alone knows. It is for us to walk together in hope because we believe that the crucified and risen Christ is with us on the way.

This beginning is at one and the same time God's gift and a responsibility, because much will be required of all of us along this road: a clear witness must be given to the Gospel, there must be humility and patience, all "triumphalism" must be excluded. Above all, no divisions can prevent us from loving each other because Christ's love knows no limits. In this love of Christ, we must seek and find the truth: seek in order to find, and find in order to seek still further, as St. Augustine says.

In concluding, I find myself moved to say: Yes, we are walking together, but our path leads us also "out of ourselves" towards our fellow men. It is said that Pope John XXIII wished this Council to bring about a change from introverted self-concern to concern for men, from *en soi* to *pour les hommes*. Is there any better way for us to meet each other than by going out from ourselves in the assurance of the forgiveness of sins, without concern for our preferences or our merits, in order to live in the world and with men in the world? It is thus that we shall be truly disciples of the Christ Who did not desire to exist for Himself but solely for the world.

We are grateful to Your Holiness, as to your predecessor, for having pointed to this twofold openness: openness to the ecumenical dialogue in truth and love, and openness to the world in humility and service.

Pope Paul VI

To the Observer-Delegates at the Second Session of
Vatican II, October 17, 1963

LOVE FOR ONE ANOTHER

This evening's meeting is a renewal, in a less formal setting,
of what was offered us the other day in the Council. But
is not the reality, the profound reality, the same? That you,
gentlemen, are here, dear brothers in Jesus Christ, at our
invitation, to be present at this important event, the Ecumenical Council.

What is simpler, what is more natural than to approach
one another, to meet, to greet one another, to know and to
speak with one another. But there is yet more: to listen to
each other, to pray for one another, and, after such long
years of separation, after such distressing controversy, to begin again loving each other. This is what makes this meeting
memorable and full of promise.

Doubtless, we would have only to repeat to you here what
we said in St. Peter's Basilica on the opening day of the second session of the Council. But here, in our library where
we receive private audiences, we will do it in familiarity and
friendliness. This setting, perhaps, has a symbolic value, that
of our desire to welcome you not only on the threshold of
our house, but in the very heart of our home.

The sincerity of our words and of our feelings permit us,
and even impose upon us this second opening of our heart
to you, and this time in the French language in which we
can, better than in the solemnity of Latin, express to you
something of the depths of our soul.

We say to you once again: thank you for having welcomed

our invitation, thank you for coming; thank you for your presence at the sessions of the Council. Be assured of our respect, of our esteem, of our desire to be on the best possible terms with you. Our attitude conceals no snare, no intention of falsifying the difficulties which stand in the way of a complete and definitive understanding; nor does it fear the delicacy of discussion nor the pain of waiting. Good faith and charity are the foundations which we offer here in your presence. The esteem which we have for you personally and for the institutions and the Christian values which you represent makes easy for us the task of approaching with you the great dialogue, a dialogue whose length no one today, given the as yet unresolved doctrinal differences, can predict. And confidence in our Lord Jesus Christ to Whom we are all bound by faith and baptism fills our heart with a gentle and strong hope.

That is not all. Perhaps we should add another word to clarify still further our state of mind in the joy which your kind visit brings to us, filled with the memory which you have just refreshed—that of our lamented and venerable predecessor Pope John XXIII.

This is what we wish to say: in what direction does our thought instinctively turn when we wish to understand clearly the encounter—on the highest level, that of the greatest responsibility—of the Catholic Church with the other Christian confessions? Our minds are tempted to turn towards the past. And there we would become entangled in the maze of history, and doubtless reopen wounds which are not fully healed.

We have not hesitated, in our discourse of November 29, to have recourse first of all to Christian forgiveness, and mutual forgiveness if possible. "Let us all give and seek forgiveness" (Horace). Our minds need this tranquility if we are to enter into friendly relationship and peaceful conversations. This is so first of all because it is Christian: "If thou art bringing thy gift before the altar, and rememberest there that thy brother has some ground of complaint against thee, leave thy gift lying there before the altar, and go home; be reconciled with thy brother first, and then come back to offer thy gift" (Matt. 5:23–24).

But it is also best to look not towards the past, but to the present and especially to the future. Others can and must pursue the study of history. We prefer now to fix our attention on what shall be rather than on what has been. We are concerned with the birth of something new, the realization of a dream. May we borrow the words of St. Paul: "Forgetting what I have left behind, intent on what lies before me, I press on with the goal in view, eager for the prize, God's heavenly summons in Christ Jesus" (Phil. 3: 13–14). Hope is our guide, prayer our strength, charity our way in the service of divine truth which is our faith and our salvation.

One must strive ceaselessly to deepen that divine truth so better to possess it and to live it more fully. "Seek in order to find, and find in order to seek still further." This quotation from St. Augustine which we have had the pleasure of hearing you cite, Professor, concerns us all. A true Christian is a stranger to immobility. And you have broached for us aspects of this matter which we would have taken care not to neglect.

We subscribe freely, on our part, to the development, to which you appeal, of a theology which is "concrete and historical," "centered on the history of salvation," and this suggestion seems to us to be worthy of thorough study. The Catholic Church has institutions which nothing would prevent from specializing in this kind of research, and can even create a new institution for this purpose if circumstances prompt it.

Before leaving you, gentlemen, may we recall still another word of your spokesman: "We are together on the way." That is to say: we have not yet reached our destination.

No more than you, dear friends, and we have mentioned

this before, do we expect miraculous and immediate solutions. The fruit for which we hope must mature slowly by study and prayer. And reconciliations which are only apparent or improvised and which cover up difficulties instead of resolving them, far from being of any help, rather retard our advance.

As for us, just as the watchman of whom Isaias speaks: "Watchman, how much longer the night?" We are on watch seeking to discern, and happy to record each time that prevenient signs of a luminous dawn appear in the depths of the night. We refer to the indications of real progress in the dialogue which has begun, of a step forward towards the reconciliation of those who are nourished by the same Gospel and in the depths of whose hearts resounds the same joyful cry of St. Paul to the Ephesians: "One Lord, one faith, one baptism, one God and Father of all, who is above all beings, pervades all things, and lives in all of us" (Eph. 4:4–6).

It is this God of mercy, the Father of our Lord Jesus Christ in Whom we believe, Whom we wish to invoke, gentlemen, in taking leave of you. It is to Him that we entrust our desires, our expectations and our hopes; it is from Him that we beg for you all peace and joy, graces and blessings. And allow us to salute you with the very words of the great Apostle whose name we have taken: "The grace of the Lord Jesus be with you! My love be with you all in Christ Jesus. Amen" (1 Cor. 16:23–24).

ECUMENICAL VOICES AT MONTREAL

In July 1963 there was held at Montreal, Canada, the Faith and Order Conference. The local ecumenical committee arranged an Ecumenical Assembly, an evening of common prayer and reflections on Christian unity at the University of Montreal, at which Protestants, Orthodox, and Catholics participated on equal terms. At that evening assembly four addresses were given by leading representatives of the three different faiths. This was the first such assembly ever to be held. Because of the unique character of the event and its ecumenical significance, we present the highlights of the four addresses.

W. A. Visser 't Hooft

General Secretary of the World Council of Churches

A SPIRITUAL DISCOVERY

Everyone who knows anything about the history of the relationships between the Churches must feel a deep astonishment about the nature of this our meeting tonight. During the last centuries the various Churches have lived in isolation. They stood with their backs to each other. The gulf between them seemed to become larger and larger. Each had developed its own spiritual world and there was practically no real communication or conversation between them.

What then is the explanation for the fact that today we can meet together, that we are here in one place and that not on the basis of common political or social interests, not on the basis of some vague religious concern, but quite specifically on the basis of our common faith in the one and only Saviour Jesus Christ? What has happened? The answer is that the ecumenical movement has happened.

About fifty years ago a group of pioneers began to work at the bringing together of the Churches. Some felt strongly that the Churches should get together for missionary or social purposes. Others felt that the time had come to create a movement for the promotion of unity in the field of doctrine and Church order. Our *Faith and Order Conference* here in Montreal stands in that tradition. The ecumenical movement grew. It found one definite expression in the World Council of Churches. But it came to penetrate all Churches.

What does it all mean? Are the Churches affected by that spirit of general indifferentism according to which clear and firm convictions are outmoded? Is this an ecclesiastical sales period in which the prices go down? Is it the night in which all cats are gray? Definitely no. The ecumenical movement is not a movement of and for the lukewarm. It is a fixed principle in our meetings that disagreements are to be recorded as honestly as agreements.

Is it perhaps rather that we are afraid and that we want to get together to face the menace of an increasingly secularized world? No—this movement is a movement *pro*, not *contra*.

The true meaning of the ecumenical movement lies in a spiritual discovery. Our eyes have been opened for the extraordinary contradiction between two facts. The fact that according to Holy Scripture the Church which is the people of God is called to manifest in this world that God has reconciled men to Himself and to each other. And the other fact that men and women who believe in the same Lord Jesus Christ find themselves separated from each other. We know that we are all responsible for this. For none of us have lived up to the word of the Lord: "He who does not gather with me, scatters." We must all repent and ask the Lord to gather us in order that we may gather with him.

Athenagoras of Elaia

Greek Orthodox Metropolitan of Canada

THE WALLS ARE CRUMBLING

What we witness tonight in this history-making togetherness is perhaps an image of things to come.

A few decades ago it was inconceivable even to hope and plan for such a kind of prayerful ecumenical gathering. Today it is a reality. Christians from the West and from the East representing the three main segments of the Christian world stand in humility under the cross of their common Redeemer to offer together prayers and thanksgivings. Our common intention is eagerly and humbly to invoke the Paraclete, the Spirit of truth, to strengthen the bonds of our brotherhood and assist us to bring about a promise that we will dedicate ourselves in the work for the realization of that divinely willed end, the unity of all the people of Christ.

The protective walls erected long ago to separate and protect ourselves from each other's intervention seem now, more than ever, unbearable, anachronistic and contradictory to what we all stand for. We must leave them and come out and confess to each other in all sincerity how we feel.

A common feeling seems to prevail nowadays in the hearts and minds of all serious and conscientious Christians: the feeling of exhaustion. We have detected the presence of this feeling within our insistence to remain isolated in self-admiration, self-justification and self-complacency.

In our zeal to protect our own views we have been preoccupied in a kind of defensive theology. The sources of Christian life and thought were searched for arguments to help disprove each other's concepts. There are numerous books in our libraries written with scholastic erudition containing exhaustive essays of polemical theology, clever, rich in conviction and often abounding in prejudice and error. Judged on the basis of contemporary thinking this type of theology is found wanting and irrelevant to what the ecumenically minded Christians consider as their primary quest. Today a new theology ascends from the depths of our Christian conscience and demands our attention; it is the theology of unity.

Though this concern is the most remarkable development in the course of our Christian experience and though its significance is vital and its scope universal, it cannot help but move within a narrow frame and often be confronted with demands sounding reaction and negative conservatism. We hear and we often repeat that regardless of all the ecumenical gatherings and dialogues our many and deep differences remain strong.

This is undoubtedly true. But it is also true that regardless of these differences we do not feel today content keeping ourselves in our own enclosures. We feel rather deeply disturbed when we define our groups as "we" and the others as "they."

This inner dissatisfaction is indeed a blessed experience, the meaning of which, broad and deep as it is, must be explained and analyzed by our new theology, the theology of unity, so that we may all grasp its significance and see it as a sign by which Christ speaks to us to do something for His wounded and suffering body, the Church. We must all hope and earnestly pray that this experience enkindle in the hearts and minds of Christian leaders and people a new enthusiasm in seeking that blessed goal which is our oneness and unity in Christ.

George Johnston

McGill Divinity School of Montreal

THE FELLOWSHIP OF CHRIST

The two words "Protestant Catholicity" will probably strike many of you as a strange and peculiar combination! You are not accustomed to think that the people sometimes called Protestants have any claim whatever, or any longing for, the blessed faith and hope and charity that you associate with Catholicity. Nevertheless, I do in fact mean to suggest that it is possible and desirable to be both Protestant and Catholic.

The Reformed congregations which emerged in the 16th century believed themselves to belong to the true Church of God by grace of the Holy Spirit of Jesus Christ. Luther and Calvin, and others who came after them, were accustomed to repeat the familiar phrase of the creeds: *Credo unam sanctam Ecclesiam*—I believe in one, holy Church. Calvin, indeed, repeated with conviction the great theme of St. Cyprian of Carthage: "He cannot have God for his Father who does not have the Church for his Mother." It is significant, too, that one of the dominant strains in the doctrine and life of the Anglican communion has been that which stresses Catholic continuity and sacramental grace. To be Protestant was not necessarily to be separatist.

On the other hand, one cannot disguise the fact that many Protestants became bitterly schismatic; so much so, that today some of their descendants repudiate their very name. The world has seen a proliferation of Protestant denominations, some established as State or national Churches, some coagulated around an individual teacher or a specific principle that ballooned out of all control. In this ecumenical age a fresh understanding of their own origins reminds them that Christian faith is Apostolic, traditional and universal because it is inspired by the Spirit of love and truth.

It is out of the Bible that many of us have been persuaded that the Church of God is one Church in many local assemblies. It need never be a monolithic giant that stifles individual, national or cultural characteristics. Christ could heal the ancient types of separation. Christ still heals, if He is given His Lordship, binding men and women of all lands in what our Russian friends call *sobornost*, the deep, loving fellowship of His Spirit. Christ in His saving power is Catholic. Christ in His divine purpose is Catholic. Mankind in its wholeness is to be redeemed, and it will be united in one, holy and Catholic communion. The Bible tells me so.

Protestants have discovered therefore that they who would serve the Lord Christ must be Catholic too in all the range of that magnificent word. Catholicity must be domesticated once more among them. True, they have not yet been led into actual reunion with their separated brethren, although a few momentous experiments are in effect or in the making. True, they are not unanimous on ways and means, and they still harbor loud minorities that oppose the very concept of reunions as treason of the first order. But who can doubt that among them there is a profound desire for the wholeness of the Church, universal in space and in time? The movement cannot be ignored, for the ultimate driving force behind it is, we believe, the Lord God Himself.

Paul-Emile Cardinal Léger

Catholic Archbishop of Montreal

WE ARE BROTHERS

On the occasion of the Fourth World Congress on Faith and Order I have been invited, an archbishop of the Roman Catholic Church of Montreal, to take part in this evening of Christian fraternity and to join with you in common prayer for Church unity. It is with joy that I accepted the invitation knowing that the words of Our Lord are especially significant on an occasion such as this: "If two of you agree over any request that you make on earth, it will be granted them by my Father who is in heaven."

We acknowledge with gratitude the sincere desire and firm will of all who are gathered here to establish unity among "those who rejoice in being united in faith to the Lord Jesus."

We know also that the work of the Conference on Faith and Order has done much to spread this desire of unity throughout the Christian world. All who participate in the work of this Conference become more conscious of their responsibilities in the presence of Christ's will that all may be one.

This unity is a gift of God and a fruit of prayer, but it is also a goal toward which must be directed all the efforts of wills cleansed of egotism and enlightened by the findings of intelligent minds subject to the demands of faith.

The Christian is called to reproduce in this life, in his spirit and his flesh, the very acts of Christ, that is to say, His Passion, His death and His resurrection. To arrive at this unity, we need more than prayer, we need the Holy Eucharist. It is through communion with His Eucharistic body that the Lord truly brings us unity by giving us His Spirit who shapes us in His image so that the Father may say in all truth, to each of the baptized: "This is my beloved son, in whom I am well pleased."

In this sense, the Eucharist appears as the center and the source of the unity of the Church and the fecundity of its life.

I know well that these affirmations may not meet with the approval of all who are gathered here. In fact, the discussions which are taking place show us that the different Churches do not have identical notions of the Eucharistic mystery. It is because of these differences that we cannot yet celebrate together the Eucharistic prayer of unity.

The fraternal meetings of Roman Catholic theologians with theologians of other Christian communions show clearly the truth of the statement made by an eminent member of the Reformed Church of France: "However serious may be that which divides us, that which unites us is greater still," for we are brothers, we have the certitude of being united to Christ. St. Paul tells us that "By baptism, we have all become one being with Christ." This is our great consolation and the source of our joy. Our mutual affection, grounded on this union in faith, allows us to entertain in our hearts a hope that God cannot permit to be empty and illusory. Following the example of the patriarch of all believers, who hoped against all hope and believed that he would be the father of many nations, we are determined to walk with gladness toward unity.

Is not this ecumenical gathering a sign of our common hope? May it also be the proof of our good will to live according to the truth, in all charity, so that we may grow in every manner towards the One Who is the head, Christ, from Whom the body derives its coordination and cohesion.

Pope Paul VI

An Address Delivered at a Meeting with Orthodox
Patriarch Athenagoras in Jerusalem, January 1964

UNITED IN A COMMON PRAYER

Great is our emotion and profound our joy in this truly
historic hour, when, after centuries of silence and expectation, the Catholic Church and the patriarchate of Constantinople meet once again in the person of their highest representatives.

Great and profound also is our gratitude to you who have
kindly left temporarily your patriarchal see in order to come
here to meet us. It is, however, first of all toward God, the
Lord of the Church, that the words of our humble thanks-
giving ascend.

An ancient Christian tradition lovingly sees as the center
of the world that place upon which the glorious cross of the
Saviour was erected and whither, "Being raised up from the
earth" he draws "all things unto himself."

It was fitting then—and Providence has permitted it—that
it should be in this place, this forever blessed and sacred
place, that, as pilgrims from Rome and from Constantinople,
we should be able to meet and be united in a common
prayer.

You have desired this meeting ever since the time of our
unforgettable predecessor, John XXIII, your esteem and affection for whom you did not conceal, and to whom, with
striking intuition, you applied the words of the evangelist:
"There was a man sent from God, whose name was John."

He too yearned for this meeting, as you well know, but
his early death prevented him from realizing the desire of

his heart. The words of Christ: "That they may be one," repeated frequently by the dying Pope, leave no doubt as to one of his most cherished intentions, those for which he offered God his long agony and valuable life.

Doubtless, on the one side and on the other, the roads which lead to union may be long and strewn with difficulties. But these two paths converge toward one another and eventually reach the sources of the Gospel. Is it not, then, a happy augury that today's meeting takes place in that land where Christ founded His Church and shed His blood for her? It is in any case an eloquent manifestation of the great good will which, thanks be to God, animates ever more all Christians truly worthy of the name: the will to work to surmount disunity, to break down barriers, the will to engage resolutely upon the path which leads to reconciliation.

Divergence of a doctrinal, liturgical and disciplinary nature will have to be examined, at the proper time and place, in a spirit of fidelity to truth and of understanding in charity.

What can and must now commence to develop is that fraternal charity, which is ingenious in finding out new ways of showing itself, which, taking its lessons from the past, is ready to pardon, more ready to believe good than evil, careful above all to conform itself to the divine Master and to allow itself to be drawn and transformed by Him.

Of such charity the symbol and example should be the kiss of peace which Our Lord has permitted us to exchange in this Holy Land, and the prayer which Jesus Christ taught us and which we shall shortly recite together.

We cannot express how touched we are by this your gesture, nor are we alone in this. The Church of Rome and the Ecumenical Council will learn with deep joy of this historic event.

As for us, we raise toward God a grateful prayer and we beg Him to help us follow along this path, and to bestow upon you and upon us, who have undertaken it with faith and confidence, that blessing which will insure happy results. With these feelings, it is not a "good-bye" that we say to you, but, if you allow us, *au revoir*, based upon the hope of other fruitful meetings in the name of Our Lord.

John A. O'Brien

"After so many years of separation, after such painful polemics, what else can we do but again love one another, listen to one another, and pray for one another?"

POPE PAUL VI

PUTTING ECUMENISM INTO PRACTICE

The profound change in relations of Protestants and Catholics which has occurred throughout Christendom in the last five years is without precedent in almost two thousand years of Christianity. The attitude of suspicion, antagonism, and hostility has changed into one of understanding, good will, and brotherhood. Virtually all sections of the Christian faith are seeking to establish closer and more meaningful contacts that will advance the cause of cooperation in civic and social affairs, as well as bring the Churches closer together.

While there were many signs which indicated that the time was ripe for such a rapprochement, the factor which probably more than any other brought those tendencies into life was the immensely warm personality of Pope John XXIII and his totally unexpected announcement that he would call an Ecumenical Council—the first in almost a century. Its purpose would be internal renewal and reform and Christian unity. What particularly captured the imagination of the world was his inviting Protestant and Eastern Orthodox observers to attend the Council. The acceptance of that invitation by representatives of most of the leading Protestant and Eastern Orthodox Churches greatly enhanced the interest in the Council and showed the earnestness of Pope John to close the gap which has so long divided the followers of Christ.

So far-reaching and even revolutionary is the change in the attitude of the members of the three major segments of the Christian faith toward one another, that it has astonished most Christians and even shocked a few. Indeed, if a Christian who had died before 1959 were to return to the earth today and witness the revolution which has taken place, he could scarcely believe his eyes. Imagine his astonishment at entering an Episcopalian Church in Boston and seeing Richard Cardinal Cushing kneeling in prayer with its rector.

Picture, too, his surprise at seeing Francis Cardinal Spellman attending for the first time a funeral service in a Presbyterian church, which he did at the funeral of Mrs. Robert F. Wagner, the wife of New York's mayor. Think, too, of the bewilderment he would experience at seeing James Cardinal McIntyre addressing a gathering of sixteen thousand Episcopalian women of the Los Angeles diocese at their annual meeting.

Fancy also his astonishment, if he were in attendance at the funeral of Monsignor Daniel Moore of St. Louis, and saw Episcopalian Bishop George L. Cadigan inside the sanctuary with Cardinal Ritter and his two auxiliary bishops, while seated just outside it were seventy-five Protestant and Jewish clergymen. This unusual tribute of esteem and friendship was paid the priest-editor who has opened the columns of the *St. Louis Review* to Protestant and Jewish news and opinion, and pioneered a column in which Catholics and non-Catholics discussed problems of common concern. It won for him in 1963 the "ecumenical cross" of the Protestant Metropolitan Church Federation of St. Louis—the first ever awarded a Catholic priest.

A survey of the nation's press shows that incidents of this nature are occurring not only in all parts of the nation but in virtually all the countries of Christendom. Thus in New Orleans, Archbishop John P. Cody initiated Operation Understanding—a three-day visit of Protestant, Catholic, Orthodox, and Jewish houses of worship. Held on December

25, 1963, and January 5 and 11, 1964, the program was designed to increase the understanding and good will between members of all these faiths.

On the first day thirty-four hundred persons visited Catholic churches, some twelve thousand visited Protestant churches on the second, and more than twenty-seven thousand visited New Orleans' six synagogues and temples on the last day. During the visits representatives of the church visited explained their faith and worship, and the explanations were received with respect and gratitude.

Rabbi Julian Feibelman of Temple Sinai, president of the New Orleans Rabbinical Council, termed it a "historic event," while his colleague, Rabbi Leo A. Bergman of Touro Synagogue, called it "a miracle." Operation Understanding is being held in many cities from coast to coast and illustrates a spirit of good will, warmth, and understanding that was strangely lacking only five years ago. Moreover, the ecumenical movement is bringing Protestant and Catholic clergymen together with a warmth and frequency that no one, a few years ago, would have believed possible.

Thus in Pueblo, Colorado, a Church Unity Week was held during which a three-hour meeting of fifty Episcopal priests and Bishop Joseph S. Minnis met with thirty-five Catholic priests led by Bishop Charles A. Buswell. In a joint statement at the close of the meeting, the bishops said: "It is the hope of all of us that our continued meeting together will break down the barriers . . . encountered in the past."

The theological discussion was followed a few days later by an interfaith Scripture service, conducted by Bishop Buswell for both clergies. Similar significant meetings were held that week, called Unity Week, January 18–25. In Seattle, Washington, a precedent was set when Archbishop Thomas A. Connolly spoke in a public forum at Gethsemane Lutheran Church. In Vancouver, British Columbia, and elsewhere throughout Canada joint prayer services between separated Churches featured unity action.

During that same Unity Week Cardinal Meyer addressed some two hundred Protestant clergymen at the Chicago Theological Seminary. He then participated in a three-part Litany of Prayer for Christian Unity, and thus established a historic milestone in Catholic-Protestant relations in the U.S.A. With the cardinal reading the invocations, the ministers thanked almighty God "for opening minds and hearts to the understanding and sharing of gifts." All then united in begging pardon "for our controversies, sometimes full of irony, narrow-mindedness or exaggerations . . . for our intransigence and our harsh judgments."

This memorable instance of fully ecumenical prayer ranks with Cardinal Léger's leading of a prayer service at the Faith and Order Congress in Montreal and with Pope Paul VI's recitation of the Lord's Prayer with the official observers of the Protestant and Orthodox Churches at the Council. The ecumenical spirit is flowing down through all the levels of Protestant and Catholic relationships.

In San Francisco the Sacred Heart High School followed out Swiss Lutheran theologian Oscar Cullmann's proposal to exchange Sunday collections, and presented a love offering for the poor to a nearby Lutheran church. The pastor reciprocated by establishing an award for the outstanding student at Sacred Heart. In the fall, twenty thousand Protestant, Catholic, and Jewish laymen in Houston will cooperate on a city-wide Church census.

Relaxing Social Tensions

The new warmth between Protestants and Catholics is reflected in the increasing acts of friendly cooperation between the Knights of Columbus and the Masons. Thus on April 5, 1964, a group of forty students from Our Lady of the Lake Seminary, Syracuse, Indiana was driven to Chicago by twelve Knights of Columbus. Each seminarian had volunteered to donate a pint of blood to the Chicago Shrine Hospital for Crippled Children.

Learning of this unusual caravan of mercy and good will, members of the state police of Indiana and Illinois offered their services as escorts. The hospital treats crippled children irrespective of race, color, or creed without charge. This was the second group of students from that Seminary to make such a donation.

Years ago when Thomas Morrow, one of the seminarians, was a child, he was treated successfully at the Shrine Hospital. "Please, God," he prayed then, "make me well so that I can be a priest and help the Shriners." The Knights of Columbus asked to serve as chauffeurs, so that they too might show their appreciation of the great work of the Shrine Hospital. "This concrete example of Roman Catholic charity," commented Editor John G. Fleck in the Masonic monthly, *News-Letter*, "should warm the heart of every Mason. It seems that we really are brothers under the skin."

The incident is typical of hundreds of similar acts of friendship, good will, and brotherhood between Masons and Catholics in general. They are prompting increasing numbers of both groups to wonder if the time has not come to re-examine the circumstances and the causes of their unhappy separation.

Trickling down to the congregational level, the ecumenical spirit has notably relaxed social tensions and quickened an interest in learning about the faith of others and in visiting their churches. Thus the Rev. Donald Prytherch of Bethel United Presbyterian Church estimates that at least one-third of all Protestant sermons now make reference to Christian unity. "This simply couldn't have happened five years ago," he said.

The ecumenical spirit spills over to the relations of Christians with Jews. Thus at a recent Lenten service at Kansas City's Country Club Christian Church, the speaker was Rabbi Alexander Graubart of Congregation Beth Shalom.

In Tulsa, Oklahoma, Jewish and Protestant scholars lecture at an eight-week Catholic Bible course.

In Church publications religious barriers have virtually disappeared. Presbyterian theologian Robert McAfee Brown of Stanford writes a monthly feature for the Catholic weekly, *The Commonweal* of New York, while Lutheran theologian Jeroslav Pelikan writes a weekly column for the *Register*, a national Catholic weekly published in Denver.

Pittsburgh's Catholic Duquesne University has established a new *Journal of Ecumenical Studies*, and the editors include Brown, Catholic theologians Gregory Baum and Hans Küng, and Lutheran George Linbeck. The Catholic weekly *The Ave Maria* recently featured an article by Lutheran theologian Martin E. Marty, and the *Christian Century* of Chicago new opens its columns to articles by Catholic theologians. In a beautiful and unprecedented expression of the ecumenical spirit, both magazines simultaneously published a series of three articles on Family Planning and the Population Explosion by the editor of this book.

What is of utmost importance is the fact that this new spirit of understanding, friendship, and warmth is permeating the great masses of people. Christian unity can be achieved only if it "takes root in the local communities," points out Bishop Reuben H. Mueller, the new president of the National Council of Churches. "Those roots are already sprouting. Instead of being the private dream of theologians and the occasional public practice of prominent clergymen, the ecumenical movement has become a spirit-changing factor in the religious life of every U.S. community."

"Every day," remarks *Time*, "more laymen join in a dialogue once reserved for ministers." Indeed one Washington, D.C. pastor points out that "some of the best discussions take place in car pools and laundromats." That this new spirit of warmth and friendliness is penetrating into the masses is evident in the results of a survey conducted by the *Minneapolis Star* and *Tribune*. The results show a marked and even striking decrease in the number of Protestants who feared that the election of a Catholic would mean that "the Pope would dictate to the President," or "the orders would come from Rome," or "the Church would be more important than the nation."

That any vestiges of such fears are continuing to fade is further evidenced by the fact that a Catholic, President John F. Kennedy, was scheduled as the main speaker in December 1963 at the General Assembly of the National Council of Churches of Christ in America at which he was to receive a special award.

At the memorial tribute that the assembly paid him instead, Rev. Dr. Eugene Carson Blake of United Presbyterian Church declared: "President Kennedy's coming to address this assembly on this night, if an assassin's hand had not prevented it, would have clearly symbolized the beginning of a *new era* of hope for Christian cooperation in the United States of America." The young President had demonstrated by his actions that he was "indeed a good Catholic," said Dr. Blake. And he added that, short as Mr. Kennedy's term of office had been, "it was long enough to make abundantly clear that those who had feared, for any reason, a Roman Catholic President had misunderstood both the man and his Church."

It is the filtering of the ecumenical spirit into the bloodstream of the masses in all countries that offers the best promise of giving roots, anchorage, stability, and reality to the age-old dream of Christian unity. Realizing this, Cardinal Cushing has accepted scores of invitations from Protestant ministers to address their congregations on the prospects for Christian unity. Typical was his recent talk at a meeting sponsored by the Sudbury Council of Protestant Churches to an audience that overflowed both the Methodist church and a nearby parish hall.

"Unless the spirit of theologians and Biblical scholars," he told the audience, "penetrates to the grass roots, the ecumenical spirit will have no roots and hence will not long survive." Referring to the huge crowds which turn out for such talks, Cardinal Cushing told a Holy Name father-son meeting: "Nothing like this has ever happened before."

Catholics, too, are opening their doors to Protestant spokesmen. In June 1962, Dr. Jeroslav Pelikan was the first Protestant ever to address the American Catholic Theological Society, and a year later became the first Protestant minister to speak on the Catholic Hour, carried on a national network. Other Protestant speakers followed him. In March 1964 at Notre Dame University, Dr. Oscar Cullmann delivered a series of three lectures to the students and faculty, and Methodist Church historian Dr. Franklin Littell addressed the monthly Clergy Conference—the first Protestant minister ever to do so.

Numerous ecumenical conferences of Protestant and Catholic theologians and Scriptural scholars have likewise been held on the campus within the past few years. Heralding this change in Catholic attitudes, the Rev. Dr. Robert J. McCracken of New York City's Riverside Church told his congregation that Roman Catholics are showing "a well-nigh revolutionary willingness to think of Protestantism as something more than a heretical schism. A new day has dawned in Protestant-Roman Catholic relations."

Similar testimony comes from the officers of the National Conference of Christians and Jews. A spokesman at the national headquarters recently remarked on the noticeable improvement of the relations between the faiths on the local levels. In a number of dioceses just a few years ago the NCCJ was anything but welcome: some bishops frowned upon their priests participating in interreligious activities. "There was a considerable anxiety," the spokesman recalled, "about a priest sharing a platform with a Protestant or Jewish clergyman." Now in many dioceses Catholic priests are encouraged to participate in these activities, and even bishops, archbishops, and cardinals are addressing their meetings.

Religious Leaders Unite

This new spirit has made itself evident in uniting religious leaders to come to grips with two major issues facing this country today: the civil rights of Negroes and world peace. In recent months priests, ministers, and rabbis have been marching, picketing, protesting, and been arrested arm in arm in upholding the struggle of Negroes for civil rights. Probably the most dramatic expression of this new unity occurred in Chicago in January 1963, when 669 delegates from sixty-seven major Protestant, Eastern Orthodox, Catholic, and Jewish organizations met at the First National Conference on Religion and Race. This unique gathering, initiated by Catholics, issued a well-reasoned and moving "Appeal to Conscience" against racial prejudice and inequality.

Carried in virtually all the papers of the nation, the Appeal said in part: "We Americans of all religious faiths have been slow to recognize that racial discrimination and segregation are an insult to God, the Giver of human dignity and human rights. Even worse, we have all participated in perpetuating racial discrimination and segregation in civil, political, industrial, social and private life. And worse still, in our houses of worship, our religious schools, hospitals, welfare institutions and fraternal organizations we have often failed our own religious commitments. . . . We repent our failures and ask the forgiveness of God. We ask also the forgiveness of our brothers, whose rights we have ignored and whose dignity we have offended. We call for a renewed religious conscience on this basically moral evil."

Another striking manifestation of the new spirit of religious understanding and brotherhood occurred in September 1963. Leading Protestant, Catholic, and Jewish clergymen appeared before a U. S. Senate committee considering the proposed nuclear test ban to plead for its ratification. These, too, united in stressing "the moral aspect of the issue" and warned that "continued nuclear testing has consequences for life on earth that must be recognized."

This new rapprochement has had a noticeable effect in lessening the bitterness and emotionalism that has long characterized the discussion on two controversial issues: birth control and federal aid for the pupils of *all* schools. Catholics are showing an increasing realization that medically approved contraceptive birth regulation is now part of the religious faith of most Protestants and are respecting their Constitutional rights to follow their religious convictions in this matter. Similarly, Protestants are showing a new sensitivity to the Catholic conscience and are respecting their convictions on what they regard as the moral method of family planning.

On the matter of federal aid, as shown by the action of the National Council of Churches of Christ, there is a new and sympathetic understanding of the claim of Catholics for federal aid in the teaching of *secular* subjects, while Catholics are becoming more sensitive to the Protestant objection to the use of public funds for the teaching of distinctly *religious* subjects. It is this new spirit of understanding and good will that offers the best hope for the solution of both these nettlesome problems, which have so long disturbed the relations of the members of the three major faiths.

A significant expression of the new ecumenical spirit occurred in Camden, New Jersey, where Monsignor S. J. Adamo, executive editor of the *Catholic Star Herald*, expressed the hope that the Church would canonize non-Catholics as specific recognition of the holy lives non-Catholics have led and are leading. As a candidate for such honors, he suggested Anne Frank, the Jewish girl murdered by the Nazis. "This," he said, "could be a benign beginning for unity and love among all people, and a beginning of the end of those feelings of superiority among so many Catholics."

In the cloistered seclusion of convents the new spirit is manifesting itself. When the World Council of Churches held its Faith and Order Conference in Montreal, Cardinal Léger requested the prayers of Catholics for the success of their meeting. Not content to pray alone with her community, Mother Françoise de la Visitation organized a prayer meeting and invited Anglican nuns to participate. The result was that, for the first time since their establishment in Montreal in 1883, the Anglican Sisters of St. Margaret joined officially with five congregations of Catholic nuns and prayed for the success of the Montreal meeting and for the fulfillment of Christ's prayer for the unity of all His followers.

In other countries similar expressions of the ecumenical spirit are occurring with ever-increasing frequency. In Bluff Point, Australia, every noon during Lent a group of "prayer partners," including Catholics, Anglicans, Greek Orthodox, Methodists, and Presbyterians, recite a prayer for Christian unity in response to the ringing of the bell of St. George's Anglican Church there. The program was initiated for Lent last year by the Rev. E. W. Doncaster, St. George's rector.

In Nagpur, India, a study circle of Catholics, Protestants, and Orthodox Christians met for a week-long session, designed to pave the way for a dialogue between Christianity and Hinduism. A feature of the meeting was the reading together in a spirit of contemplation and prayer, of passages from the Bible and the Upanishads, the Hindu holy book. In Madrid, *Ya*, Spain's leading Catholic newspaper, reported that "for the first time here Protestants, Eastern Orthodox and Catholics prayed together for Christian unity." The meeting occurred during the Church Unity Week.

In Moscow Patriarch Alexei, supreme head of the Russian Orthodox Church, spoke out in favor of further contact between Roman Catholicism and Eastern Orthodoxy. Such contacts, he said, could "lead to a dialogue between the Churches" and thus help to hasten the realization of Christian unity. In Munich Cardinal Doepfner urged that Protestant and Catholic scholars work out a text of the Lord's Prayer that would be acceptable to all Christians.

Even more significant is the authorization by the Catholic bishops of Scotland for official use of the Revised Standard Edition of the New Testament, prepared by Protestant scholars, with a few additional footnotes. This is in line with the proposal made by the Jesuit-edited *America,* that Catholic and Protestant Scriptural scholars work out jointly a translation of the New Testament that could be used by all Christians and thus give further impetus to the striving for complete Christian unity. In Germany, France, Austria, Belgium, Switzerland, and Holland, the ecumenical movement is further advanced than in the United States, and instances of ecumenical activity are of weekly occurrence in most of those countries.

"Nothing Is Insurmountable"

The climax of all the expressions of the ecumenical spirit was the meeting of Pope Paul VI and Ecumenical Patriarch Athenagoras I of Constantinople in Jerusalem. "This moment, Your Holiness," said the Patriarch, "is one of the most significant for mankind. Humanity at its highest spiritual level has the opportunity at last to guide the world toward peace."

"Your Holiness," replied the Pope, "we must bring our Churches closer together. It will not be easy, but we are already on the right road. Nothing is insurmountable in our striving to unite mankind, but we must unite beforehand." Thus spoke the highest-ranking prelates of Roman Catholicism and of Orthodoxy, the branches of Christianity sundered in the great schism of 1054. It was the first encounter of Pope and Patriarch since a tentative reconciliation in 1439, and it was truly a meeting of brothers.

Each embraced the other with warmth and affection and exchanged the kiss of peace. The picture of that embrace was featured in newspapers throughout the world, while millions in many countries witnessed the moving scene on their television screens. That picture shows more vividly and

66666

movingly than a score of books the almost incredible and miraculous change in the attitude of divided segments of Christianity toward one another. That embrace symbolizes the sincerity, warmth, and reality of the movement for Christian unity.

Is such unity really possible? The answer must steer a midway path between dewy-eyed optimism and cynical pessimism. Christian realism is characterized by hope, and that hope rests, we believe, on the following three foundations. First, the basis of the Christian faith is the Gospel of Christ, and His teachings possess a unity that must ultimately be reflected in the faith of all His followers. Second, the human mind responds to the same basic laws of evidence and of logic, and the dispassionate consideration of the evidence in the light of reason leads to a common conclusion. Third, we have Christ's word that He wants unity and prayed for the unity of all His followers. In the power of God lies the best hope for the ultimate achievement of Christian unity.

What is impossible for men is simple and easy for God. The foolishness of God is wiser than our wisdom and His weakness is stronger than our strength. Only God can bridge chasms so deep and so ancient. Through humble and persistent prayer, Christians believe, God will be moved to make up for our deficiencies, our awkwardness and ineptness, and thus fulfill the prayer of Christ "that all may be one." In penitence, humility, trust, confidence, and persevering prayer, we shall do our best and leave the outcome in the hands of the God Who assured us that no prayer uttered in the name of Christ will go unanswered.

F36